Islamic Social Finance

The current dynamics of world economy show remarkable changes in the socio-economics of credit provision and entrepreneurship. If the emergence of the sharing economy is fostering innovative models of collaborative agency, networking and venture business, economic actors are also looking for a more sustainable development, able to foster profitability as well as community welfare. This book investigates Islamic social finance as a paramount example of this economy under change, where the balance between economic efficiency and social impact is contributing to the transformation of the market from an exchange- to a community-oriented institution.

The collected essays analyse the social dimension of entrepreneurship from an Islamic perspective, highlighting the extent to which the rationales of "sharing," distribution and cooperation, affect the conceptualization of the market in Islam as a place of "shared prosperity." Moving from the conceptual "roots" of this paradigm to its operative "branches," the contributing authors also connect the most recent trends in the financial market to Shari'ah-based strategies for community welfare, hence exploring the applications of Islamic social finance from the sharing economy, FinTech and crowdfunding to microcredit, waqf, zakat, sukuk and green investments.

An illuminating reference for researchers, practitioners and policy-makers dealing with the challenges of a global market where not only is diversity being perceived as a value to be fostered, but also as an important opportunity for a more inclusive economy for everybody.

Valentino Cattelan specializes in Islamic law, economics and finance, and his research activity covers aspects of legal pluralism, property rights theory, history of capitalism, law of Islamic finance, comparative law and social finance.

Islamic Business and Finance Series
Series Editor: Ishaq Bhatti

There is an increasing need for western politicians, financiers, bankers, and indeed the western business community in general to have access to high quality and authoritative texts on Islamic financial and business practices. Drawing on expertise from across the Islamic world, this new series will provide carefully chosen and focused monographs and collections, each authored/edited by an expert in their respective field all over the world.

The series will be pitched at a level to appeal to middle and senior management in both the western and the Islamic business communities. For the manager with a western background the series will provide detailed and up-to-date briefings on important topics; for the academics, postgraduates, business communities, manager with western and an Islamic background the series will provide a guide to best practice in business in Islamic communities around the world, including Muslim minorities in the west and majorities in the rest of the world.

Labor in an Islamic Setting
Edited by Necmettin Kizilkaya and Toseef Azid

Islamic Macroeconomics
A Model for Efficient Government, Stability and Full Employment
Raja Almarzoqi, Walid Mansour and Noureddine Krichene

Dilemmas and Challenges in Islamic Finance
Looking at Equity and Microfinance
Edited by Yasushi Suzuki and Mohammad Dulal Miah

Islamic Social Finance
Entrepreneurship, Cooperation and the Sharing Economy
Edited by Valentino Cattelan

For more information about this series, please visit www.routledge.com/Islamic-Business-and-Finance-Series/book-series/ISLAMICFINANCE

Islamic Social Finance

Entrepreneurship, Cooperation and the Sharing Economy

Edited by Valentino Cattelan

LONDON AND NEW YORK

First published 2019
by Routledge
2 Park Square, Milton Park, Abingdon, Oxon OX14 4RN

and by Routledge
52 Vanderbilt Avenue, New York, NY 10017

First issued in paperback 2020

Routledge is an imprint of the Taylor & Francis Group, an informa business

British Library Cataloguing-in-Publication Data
A catalogue record for this book is available from the British Library

Library of Congress Cataloging-in-Publication Data
Names: Cattelan, Valentino, editor.
Title: Islamic social finance : entrepreneurship, cooperation and the sharing
economy / edited by Valentino Cattelan.
Description: 1 Edition. | New York : Routledge, 2019. | Series: Islamic business and
finance series | Series: Islamicfinance | Includes bibliographical references and index.
Identifiers: LCCN 2018012967 | ISBN 9781138280304 (hardback) |
ISBN 9781315272221 (e-book)
Subjects: LCSH: Finance–Religious aspects–Islam. | Finance (Islamic law) |
Social responsibility of business–Islamic countries. | Sharing–Religious
aspects–Islam.
Classification: LCC HG187.4 .I8366 2019 | DDC 334/.2091767–dc23
LC record available at https://lccn.loc.gov/2018012967

ISBN 13: 978-0-367-58805-2 (pbk)
ISBN 13: 978-1-138-28030-4 (hbk)

Typeset in Times New Roman
by Out of House Publishing

Contents

Illustrations

Figures

Table

Contributors

Valentino Cattelan is a scholar in Islamic law, economics and finance, and his research activity covers aspects of legal and financial pluralism, Islamic contract and commercial law, property rights theory, Islamic finance regulation, comparative law and social finance. In particular, Dr Cattelan's research focuses on the substantive spirit of Islamic law and its application in contemporary financial markets: in this way his work intersects law, economics, ethics and religion, with a particular emphasis on the comparison between the rationales of conventional capitalism and Islamic economics. After the completion of his PhD in Law & Economics (University of Siena, 2009), he has held research positions at the University of Rome Tor Vergata, the Oxford Centre for Islamic Studies (University of Oxford, UK), IE Business School (Madrid) and he has served as a Visiting Research Fellow at the Department of Law & Anthropology of the Max Planck Institute for Social Anthropology in Halle/Salle (Germany). He is the editor of the volume *Islamic Finance in Europe: Towards a Plural Financial System* (2013, Edward Elgar).

Rami Abdelkafi is a Senior Research Economist and Training Specialist at the Islamic Research and Training Institute (IRTI). He joined the Islamic Development Bank (IDB) in August 2008 and has accumulated an important experience in the field of economic development. Prior to this, Dr Abdelkafi worked as an Assistant Professor at the University of Sfax in Tunisia. He earned a Doctorate in Economics from the University of Nice, France, in 2002. His areas of expertise are economic growth and development, Islamic economics and finance and macroeconomic policies.

Mohamed Ariff has worked full-time for 26 years at AACSB-accredited business schools (National University of Singapore; Monash University; Bond University; University Putra Malaysia). He has held senior university administrative positions as well as executive positions including in a central bank (Singapore). He worked as Professor/Fellow at Harvard (1994), Tokyo University (1989, 1991, 2008), UCD Dublin (1992, 2004), among others. He is an active researcher in financial economics with contributions in 163 journals (58 ISI): *JIFMI&M, JBFA, AE, JIMF, JFSR*, etc. and is a series editor for Edward Elgar's *Islamic Finance Series*. He has consulted for three stock exchanges, a securities commission, UNESCO, ADB and private corporations. His work on Islamic finance is an area of continued contribution. He can be contacted on the following e-mail address: ariff13@gmail.com.

Houssem eddine Bedoui is a Global Lead Islamic Finance Expert at IDB. As part of his work at the Islamic Development Bank, he actively contributes to the structuring, launch and implementation of innovative products and processes for the market. Besides, Dr Bedoui has several entrepreneurial experiences putting Islamic finance principles and products into practice. Prior to his job at the IDB, he was a consultant in Europe in management advisory and ethical/sustainable finance, and worked with many think tanks to develop Islamic finance in France. He has a Master's from Telecom SudParis Engineering School (INT), France; an MBA from IE Business School (Spain); a PhD from ENS (École Normale Supérieure, France); he is also an Alumni from Harvard Kennedy School (CID, Center for International Development). Dr Bedoui is the co-editor of IRTI's French journal. His research interests comprise Islamic capital markets, fintech, social entrepreneurship and finance, competitiveness and Islamic banking; he has published in several academic journals and presented his research works at various international conferences.

Fatima Z. Bensar is a financial consultant at Management Solutions. She has professional experience in the banking industry across Spain and the United States. In parallel, she is a Research Associate at the Saudi-Spanish Center for Islamic Economics and Finance at IE Business School. She holds a degree in Business Administration from Universidad de Alcalá (Madrid) and she is currently studying towards a Master's in Business Consulting with a focus on banking at Universidad Pontificia Comillas (Madrid).

Mohd Ma'Sum Billah (PhD Insurance, IIUM, Malaysia) is Professor of Finance, Islamic Economics Institute, King Abdul Aziz University, Saudi Arabia (www.drmasumbillah.blogspot.com). Professor Billah has served/contributed to both academic and corporate industries for more than 20 years with management, teaching, research, solution provision and sharing of strategic and technical thoughts towards the advancement of Islamic insurance (*takaful*), in particular, and Islamic finance, in general, besides *halal* standards. In addition, he has also been affiliated with corporate, academic and financial industries besides NGOs in his capacity as a member of the board, advisor, strategic decision maker, transformer and reformer with strategic solutions. Among the areas of his interest/contributions are: Islamic insurance (*takaful*), finance, crowdfunding, investment, capital market (*sukuk*), social finance, petroleum finance, FinTech and digital currency standards.

Masudul Alam Choudhury (PhD University of Toronto; MPhil Quaid-e-Azam University) is Professor at the Department of *Shari'ah* and Economics, Academy of Islamic Studies and Professor and International Chair, Postgraduate Programme in Islamic Economics and Finance, Faculty of Economics, Trisakti University, Jakarta, Indonesia. He is a rare scholar in the field of Islamic economics and finance whose work has been recognized in both Western as well as Muslim academic circles as playing an influential role in defining the discipline of Islamic finance and economics. He is the first academic in his field to address the original methodology of *tawhid* as ontological law in the development of a theory of meta-science within the *Qur'anic* epistemological framework of Unity of Monotheistic Knowledge. Professor Choudhury is widely and reputably published.

Mohammad Shahadat Hossain (Professor, Department of Computer Science, Chittagong University, Bangladesh) received MPhil and PhD degrees in Computation from the University of Manchester's Institute of Science and Technology (UMIST), UK, in 1999 and 2002, respectively. He is a Professor of Computer Science and Engineering of the Chittagong University (CU), Bangladesh. His interest of research includes the development of evolutionary computing techniques to support the computer model of *tawhidi* epistemology. In addition, the investigation of pragmatic software development tools and methods, for information systems in general and for expert systems in particular, are also his areas of research. He has published 90 scholarly articles and three books.

Charilaos Mertzanis was educated at the Aristotle University of Thessaloniki (Greece) and the New School for Social Research (USA), where he studied as a Fulbright and a NATO fellow. He is currently an Associate Professor of Financial Economics at the American University in Cairo. In the past, he served as Director of Research of the Hellenic Capital Market Commission for 17 years. He has published several scholarly articles on finance, corporate governance, macroeconomics, economic philosophy and history. He has held various professional appointments, participated in several international policy-making groups (OECD, EC, ESMA) and provided advisory services on financial policy development to several national governments in developing countries.

Marianella Piratti holds a PhD in International Law and a Master's in Political Sciences from the University of Padua. She has served as a visiting researcher at the IREMAM/MMSH in Aix en Provence and the University Ben Youcef Ben Khadda of Algiers. Dr Piratti currently participates in the research activities of the University of Padua; she is affiliated to CESTUDIR (Centre for Human Rights Study, University of Venice) and she is a member of ICLARS (International Consortium for Law and Religion Studies). Her research interests cover international law, comparative constitutional law and Islamic law, as well as human rights, sustainable development and environmental protection. Among her publications: 'La tutela dell'ambiente in una prospettiva islamica. Lo statuto degli animali', in Gazzola, M., and Turchetto, M. (eds, 2016) *Per gli Animali è Sempre Treblinka*. Milano: Mimesis, pp. 201–218; and 'Il diritto dell'ambiente in Algeria, profili generali e fiscalità ambientale', in Antonini, L. (ed., 2010), *L'Imposizione Ambientale nel Quadro del Nuovo Federalismo Fiscale*. Napoli: Jovene, pp. 341–365.

Ari Pratiwi (Lecturer, Paramadina University, Jakarta, Indonesia and Human Resource Development, IBM Indonesia, Jakarta, Indonesia) obtained her doctoral degree from Trisakti University, Jakarta, Indonesia. She specialized in the field of Islamic economics and finance under the supervision of Professor Dr Masudul Alam Choudhury. Dr Pratiwi proved to be an expert in the computational techniques of the *tawhidi* circular causation simulation model. She is now employed as a software client architect with IBM Indonesia and teaches as a lecturer in the Graduate Management School of Universitas Paramadina Jakarta. Dr Pratiwi has a number of scholarly articles in SCOPUS listed journals and scholarly books.

Atiq-ur-Rehman is Assistant Professor of Econometrics at Pakistan Institute of Development Economics, Islamabad, Pakistan's leading university in economics. Before joining PIDE, he served at International Islamic University, Islamabad in a similar position. He holds a PhD in Econometrics from International Islamic University, where he wrote his thesis under the supervision of Dr Asad Zaman. Dr Rehman teaches Econometrics and Statistics, especially theoretical and time series econometrics and statistical research methods. His published research relates to Development Studies, Islamic Economics, Islamic Banking and Finance, Monetary Economics and Econometrics. He has supervised a large number of students in their MS/PhD theses and has presented his research in several international events.

Gonzalo Rodríguez is currently the General Coordinator of the Saudi-Spanish Center for Islamic Economics and Finance at IE Business School, Madrid. Previously he was a lawyer at Triodos Bank, the leading ethical bank in Europe and legal adviser at Garrigues Abogados (the Iberian peninsula's leading tax and legal services firm in terms of professional headcount and billings). He received his MAJ (LLM) from IE Business School, a degree in Law from Universidad Autonoma de Madrid, and an International Executive Programme in Islamic Finance at IE Business School. He is currently studying for a degree in Political Science at the Universidad Complutense de Madrid.

Germán Rodríguez-Moreno is Associate Professor in Islamic Finance at IE Business School, Madrid. He has developed an expertise in *takaful* (Islamic insurance), *waqf* (Islamic charitable trusts) and other aspects of Islamic finance. He is a member of the Observatorio de Finanzas Islámicas (Islamic Finance Observatory) in Spain. He has lived in Madrid since July 2008. City of London trained, Mr Rodríguez-Moreno is an English solicitor with 20 years of experience as a corporate lawyer doing M&A work all around the world. He is a former Head of Legal at Aviva, a large international insurance company. Prior to qualifying as a lawyer, he obtained a First Class BA (Honours) and an MSc in Politics at Stirling University, Scotland. He then worked as a freelance journalist, during which time he co-authored a book (for the non-profit organization Article 19) on censorship in Mexico, published by Human Rights Watch.

Foreword

A just economy calls for fair distribution by making everyone morally responsible to care about – and share with – each other. One's natural right is to be
socio-economically sound with basic satisfaction. The world is witnessing a
significant number of populations in almost every corner of the globe that
are experiencing growing poverty, struggling to maintain their day to day life
with reasonable economic satisfaction. Referring to the UNDP Report 2014
(*Sustaining Human Progress: Reducing Vulnerabilities and Building Resilience*)
and the estimates of wealth distribution for the period 2008–2013, globally '1.2
billion people (22 percent) live on less than $1.25 a day. Increasing the income
poverty line to $2.50 a day raises the global income poverty rate to about
50 percent, or 2.7 billion people' (p. 19). Also the World Bank Report *Poverty
and Shared Prosperity 2016 – Taking on Inequality* confirms the persistence of
vulnerability to poverty for nearly the half of the world's population.

Although today's world is to some extent dominated by the self-oriented
spirit of capitalism, a growing concern is emerging, both among public
authorities and private actors, about the need for sustaining the poor, the
unemployed and the destitute, so to ensure that everyone can enjoy basic
economic rights. Among the effective measures that have been taken in the
mainstream economy, one can refer to micro-credit, social financing, ethical
funds, social business, trust funds and other socio-humanitarian economic
missions.

Alternatively, under the *Shari'ah* principles, this humanitarian concern in
caring for the poor, helpless, destitute and underprivileged is realized through
instruments like *zakat* (alms-giving), *waqf* (endowment), *tabarru'* (donation),
ibra' (waiver), *sukuk al-waqf* (charitable bond), crowdfunding and *sadaqah*
(charity), that aim at fighting poverty while creating an economically self-
reliant community, hence laying the foundations of Islamic social finance.
The social financing model under *Shari'ah* principles does not mean to position itself as a mere charitable platform in financing the poor and the needy
for their temporary needs only, but its scope and objectives are significantly
greater than might have ever been thought traditionally. A result-oriented
Islamic social financing model is, indeed, a vehicle integrated with divine

ethical principles in creating an enterprising and a micro-entrepreneurship-based community by targeting the poor, destitute, helpless, underprivileged and unemployed.

It is thus timely that Valentino Cattelan has initiated this meaningful volume under the heading of *Islamic Social Finance*, collecting a series of specialized essays contributed by several internationally renowned scholars with their own subject specialization. The contributors of this book have treated the chapters with talented inputs gathering *Shari'ah* normative and corporate understanding, issues related to contemporary phenomena, technicalities, challenges and the way forward, thus enabling the readers to face existing concerns and explore proper solutions for the development of this growing market niche.

The book presents 11 essays with specialized issues after an introduction (Chapter 1), all of which facilitate a detailed understanding of the social financing model under the *Shari'ah* ethical and socio-economic principles, both from a conceptual perspective (Part I) and an operative approach (Part II). The strong interrelation between the theory and the practice is certainly a merit of this volume, as it highlights in this way the concrete practicability of the principles underlying Islamic social finance in the real economy.

Each essay focuses on a specific issue with possible paradigm and modelling structure. All the contributions deal with solutions of community-related financing plans fostered by divine-inspired value in strategizing the creation of an economically sound community within the holistic spirit of care and cooperation. The Islamic financing model shall in no situation be ignored in integration with the *tawhidi* spirit (i.e. the unity of God's creation) thus, the social financing paradigm under *Shari'ah* principles shall be understood and implemented by complying this *tawhidi* concern, as Chapter 2, in Part I of the book, appropriately shows.

In some cases it has been observed that, in social business, social financing, micro-entrepreneurship and ethical financing under a *halal* shield, the main concern in practicality is an economic or a political goal while keeping the divine or ethical value as a secondary one by paying lip service to it only. But, in actual fact, the prime objective of an Islamic entrepreneurship or social financing model is that the *Shari'ah* objectives (*maqasid al-Shari'ah*) have to be strictly observed in both modelling and managing Islamic financial operations besides keeping up with *halal* socio-economic concerns (Chapter 3).

What should be a development theory in designing and operating an Islamic social financing structure? It is the precise purpose of this book to provide a guideline for researchers, product specialists and practitioners, in the light of the general spirit of Islam as depicted above.

Indeed, social financing under the *halal* banner is not a new research field, but different players have adopted till now different tools in designing Islamic social financing products and services, financial engineering has progressed in the last decade and new challenges have emerged. Therefore, it is important for every provider to design products by reviewing the existing tools while adapting appropriate ones and considering the socio-economic phenomena of concerned markets. This corporate culture may create a new dimension in making a sustainable community's future. Accordingly, this book touches upon issues related to collaborative governance, social capital (Chapter 4) as well as the challenge of a proper conceptualization of the sharing economy according to the semantics of Islamic economics and finance (Chapter 5), highlighting the importance of new Islamic tools and their implication in designing desirable and result-oriented social financing products and services under *Shari'ah* principles.

For a result of an oriented social financing structure under *Shari'ah*, it is of utmost importance that the aforementioned *tawhidi* foundation, the fundamental objectives of *Shari'ah*, principles of collaborative and social capital and tools of financial innovations, also through new technologies and the sharing economy, are fully integrated in the operative dimension of the market. Part II of the book explicitly addresses this objective.

In fact, a just economy with rightful distribution advocates sharing and fostering. Hence a *halal* social financing model totally embraces a paradigm that promotes cooperation with due care towards lawful achievement and just allocation. In the *halal* market segment, with cooperation at its grassroots, this paradigm moves from traditional to online and then to the real market, re-formulating the global debt market through interest-free and asset-backed risk sharing financial instruments (Chapter 6), for the Islamic social financing model to be nourished to climb to its glorious destination. *Sukuk* is the fastest growing segment in Islamic finance. The instruments used in designing *sukuk* products need regular innovative revision in discovering possible new instruments for a better programme by looking at the socio-economic dimension of the contemporary world. Thus, Chapter 6 demonstrates the operative advantages of these new instruments, which may also facilitate to tap existing and virgin markets.

Islamic social finance can also be fostered by a financing model that unlocks the social impact of Islamic entrepreneurship via crowdfunding (Chapter 7). It is essential under the *Shari'ah* objectives that a financing initiative shall concern both commercial return and socio-economic impact equally; thus the chapter indicates how financing contributes to social integrality. Crowdfunding is a growing segment in today's Islamic finance and is another sub-model of Islamic social finance, which can contribute to poverty eradication, socio-community development and other humanitarian concerns. The chapter focuses on a *halal* crowdfunding model that may be an added value in today's reality also through the use of new technologies.

In this direction, Chapter 8 expressly deals with the rise of FinTech, that is to say the development of new financial technologies, as an emerging area of market growth for Islamic finance. It is of remarkable relevance that the new tools offered by financial technologies are appropriately integrated in the Islamic social financing model, and the book offers aspects of reflection also in this regard.

Furthermore, since the rise of economic consciousness about the need for sustainability has become part of the global debate, Chapter 9 considers Islamic green finance with its background rooted in Islamic religion as the appropriate social-oriented segment of Islamic finance in the direction of an economic development balanced with environmental protection. Both theoretical and operative aspects of Islamic green finance are given equal attention in the investigation by the authors of the chapter.

Another interesting contribution (Chapter 10) is dedicated in this book to the *salam* micro-financing model in view of community development. It is a timely study, since the model may be a useful guidance in designing a product to care about the community's education, shelter, healthcare, and a variety of economic needs.

Takaful ('Islamic mutual insurance') is another tool to eradicate poverty through collective protection. The volume looks at this tool by proposing a *waqf*-based model for *takaful* for the purpose of social entrepreneurship and the coverage for the needy community against any catastrophe (Chapter 11).

To conclude, the comprehensive investigation of Islamic entrepreneurship provided by the book also covers *zakat*, interpreted not as a way to create beggars by giving mere charity, but in the light of its true objective of eradicating poverty, thus providing a solution to the unemployed and caring about the needy with a long-term plan so to contribute towards creating an eco-sustainable and entrepreneurship-based community with self-reliance. The final chapter (Chapter 12) of this volume precisely establishes the idea that *zakat* is not a mere charity-giving platform, but a tool for socio-humanitarian entrepreneurship within a holistic approach.

Considering the noteworthy and all-encompassing study of Islamic social finance that the readers will find in the present book, this volume can be seen as the result of a remarkable effort by Valentino Cattelan and all the contributors, an effort which is certainly timely to meet the global market demand of academia, researchers, industrialists, professionals and students. In this regard, the volume will definitely prove a useful reference for the understanding and promotion of the Islamic social finance model in the contemporary practice of entrepreneurship, cooperation and the sharing economy in Islamic finance, as well as a guide to facilitate a socially oriented change in the global market as a whole.

Prof. Abdullah Qurban Turkistani, PhD
Dean, Islamic Economics Institute
King Abdul Aziz University
Kingdom of Saudi Arabia

1 Introduction

Islamic social finance and the importance of roots

Valentino Cattelan

1. *La Grande Bellezza*

Academic volumes that start with a reference to the editor's personal experiences have never been my cup of tea. But, for some reason, my brain usually works by associating my research interests with books of other disciplines as well as the humanities in general, if not novels or artworks that I encounter in real life.

In this case, while editing the present volume, I spent some spare time watching *La Grande Bellezza* ('The Great Beauty') and I came across there, in a scene of the movie, what I believe can be regarded as the ultimate sense of this book: that is to say, that *roots are important*.

I trust then that the reader (who may dislike digressions to editors' personal lives as much as I do) will tolerate this allusion, to the benefit of explanation.

'The Great Beauty' is a 2013 Italian art drama film directed by Paolo Sorrentino, winner of Best Foreign Language Film at the 86th Academy Awards, as well as of the Golden Globe and the BAFTA Award in the same category. Its style is reminiscent of the work of great Italian film directors such as Luchino Visconti and Federico Fellini, with the splendour of photography, the superb psychological investigation and a symbolism that in *La Grande Bellezza* plays a game of mirrors between the stunning beauty of Rome, where the plot is set, and the contradictions of existence, balancing 'the glorious with ordinary human tragedy' (Garrett, 2017).

The protagonist of this game is an ageing socialite and journalist, Jep Gambardella, a libertine, sarcastic and cynical man who, after publishing during his twenties a celebrated novel, *The Human Apparatus*, has immersed himself in a decadent life of parties and futile experiences. Many other eccentric characters gather around Jep, all of them pretending to be fully satisfied with their lives but sharing, in reality, a deep feeling of solitude that dominates an everyday existence 'in which anguish follows joy, … [and] routine and surprise shadow each other' (Garrett, 2017): characters whose energies seem to be consumed in vain.

However, a person remains outside of this futility: a very old nun who works in poverty in Africa, Sister ('Suor') Maria, who is considered a saint.

'La Santa' (as she is often named in the movie) visits Rome after a long time, and since she read and liked Jep's novel, she asks to meet him. Jep's editor arranges a rich dinner with other guests, even if Suor Maria's attendant warns everybody that she has a very rigid diet: her only food are edible roots. At a certain point she disappears from the dinner and in the early morning Jep finds the saint on his terrace, surrounded by a flock of flamingos: they are having some rest, before continuing their migration. At that point Suor Maria asks Jep why he did not write another book. 'I was looking for the great beauty, but I did not find it', he replies. Suor Maria then responds with a touch of spiritual wisdom, explaining why she only eats roots.

SUOR MARIA: Do you know why I only eat roots?
JEP GAMBARDELLA: No... no, why?
SUOR MARIA: Because roots are important.

(La Grande Bellezza, 2013)

She smiles, blows and immediately afterwards, in a scene of pure enchantment, all the flamingos flow away towards the sunrise. At the end of the movie, the saint climbs the steps of a sanctuary, exemplifying her 'roots' of discipline and faith; Jep, on a yacht trip, goes back to the places of his youth and, in the memory of his 'roots', he seems to discover renewed inspiration.

Clearly, by reminding Jep of the importance of roots, 'roots' of any kind, 'la Santa' gives him the symbolic recipe for the *real* great beauty, so as to avoid living in vain. 'Feeding oneself with roots', in order to remember the true meaning of life, implies that 'one does not simply want to be ambitious or dedicated, always seeking, always struggling. One wants friendship and love and spiritual fulfilment' (Garrett, 2017).

2. Risk, *razaqa* and the 'roots of understanding' (*usul al-fiqh*)

La Santa's advice can be addressed also to the actors of contemporary capitalism, a Rome of 'glory' for the rich and 'ordinary human tragedy' for the poor.

Here, in a world of constant competition, where energies are dissipated without caring about long term sustainability, revisiting the social roots of entrepreneurship acquires the meaning of not consuming natural and human resources in vain, so to recognize how the perpetual struggle for wealth becomes worthless and futile if benefits are not shared at a community level, and the 'spiritual fulfilment' of a common welfare is lacking.

Certainly, contemporary capitalism is also a world of change, where remarkable innovations are appearing in the socio-economics of property management, credit provision, as well as in the conceptualization of entrepreneurship.

Only recently have international bodies re-affirmed the necessity to comply with *Sustainable Development Goals* (SDGs), as listed by the United Nations

Resolution of 25 September 2015. But, while a stronger consciousness is emerging about the need for social investments that link profitability with community welfare, property structures and relations are also experiencing deep transformation due to the impact of the new technologies and the digital revolution. The so-called 'sharing economy', with its innovative models of collaborative agency, networking and venture business, is radically changing our way to interact in the market, if not even our way to think about work, about ownership, economic value and, in the end, about our social fabric.

Navigating this changing economic and social identity represents a risky enterprise that can be undertaken only by setting sail from sound roots.

In this regard, one should preliminarily note that if 'the Latin *resecare, resicum, risicum, riscus* are the direct precedents for the Italian *risicare*, meaning "to dare", ... a more ancient etymology of the word "risk" ... remains uncertain' (Cattelan, 2014, p. 2). In fact, although the Latin forms 'may have derived from the Greek ριζα, meaning "root", "stone", "cut of the firm land", which was also used as a metaphor for a "difficulty to avoid in the sea" ', the origin of the word also 'seems to find (at least phonetically) an equivalent in the Arabic *rizq* (رزق), from which the word "risk" may derive too' (*ibidem*).

The significance of 'roots' as a symbolic means of security from the perils of everyday life, the ones that may also dissipate the efforts of genuine economic work, acquires in the Arabic notion of *rizq* a connotation of fundamental significance to understand the ultimate sense of entrepreneurship in Islam, and its relevance for a functioning community. In fact,

> if *rizq* on the one side expresses the idea of 'fortune', 'profit', 'gain', 'blessing' ..., on the other side ... this fortune is depicted and conceived in Arabic language in the particular sense of 'a sustenance that is given by God for livelihood' (Wehr, 1994). Accordingly, the verb *razaqa* is always used in the sense of 'God providing somebody with means of subsistence'; الرزاق *ar-Razzaq*, 'the Maintainer', 'the Provider' is one of the ninety-nine attributes of God; and مرزوق *marzuq* is the 'person blessed by God', thus 'fortunate', 'prosperous', 'successful'.
>
> (Cattelan, 2014, p. 3)

So, if good work leads to deserved profits, the 'root' of these gains necessarily comes from assuming the *risk* of an economic activity whose potential outcomes are provided by Allah as God's blessing (*rizq*). At the same time, 'good work' is not without responsibility towards others (as if seeking gain would be a perpetual struggle of competition): on the contrary, Islamic entrepreneurship is governed by the principle *al-kharaj bi-l-daman*, that is to say, *profit* (in the sense of what is someone's due, what someone needs, deserves: see Wehr, 1994) *relates to liability*, i.e. the risk of potential loss for which he also becomes responsible and has to give 'security' (from the root ضمن *damina*) to others.

As well-known, to 'secure' justice and sustenance for all His believers that pursue a legitimate profit, God has provided clear Guidance through the Revelation of *Shari'ah*.

And, if one broadens the interpretation followed in these pages from economic to legal science, the 'importance of roots' leads the reasoning immediately to the 'science of understanding' *par excellence* in Islam, the discipline of *fiqh*, with its foundational 'principles', 'roots', the *usul al-fiqh*, and in particular the Holy *Qur'an*.

As the primary source of the *Shari'ah*, the *Qur'an* offers solid 'roots' for the performance of entrepreneurial activities balancing available resources, human needs and desires, so not to 'devour' each other's wealth and struggle 'in vain' by transforming the market into a place of scarcity, division and competition, where the 'glory' of the rich and the 'tragedy' of the poor shadow each other.

> Q. 2:275 – Those who consume *riba* [interest, usury] will not stand [on the Day of Resurrection] except as one stands who is being eaten by Satan into insanity. That is because they say, 'Trade is [just] like interest', whereas Allah has permitted trading and forbidden *riba*. [...] (see also Q. 2:276–281).
>
> Q. 3:130 – O you who believe! Devour not *riba*, doubling and multiplying [the sum lent], but fear Allah; that you may [really] prosper.
>
> Q. 4:29 – O you who believe! Do not consume one another's wealth unjustly but only in [lawful] business among you by mutual good-will. And do not kill yourselves [nor kill one another]. Surely, Allah is Most Merciful to you!

The precepts that can be found in the *ayat* above are explanatory of a specific conception of the market as a place of mutual cooperation and common welfare, where human beings' lives are not intended to be spent 'in vain', by consuming one another's wealth in the meaningless search for unjust profit (on the idea of *riba* as illegitimate gain, see Saleh, 1992), but where solid 'roots' can guarantee prosperity for everybody.

It is in this light that the notion of entrepreneurship, with its social and human value, can be fully comprehended in the domain of Islamic economics, and be explored with regard to its all-encompassing implications for the current evolution of an Islamic financial market 'well-rooted' in the *Shari'ah*.

3. Introducing this book: the meaning of 'sharing' in Islamic entrepreneurship (Part I of the volume)

The importance of the roots of *Shari'ah* and God's sustenance to understand the social dimension of Islamic finance constitutes precisely the conceptual background of this book.

In particular, the originality of this volume lies in the contextualization of Islamic finance within the transformative nature of the contemporary global economy where

- if, on the one side, stronger attention is emerging with regard to issues of sustainability, community development and social impact,
- on the other side, a radical transformation is affecting market relations, due to the digital revolution and the new opportunities offered by the so-called 'sharing economy' in the realm of financial services.

Investigating Islamic social finance at the intersection of this concurrent phenomena has not been an easy task, and my editorial work has benefitted immensely from the contributions by all the talented scholars involved in this project.

In fact, if contemporary Islamic finance has necessarily to be studied within the broader dynamics of evolution that belong to the global economy, its paradigm does hold distinctive 'roots' in the *Shari'ah* (as expression of God's benevolence) which *substitute* (and not simply rectify: see Cattelan, 2013) those of conventional capitalism in the conceptualization of the market as a socio-economic community. It is by adhering to the substantive spirit of *Shari'ah* in the understanding and the application of Islamic finance (so to 'pave the road for developing financial products that may be marketed more effectively to Muslims and non-Muslims alike': El-Gamal, 2006, p. 25) that this volume has been conceived.

In particular, Part I collects four essays that analyse the social dimension of entrepreneurship from an Islamic perspective, highlighting the extent to which the rationales of 'sharing', in terms of abundance, distribution and cooperation, affect the conceptualization of the market in Islam as a socio-economic community of shared prosperity.

Entrepreneurship in Islam is a means to achieve common welfare, where the exercise of human freedom is 'rooted' in the recognition of God's absolute ownership on everything and the ontological unity (*tawhid*) of the creation. This ontological unity represents as well the core epistemological instrument that can nourish the effective implementation of Islamic social finance as direct result of God's sustenance. Prof. Choudhury, Dr Pratiwi and Prof. Hossain provide in Chapter 2 a scholarly investigation of this epistemic approach, moving from the abstraction of the wellbeing function in Islam to its quantitative analysis through statistical data, hence giving solid theoretical foundations to the discussion.

Within the *tawhidi* framework, by assuming the role of the human being as God's representative (*khalifah*) on earth, Dr Atiq-ur-Rehman focuses on the fundamental interrelation between the objectives (*maqasid*) of *Shari'ah* and Islamic social finance. He describes the *maqasid* (securing of faith; protection of life; safeguard of intellect; security of progeny; preservation of wealth) as the pillars of human welfare (*falah*) and, correspondingly, he specifies which provisions are upheld by Islam to this aim (Chapter 3).

The core rationale of shared prosperity and the notion of risk-sharing inherent in the Islamic value system are later explored by Prof. Charilaos Mertzanis in relation to the complementarity of communities, markets and states to achieve efficient economic organization. In this regard, Chapter 4 investigates social capital and collaborative governance in relation to a decision-making approach where 'sharing' has the potential to foster the social impact of entrepreneurship.

To conclude Part I and the theoretical study of the social dimension of entrepreneurship in Islam, I look in Chapter 5 at the sharing economy (as the new 'text' of market relations brought about by the digital revolution) by comparing the different meaning-*s* that 'sharing' holds in the 'languages' of conventional capitalism and Islamic economics, and more precisely when parameters of scarcity, division and competition are replaced with assumptions of abundance (thanks to the balance, *mizan*, between available resources, human needs and desires), distribution and cooperation among economic agents.

By 'rooting' the understanding of Islamic social finance in this background, the volume then proceeds to the operative implementation of strategies of shared prosperity, to which Part II is dedicated.

4. Feeding the global economy on Islamic social finance (Part II)

Moving from the understanding of the market in Islam as a place of shared prosperity to the applicative dimensions of this conception, Part II of the volume deals with relevant cases and instruments of social impact entrepreneurship, connecting current trends in the financial market to *Shari'ah*-rooted strategies for local and community development.

In Chapter 6, Prof. Mohamed Ariff offers a comprehensive outline of the global market of *sukuk* as certificates for fund mobilization grounded on asset-backed debt financing, highlighting their related advantages in terms of financial stability, limitation of debt overhang and infrastructural development. Accordingly, the contribution demonstrates the importance of *sukuk* as an alternative to lending interest-based financial tools, through a shared development grounded in the real economy.

Issues of fund mobilization represent the core topic of Chapter 7, where Dr Houssem eddine Bedoui and Dr Rami Abdelkafi look at the challenge of fundraising to promote an effective model of social finance able to foster Islamic entrepreneurship. To this objective, after discussing in general the problem of fundraising in the private sector, their attention goes to the potential of crowdfunding platforms (via donation, reward, debt and equity models) to unlock Islamic entrepreneurship within the growing sector of the sharing economy.

The domain of the sharing economy, of which crowdfunding constitutes one of the most popular examples, is later contextualized by Fatima Z. Bensar and Gonzalo Rodríguez in the broader paradigm shift that the financial system, in general, and the Islamic eco-system, in particular (as part of the global economy), are experiencing today through the latest developments of the realm of FinTech – financial technology (Chapter 8). This paradigm shift is discussed in relation to crowdfunding; online *zakat* and *waqf*; Islamic wealth management; and the applications of the blockchain technology in Islamic finance (e.g. smart contracts, identity authentication and cryptocurrencies).

The notion of shared prosperity as the substantive spirit of Islamic social finance also sheds light on the contents of the four final chapters collected in the volume.

In Chapter 9, Dr Marianella Piratti and I investigate Islamic green finance as a significant market innovation both in the light of environmental sustainability and *Shari'ah* standards. To this aim, after referring to the Islamic tradition on environment protection, its principles, precepts and key institutes as 'roots' for Islamic green finance, the contribution focuses on the research agenda of contemporary Islamic economics, and depicts green *sukuk* and *awqaf* as further 'branches' of Islamic social finance that are able to match objectives of sustainable development with *Shari'ah*-compliance criteria.

Later on, Dr Atiq-ur-Rehman examines microfinance for household enterprises as one of the most effective strategies for poverty eradication and rural development. In Chapter 10 he suggests that some persistent deficiencies in this domain (i.e. insufficient entrepreneurial skills of the recipients; use of funds for purposes which are not related to income-generating activities; danger of a debt trap when the borrower is not able to repay the debt; scarce impact on the poorest among the poor) can be overcome by *salam* financing, which is presented as a viable tool for securing the social objective of micro-credit and as a strategy of financial inclusion.

To fulfil the purpose of social entrepreneurship through solid 'roots', Germán Rodríguez-Moreno looks at the possible convergence between two traditional institutes of Islamic law and economics, namely *waqf* and *takaful*, to foster mutual participation, cooperation and shared prosperity. In particular, Chapter 11 critically evaluates: (i) the concept of *tabarru'*, which is central to understand *takaful*; (ii) the principles governing *waqf*, particularly those of charitable purpose and irrevocability; (iii) the principle of profit-sharing in a relationship of this nature; (iv) the regulatory requirements of a *takaful* undertaking; and (v) the corporate governance underlying the relationship between *waqf* and *takaful*.

To conclude, Chapter 12 by Prof. Mohd Ma'Sum Billah deals with *zakat* as a divine obligatory tax in Islam which is imposed on the wealthier and is aimed at poverty eradication and shared prosperity. More precisely, Prof. Billah argues that *zakat*, when conceptualized within the general objectives of Islamic law (*maqasid al-Shari'ah*), can be seen as an instrument for general human welfare for all the members of the community, where economic development is fostered also through micro-entrepreneurial mechanisms with an underlying humanitarian impact. In this light, the study indicates the mechanisms to facilitate the implementation of *zakat* in relation to entrepreneurial objectives also through cooperatives, *takaful* and capacity building, and provides some final recommendations for a model of poverty eradication compliant with the *maqasid al-Shari'ah*.

By looking at the 'roots' of Islamic social finance (Part I) and by nurturing its 'branches' (Part II) within the transformative nature of the contemporary global economy, I trust that this volume will offer valuable conceptual tools to the readers, so to provide an illuminating reference for researchers, practitioners and policy-makers dealing with the challenges of a market where not only is diversity being perceived as a value to be fostered, but also as an important opportunity for a more inclusive welfare for everybody.

Indeed, to feed this future of shared prosperity, sound roots will be of primary importance.

References

Cattelan, V. (2013) *Shari'ah* economics as autonomous paradigm: theoretical approach and operative outcomes. *Journal of Islamic Perspective on Science, Technology and Society.* **1**(1), pp. 3–11.

Cattelan, V. (2014) In the Name of God: managing risk in Islamic finance. *Eabh Working Papers Series* [online]. Paper no. 14–07. Available from: www.eabh.info/publications/eabh-papers [Accessed 14 September 2017].

El-Gamal, M.A. (2006) *Islamic Finance: Law, Economics, and Practice.* Cambridge and New York: Cambridge University Press.

Garrett, D. (2017) *The Great Beauty*, an exceptional film by Paolo Sorrentino, starring Toni Servillo. *Offscreen* [online]. **21**(8). Available from: http://offscreen.com/view/la-grande-bellezza-paolo-sorrentino [Accessed 28 September 2017].

La Grande Bellezza (2013) Directed by Paolo Sorrentino. [DVD]. Indigo Film, Medusa Film, Babe Films, Pathé.

Saleh, N.A. (1992, 2nd ed.) *Unlawful Gain and Legitimate Profit in Islamic Law: Riba, Gharar and Islamic Banking.* London: Graham & Trotman Ltd.

United Nations (2015) *Transforming Our World: The 2030 Agenda for Sustainable Development.* Resolution adopted by the General Assembly on 25 September 2015, A/RES/70/1.

Wehr, H. (1994) *A Dictionary of Modern Written Arabic*, ed. by J.M. Cowan (IV ed.). Wiesbaden: Harrassowitz; Urbana, IL: Spoken Language Services.

Part I

Islam, shared prosperity and the market as socio-economic community

2 From the ontology of *tawhid* to Islamic social finance

Conceptualization and application

*Masudul Alam Choudhury, Ari Pratiwi
and Mohammad Shahadat Hossain*

1. Background, methodology and objective of this chapter

Islamic financing methodology, like all other areas of economic knowledge, is deeply entrenched in moral and ethical issues. But what is the primal premise upon which all moral and ethical issues behind Islamic economics and finance are grounded and from which a universal and unique constructive worldview can be derived? Such a worldview gives shape and form to two aspects of interdependent knowledge. On the one side, the realm of abstractions that establish foundational thought about the nature of reasoning, mind and the universe, evolve together in a synchrony of unity. In Islam, the universal unity, *tawhid*, as the monotheistic belief in the Oneness of God and the emergent law of unity of knowledge of all the creation depends on God's Will and Grand Design. On the other side, the applied perspective of such a foundational understanding of the unity between all things by the underlying meaning of *tawhid* takes the form of participatory unity of being and becoming by organic interaction between the good things of life, and the converse is the opposite case. This means to derive, construct and explain the generality and details of the world-system that we study as being organically interdependent in its variety of particular issues and problems.

These two perspectives of the unity of knowledge universally and uniquely characterize the holism of abstraction and application and then acquire a crucial methodological value in Islamic economics and finance, and consequently Islamic social finance.

In contrast to the Western worldview and its secular approach, that disaggregate economic theory and practice from the unity of the world-system, Islam recognizes the *tawhid* of God's creation as the core epistemological foundation of both abstract and operative knowledge. In this sense, a radical distinction denotes the Western and Islamic methodologies in all their details, as well as in their explanation of the universe and its structures, where the analytical investigation of such details is pursued in the light of the inherent differentiations between the two worldviews.

Our objective in this chapter is to explain the substantive meaning of morality and ethics governing the universe in reference to the foundation of the unity (*tawhid*) of knowledge in Islam and outline its consequent impact on the empirical dimension of Islamic social finance.

In particular, the discussion will embrace a method called inter-causal relations between interdependent variables of a vector of selected ethically induced variables. Such interdependencies (that make every one of the variables circularly endogenous, showing pervasive complementarities) are based on the philosophy of *consilience* as unity of knowledge (Wilson, 1998). Examples here will be made with regard to charity as an attribute of sharing in financing the target grassroots of the poor, the needy and the underprivileged by the wealthy who have the responsibility to relate with and address the problem of social deprivation. The interdependent relations of such endogenously circular inter-causality based on the epistemic worldview of consilience convey the ethical nature of consilience between the charity variable (that plays its financing role for the ethical purpose at the grassroots) and among others (who must extend such ethical responsibility towards establishing an equalitarian society). The imminent meaning of morality and ethics in respect of the methodological worldview of the unity of knowledge feeds into the characterization leading to the conceptual and quantitative measurement of the objective criterion that arises from the premise of unity of knowledge. We name this objective criterion as the *wellbeing function* (see later in Section 2.4).

Wellbeing is the objective criterion of the holistic ontological design of monotheism in terms of its principle of organic unity of knowledge inducing the generality and particular of the world-system. The example of the former type is the universal ontology of monotheism. The example of the latter type is the field of ethics, economics, finance, science and society (Choudhury, 2007). The evaluation of wellbeing takes place in the interactive, integrative and evolutionary learning dimensions of knowledge, space and time. It goes through two stages of its evaluation. First, wellbeing is expressed as an abstraction that induces in its representative variables the parameter of unity of knowledge. The second stage is the quantitative empirical estimation and simulation of the abstract functional form of the wellbeing criterion.

Accordingly, in this chapter, these two steps and all the implications of the monotheistic unity of knowledge with regard to Islamic social finance are studied in a combined way, through the concept of *wellbeing*. Such a concept as objective social criterion is also employed by Amartya Sen (1987), who avoids the use of the term 'welfare' in his deontological theory of ethics.

By employing the wellbeing function as objective criterion derived from the *tawhidi* methodological worldview, this chapter is divided into two parts. In Part I, formulation of the abstract type of the wellbeing function is done in the light of the monotheistic (*tawhidi*) meaning of organic unity of knowledge and its embedding in the variables of the generalized and particular sub-systems of the world-system as background for Islamic social finance. Later on, Part II deals with the quantitative empirical part that translates the abstraction of Part I into statistical model-selection for estimation and simulation with the use of statistical data. The intent is to show how ethics (now meaning organic unity of inter-variable causality) is embedded in the study of Islamic social finance as endogenous (systemic) phenomenon.

Because of the central endogenous role of charity variables as ethical ones among Islamic financing instruments, we show all the grassroots development variables to be functionally induced by the non-parametric nature of ethical consciousness. However, we also show in the conceptual and empirical forms of the objective criterion function that the ethical non-parametric variable and its induction of the observed variables are quantitatively estimable in a mathematical system-model. We formalize this system-model by its epistemological foundations of the ethical conception in the *Qur'an* and the *Sunnah*. In a nutshell, the conceptual form explains the underlying methodology, while the quantitative formulation of the system-model gives the objective criterion of wellbeing its empirical form.

2. Part I. Grounding Islamic social finance on the unity of knowledge in Islam: an outline of the *tawhidi* framework and its scope in formalizing the wellbeing function

2.1. *The current debility of Islamic economics and finance methodology*

The field of Islamic economics and finance as we have inherited from the mainstream background has sorrowfully failed in its conceptual and applied creativity. The main reason for this debility relates to its incapability to lay the essential groundwork of a moral and ethical transformation from a methodological perspective. In fact, Islamic economics and finance in its moral and ethical context has regrettably relied upon mainstream theories and methodologies and their underlying assumptions based on Western concepts of economic rationality and culture. But such prevailing understanding is contrary and distinct from the endogenous nature of the Islamic theory of knowledge and its application in the construction and practice of the unified world-system both in general and in particular.[1]

This chapter will prove in substantive terms that the indispensable foundation of the Oneness of God explained by the primal ontology of the unity of monotheism and the world-system termed as *tawhid* in the *Qur'an* has not been coherently understood and applied by the promoters of Islamic economics and finance. Thus the present emergent Islamic economic and finance methodology has not been able to embrace a revolutionary shift beyond its own laws, structures and formalism and into the search for the socio-scientific theory of 'everything' (Barrow, 1991) in the *tawhidi* framework.

Consequently, because of the absence of the methodological foundation of *tawhid* as primal ontological law and its explanatory functioning in the world-system, the conception of Islamic ethics and the promotion of a socially oriented Islamic finance has remained an exogenous phenomenon in Islamic intellection and the Muslim world-system. In the same way, the endogenous nature of moral and ethical embedding in every systemic holism of the *Qur'an* has remained subdued. On this missing understanding of the primal ontological law of *tawhid* and the world-system, Auda (2008) writes that a systemic understanding of Islamic law ought to be recast around the attributes of systemic features. These features comprise 'cognitive nature of systems, wholeness, openness, interrelated hierarchy, multi-dimensionality, and purposefulness' (p. 45).

Hence, the missing episteme of the primal ontological law of *tawhid* as unity of monotheistic knowledge in Islamic methodology has caused polemical blunders in formalism, model building and data mining (Choudhury, 2016a and 2016b; Choudhury and Hoque, 2018). For instance, the databank on macroeconomic indicators of Muslim countries provided by SESRIC[2] consists of interpolated and extrapolated figures, with the results of econometric estimation turning out to be incoherent for any analytical and policy study on *ummah* reconstruction. Likewise, the study by Choudhury and Hoque (2018) has detected an incongruous case of constant *zakat/waqf*-ratios throughout Malaysia.[3] This is an illogical statistical case.

Thus, the foundational issue of the correct Islamic methodology premised on *tawhid* as the primal ontological law of unity of knowledge is indispensable for projecting the correct Islamic methodological worldview in 'everything'. This worldview encompasses the methodologically derived formalism, the model of unity of knowledge in connection with the unified nature of the world-system, and the derived objective criterion across learning processes that are generated by inter-causality between variables and entities. Altogether, the methodological entirety spans the continuum of knowledge, space and time in multi-dimensions. The entire methodological formalism can be explained in the light of the precepts of morality and ethical values as these are formed and discursively derived from the *tawhidi* episteme[4] of the unity of knowledge and the nature of the unified world-system both in its generality and its particulars.

In this chapter, as elucidated elsewhere (Choudhury, 2006), the *tawhidi* methodological worldview is explained not only to advance the ineluctable foundation of the divine unity of knowledge as the primal ontological law. The singular *tawhidi* precept of the meta-scientific methodological worldview also presents a unique and universal way of argumentation and explanation in the meta-scientific inquiry. Within this extensive inquiry, Islamic economics, finance, science and society assume their distinctive character. The distinctive centrepiece of *tawhid* as the primal ontological law and its powerful explanatory nature in the world-system contrary to the modern approach to the *Shari'ah* can be read from Hallaq's (2009) words as follows:

> Yet, whereas pre-modern *usul al-fiqh* emerged out of a constellation of legal communities that shared a particular vision of the universe and a highly integrated legal episteme, any conception of a modern *usul* theory faces the challenge of division along lines that are local, regional, ethnic, national and etatist – all of which stand in opposition to the meaning of Muslim community, at least that community which survives in the modern Muslim imagination.
>
> (p. 501)

This extract summarizes the difference between the eschatological meaning of reality in accordance with the *tawhidi* approach and the systemic divided tradition that characterizes the modern perspective on *Shari'ah*.

2.2. *Definitions of critical terms in the epistemology of the unity* (tawhid) *of knowledge*

In this chapter, the substantive meaning of morality and ethics and the conceptual and quantitative formalism and evaluation of the objective criterion of the wellbeing function need some preliminary critical explanations, through which it becomes possible to embrace the Islamic methodological worldview emanating from the epistemology of the unity (*tawhid*) of knowledge. Accordingly, this epistemic foundation then causes the moral and ethical embedding in what is a *tawhidi*-based Islamic economy (Choudhury and Rahim, 2016), and Islamic social finance as its concretization.

The following paragraphs outline some of the critical terminologies underlying key methodological concepts that are necessary for the understanding of the moral and ethical embedding nature of Islamic economics and finance, as well as its conceptual background and applied nature in Islamic social finance.

The methodology and formal characterization emerge from the unique and exclusive primal ontological law of *tawhid* as the foundation of monotheistic oneness and its meaning and functioning in the construction of the unified world-system in generality and details. Then, Islamic economics and finance become particular fields of the generalized methodological study, and Islamic social finance their direct result in applied economics, where morality and ethics are generalized worldviews in their methodological embedding of the extensive universe of meta-science. Following this approach, we first take the sequence of necessary definitions and explanations to outline the complete methodological worldview of unity of knowledge according to *tawhid* and its application to the world-system (Section 2.3). Next, we will treat the emergent formalism as an expression of the meta-science of primal ontological law of *tawhid* and its application to the generality and details of the world-system. Here we will define the wellbeing function (Section 2.4) and its methodological evaluation by means of inter-variable circular causation equations. Third, we complete the methodology within an intra-system learning process (Section 2.5).

2.3. Tawhid *as the primal ontological law of unity of knowledge* (consilience) *in 'everything'*

We denote the monotheistic oneness of divine knowledge as a *supercardinal topology* (Maddox, 1970; Rucker, 1982). Briefly, the supercardinal space is a mathematical topology of completeness of knowledge. Its dimension is *unbounded* but *closed in an unbounded open space*. These properties of supercardinality enable mathematical analysis in abstract space of a substantive meaning of knowledge between Truth (T) and Falsehood (F), where Ω defines Truth (T), Falsehood (F) and the temporarily *undecidable* by human understanding (U).

Ω thus encompasses (T,F,U) and all explainable relations. Such a wide class of relations is denoted by G[Ω(T,F,U)]. The *topological properties* are,

(i) $T_i \in T \Rightarrow \cup_i T_i \in T$; $\cap_j T_j \in T$; $\cup_i \cap_j (T_i,T_j) \neq \varphi \in T$
(ii) $F_i \in F \Rightarrow \cup_i F_i \in F$; $\cap_j F_j \in F$; $\cup_i \cap_j (F_i,F_j) \neq \varphi \in F$; $\lim_\theta [\cap_j F_j \in F] = \varphi \in F$; $\lim_\theta [\cup_i \cap_j (F_i,F_j)] = \varphi \in F$; '$\theta$' denotes learning derived from the episteme of unity of knowledge. 'i,j' are denumerable finitely or infinitely
(iii) $\lim_\theta [U(\theta)] = T$ or F; followed by the properties (i)–(ii)
(iv) $T \cup F \subset \Omega$
(v) $T \cap F = \varphi \subset \Omega$
(vi) $T \cup \cap F = F \cup \cap T = \varphi \subset \Omega$

The properties (i)–(vi) are repeated for the following case respecting f(T,F) and G(f(T,F)) in the limiting case of discursive learning by knowledge-flows, 'θ'. By virtue of property (vi),

(vii) $H(T,F) = g(T) \cup f(F) \subseteq \Omega$, along with all the relational sets of T and F
(viii) $g(T) \cap f(F) = \varphi \subset \Omega$
(ix) $Q[T \cup \cap F] = Q[F \cup \cap T] = Q_1(T) \cup \cap Q_2(F)] = Q_1(F) \cup \cap Q_2(T) = \varphi \subset \Omega$

The important inferences we derive from the supercardinal definitional formalism on topology are first that any kind of relationship in respect of (T,F,U) denoted by 'θ' in Ω and thus in G(Ω) forms a topology by its distinct meanings corresponding to (T,F,U). Second, property (i) implies that pervasive complementarity exists only in the case of Truth. Morality being T, any of its subset T_i is an ethic. Thereby, both T and its relational subsets form pervasively complementary domains of meaningful attributes in the case of the epistemic operation of the *tawhidi* law denoted by Ω.

The inter-relational nature of 'θ' in Ω mapped by functions H,g,f,Q_1,Q_2 forms the compound functions of the type, $\Omega \rightarrow S \rightarrow L$: '$\theta$'. By extension, as '$\theta$' embeds worldly variables there arises the symbolic representations $x(\theta)$ as vector, matrix, tensor and other mathematical forms (Kupka and Peixoto, 1993). The tuple $(\theta, x(\theta))$ spans the dimensions of knowledge and space that is induced by knowledge. Besides, if the knowledge-induced spanning is taken over time of intertemporal occurrence of events then the continuum of events spanning the knowledge, space and time dimensions is described by E = $E(\theta, x(\theta), t(\theta))$. The embodiment of '$\theta$' in E(..) explains the moral and ethical nature of an interactive and integrative knowledge formation by way of $\Omega \rightarrow S \rightarrow L$: '$\theta$'. The interactions and integration between variables and their relations are further extended by evolutionary learning as system and cybernetic processes.

2.4. Deriving the unity of knowledge from the ontological law of tawhid: the wellbeing function

The nature and structure of deriving knowledge from the primal ontological law of *tawhidi* unity of knowledge can be now formalized as follows:

$$[\Omega \quad \rightarrow \quad S] \quad \rightarrow \quad L:\theta^* \rightarrow \quad \theta \quad \rightarrow \quad x(\theta) \quad \textbf{(1)}$$

primal ontology	primal epistemology	discourse with the learned	functional epistemology	functional ontology

$$[\Omega,S] \quad \rightarrow \quad \theta^* \quad \rightarrow \quad \theta \quad \rightarrow \quad (\theta,x(\theta))$$

primal ontology of *tawhid* as law of unity of knowledge (consilience)	$\rightarrow$	derivation of knowledge from the primal ontology of unity of knowledge of abstraction	$\rightarrow$	construction of the unified world-system according to the episteme of unity of knowledge (pervasive inter-variable complementarities manifest by interaction and integration in discourse)

The principle of pervasive complementarities explained by the multivariate inter-causality of organic relations between them reflects the implication of unity of knowledge. In analytical form this phenomenon is explained by the system of organism relations generated by the embedding of the relational knowledge-flow parameter, 'θ'. In the *Qur'anic* meaning of monotheistic consilience, working its moral and ethical meaning in the world-system, the principle of pervasive complementarities is explained by the verse Q. 36:36.[5]

We write the formalism of systemic continuum of unity of knowledge of the *tawhidi* ontological law functioning on the world-system as follows in continuation of expression **(1)**: W(.) denotes the well-defined conceptual form of the wellbeing function induced by 'θ' by way of continuity and openness of the evolutionary learning events denoted by $\{E(\theta,x(\theta),t(\theta))\}$. Deriving W(.) as the abstracto-empirical version of knowledge induction involves the following methodological stages:

$$\text{Expression (1)} \ldots \rightarrow \text{Simulate }_{(\theta,x(\theta),t(\theta))}[W(\theta,x(\theta),t(\theta))], \qquad \textbf{(2)}$$

signifying degrees of inter-variable complementarity

Subject to circular causation relations explaining endogenously organic inter-variable relations,

$$x_i(\theta) = fj(\theta,x_j(\theta),t(\theta)), \quad x(\theta)\text{-vector} = (x_i,x_j)[\theta]; \text{ with } (i,j) = 1,2,..,n \text{ (say)},$$
$$i \neq j. \qquad \textbf{(3)}$$

$$\theta = F(x(\theta),t(\theta)). \qquad \textbf{(4)}$$

'F' and 'f' are appropriate estimable functions. We use the natural logarithmic forms for these functions.

This expression signifies the quantitative estimable version of the *wellbeing function* as W(.). Expressions **(1)–(2)** give the ontological formative ground-work for the development of the objective criterion of this holism in the form of the wellbeing function. This epistemic expression is shown in **(1)–(2)**. The quantitative empirical expression of the wellbeing function that is viable to statistical evaluation is shown by equation **(3)**. This system of equations establishes the inter-variable causality to study complementarities of unity of knowledge embedded in the variables. Expression **(4)** is the quantitative empirical representation of the first stage abstract form of the wellbeing function W(.), such that W(.) and '$\theta = F(x(\theta))$' expressions are monotonic positive transformation of each other in the same selected variables, $\{x(\theta)\}$. While W(.) is of the conceptual form; 'θ'-function is the quantitative approxi-mation of W(.), the conceptual form of the wellbeing criterion. The wellbeing criterion is commonly referred to in the Islamic literature as *maslahah*.

Now we derive some important inferences from expressions **(2)–(4)** in connection with expression **(1)**. First, these expressions ending with expression **(4)** relate to a comprehensive process of intra- and inter-systemic learning either taken singly or within a group of several systems combined together.

The learning process is fully characterized by the epistemological deriv-ation of (θ^*, θ) by interaction **(I)** denoting discourse leading to integration **(I)** (consensus) and waiting for further change in these characterizations by evo-lution **(E)** across systems in $\{\theta\}$-induced learning processes.

The **IIE**-learning process (as an abbreviation of the previous terms) depicts the properties of process-oriented continuous learning in the *tawhidi* holistic worldview. The **IIE**-learning process thus forms the entire dynamics of the evolutionary learning process over history as the locus of events, as defined earlier. We thus go into the third stage of the complete methodology within intra-system learning process.

2.5. *Evolutionary learning and sustained continuity of the IIE-processes*

In the previous expressions, the stages **(1)–(4)** repeat themselves at subsequent events in an evolutionary continuum, from which an evaluation of the wellbeing function can be made by estimation followed by simulation as in the formula

$$\text{evaluate }_{(\theta, x(\theta), t(\theta))}[W(\theta, x(\theta), t(\theta))], \tag{5}$$

that signifies degrees of inter-variable complementarities as evidence of the unity of knowledge attained in degrees of evolutionary learning.

Expression **(5)** is evaluated subject to circular causation relations explaining endogenously organically inter-variable relations at each evaluation point, i.e. at each event in knowledge, space and time dimensions. These circular causation relations of degrees of organic inter-variable complementarities are the following ones:

$$x_i(\theta) = fj(\theta, \mathbf{x}_j(\theta), t(\theta)), \ \mathbf{x}(\theta)\text{-vector} = (x_i, \mathbf{x}_j)[\theta]; \tag{6}$$

with $(i,j) = 1,2,..,n$ (say), $i \neq j$.

The quantitative empirical form of the monotonic transformation of the well-being function is denoted by

$$\theta = F(\mathbf{x}(\theta), t(\theta)) \tag{7}$$

Events, $E(\theta, \mathbf{x}(\theta), t(\theta))$ are repeated in the knowledge, space and time dimensions. When time is replaced by cross-sectional data and questionnaire survey, information can be used in the event-wise evaluation. It is also possible to inter-mesh time-series and cross-sectional/survey data for comparative evaluation purposes. The inter-meshing method is explained later on.

The historiography (**HH**) of events in every case of time-series, cross-sectional data and surveys with simulated changes in the data is defined in continuity and well-definition of inter-variable causal relations across knowledge, space and time dimensions as shown in Figure 2.1.

The complete representation in respect of the *tawhidi* methodological worldview in its primal ontological state and worldly application in the evaluation and simulated moral construction of the generality and particulars of the world-system under study, and then towards Islamic ethical finance, is explained in Figure 2.1. This figure encapsulates the epistemic meaning of the unity of knowledge and its consilience relationship with the world-system in terms of the Foucauldian definition of 'episteme' (see note 4) in his architecture of knowledge and its applications. The precept of morality and ethicality in reference to its system relational worldview of organic unity of being and becoming in social construct is also summarized in Figure 2.1. Morality and ethics as systemic organic relations of unity of knowledge exhibited in terms of inter-causal relations are reflected in every part of the unified understanding. These take the form of unity of knowledge by integrating the *a priori* and *a posteriori* reasoning. Such systemic and ontological unification between *a priori* and *a posteriori* reasoning annuls the Kantian form of heteronomy of divisiveness and dualism (Bhaskar, 1978).

Figure 2.1 furthermore points out that the events as Signs of Allah[6] are continuous in knowledge, space and time dimensions. Therefore, while moving into the greater subtlety of truth and reality arising from the primal ontological law $[\Omega,S]$, the knowledge that is supercardinal, as explained earlier, remains relative and in the **IIE**-learning process to the limit of human extent of acquiring full and complete comprehension. This is not to say that the primal ontological law remains in process dynamics. Rather, it is the extent of its knowing capability subjected to the limits of worldly knowledge that makes $[\Omega,S]$ the continuing experience in the learning processes. Unless this inference is upheld within the *tawhidi* methodology of epistemic oneness, each event, and thus Signs of Allah will remain discontinuously isolated. The

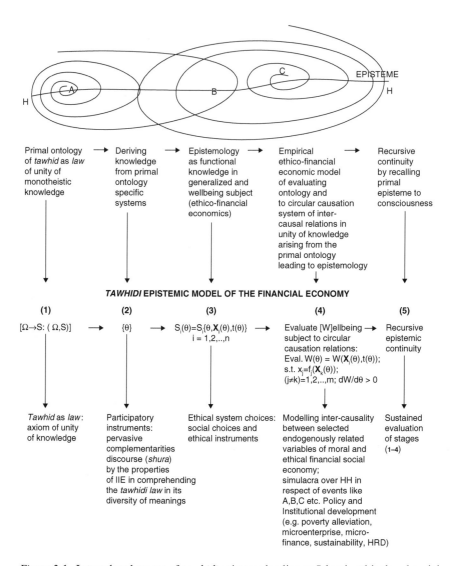

Figure 2.1. Interrelated stages of *tawhidi* episteme leading to Islamic ethical and social finance

continuity of events as Signs of Allah would also remain disjointed, and hence so in the oneness of evolutionary learning. This would be contradictory to the epistemic ontological law, and thereby, to the entire *tawhidi* methodology prevailing in 'everything'.

The continuous linkages between one event and other ones, intra- and inter- systems, are reflected via the route of simulacra of evolutionary changes in {θ} at the end of a process. The simulated level of evaluated knowledge function as wellbeing (*maslahah*) advances the continuous level of conscious understanding of unity of knowledge between *tawhid* and the world-system. The consequent level of acquired knowledge of *tawhid* causes the continuous reawakening of the primal ontological law of *tawhid* in the world-system. The *tawhidi* worldview is thus changed (raised or diminished) in human intellection, and thereby, in relation to the emergent details of the world-system. In earlier works (Choudhury, 2006) on *tawhidi* methodology a persistent limit was present in not allowing for the overall process (expressions **(1)**– **(4)**) of the *tawhidi* abstraction and empiricism to be interrelated and continuous in the historiography **HH** as in Figure 2.1. **HH(θ)** – now induced by its evolutionary learning dynamics of {θ} – is the holistic trajectory of the entire ontological learning space of the *tawhid*.[7] But in the incessantly evolutionary learning universe the incompleteness of abstracto-empirical human consciousness must place the supercardinal knowledge of [Ω,S] subjected to human limitations.

The inherent nature of continuity of the organic relationship among all things in the light of the primal ontological law of oneness is the essential nature of the historiography **HH(θ)**. Thereby, morality and ethics, as of θ∈[Ω,S], expound the permanent nature of 'everything' by the manifestation of inter-causal organic complementary relations between variables.

Formally, we represent the epistemic derivation of a generalized model of ethicized events by the details of Figure 2.1. The circular causation system of inter-variable endogenous relations resembles Myrdal's social causation model (Toner, 1999). The whole process-based orientation of the **IIE** characterization resembles the model of social becoming as a dialectical knowledge-centred learning; but with the substantive difference of evolutionary convergences[8] under the impact of the praxis of *tawhidi* unity of knowledge (Choudhury, 2011). The same properties do not form features of any rationalist type of dialectical evolutionary worldview (Campbell, 1987; Popper, 1965; Resnick and Wolff, 1987).

2.6. The tawhidi *methodological worldview applied to the domain of ethical and social finance: transiting to the abstracto-empirical Part II of this chapter*

Before setting up the initiating methodological issue in conceptual formalization of ethics in financial economic theory, and hence in Islamic social finance, we need to appreciate the importance of an epistemic approach in reformulating the financial theory of efficient capital markets.

A common objective criterion of traditional financial theory of the firm is the maximization of shareholders' wealth. In such an objective criterion, the capitalization of dividends is done by the genre of present-valuation of streams of future dividend flows under uncertainty and the choice of discount rates, dividend growth rates and speculative attitude to future risk and uncertainty that would define the firm's choice of capital structure between equity and debt with inverse tax implications on corporations (Modigliani and Miller, 1958).

To analytically change this corporation viewpoint arising from the ethically benign criterion of maximization of the value of the corporation in terms of shareholders' wealth, we need to alter the model of valuation of the firm's assets with a portion devoted to social distribution. Thereby, important ethical issues have emanated, such as corporate social responsibility, good corporate governance and stakeholders' model of social participatory choices (Lozano, 2000; Vanek, 1971). Yet above all these there is the need for replacing the axiom of economic rationality that governs market and agent specific maximizing behaviour.

Such socially inclusive attitudes cannot change unless there is the epistemic consciousness of the organic unity (*tawhid*) of knowledge between social preferences and corporation attitude. Choudhury (2014) refers to such induction of ethical values in corporation choices as conscious corporate social responsibility. It is the epistemic prelude and consequence of consciousness that initiates an endogenous adaptation of choices in the ethical field of social consideration through the aforementioned *wellbeing function* as new objective criterion for financial theory.

Having gone through Part I, which is the indispensable part on the formulation of the abstract theoretical nature of the ontological law of monotheism (*tawhid*) acting as the divine unity of knowledge in the generality and details of the pairing multiverse, we now complete Part II of the total ontological formalism. The objective here is to highlight the applied impact of the wellbeing function for ethical and social finance in Islam.

Part II is thereby a statistical evaluation of the quantitative empirical form of the wellbeing function in the form, $\theta = F(x(\theta))$, subject to the series of circular causation equations signifying inter-variable causality as the mark of degrees of pervasive complementarities possibly attainable or constructible between the selected variables. This empirical approach of statistical estimation undertakes a comprehensive dealing of the complementarities involved, through selected variables that are embedded in knowledge parameter to carry on the empirical task. Part I, emanating from expression **(1)**, now embodies the embedding of the parameter 'θ' consonant with the ranking of the selected variables in terms of their importance in wellbeing. Then all such evaluated 'θ'-related variables are averaged to signify complementarities between the variables that are induced by the empirical version of unity of knowledge in terms of the corresponding {θ}-variables. Throughout the theoretical and empirical parts ethics is signified by the property of organic unity of knowledge shown by the relationship of pervasive complementarities between the selected variables. Such endogenously structured variables corresponding to the averaged 'θ' variables (see Table 2.1 later on) bring out the higher meaning of charitable purposes in Islamic social finance, which is wellbeing-bestowing by its attributes of being and becoming.

3. Part II. Empirical method (formalism)[9] for Islamic social and charitable financing derived from the epistemic unity of knowledge and the wellbeing function

Expression **(1)** in its details denotes the functional ontological form that is derived from the epistemic methodology shown in the chain of unity of knowledge and its impact on the generalized and particular world-systems. We take the latter in the form of an example of modelling the ethico-financial economics in the light of Islamic social finance. We explain and evaluate this illustrative empirical case below.

The explanation made here is that, in the Islamic case of charitable financing within a total portfolio, the methodology of consilience (epistemic unity of knowledge) leads the empirical model to test out the degree to which inter-variable complementarities exist or can be constructed by changes in the coefficients of the circular causation relations and the wellbeing function. The wellbeing function is thus defined as an ethico-financial economic index. It reads the degree of complementarities (participation) between the selected variables in accordance with the ethico-financial economic implication of the epistemic unity of knowledge. The variables selected are some key ethical indicators of Islamic charity for grassroots development. The institutions that engage in such financing have traditionally practiced such philanthropic giving as individual modes of financing. The argument contrarily made in this chapter is that a jointly interactive model of financing between the philanthropy variables would be more effective in generating better measures of wellbeing index as opposed to pursuing independent financial dealings.

The following variables are selected for this illustrative empirical work. F denotes Islamic banking financing, with M referring to *mudarabah* financing as model for profit-sharing. Z denotes *zakat* as the philanthropy of a 2.5 per cent (according to Islamic law) taken on the net value of wealth of individuals, shareholders, and firms in any Islamic fiscal year. 'θ' denotes the average degree as ranks of the philanthropic variables. The method of computation of such 'θ' values is shown in Table 2.1, which also computes the average 'θ' column to estimate the circular causation relations.

Estimating ethically induced inter-causal relations of financing variables

The symbols in Table 2.1 are defined as follows:

> lnF: natural logarithm of Islamic banking financing
> lnM: natural logarithm of Islamic banking profit-sharing (*mudarabah*) financing
> lnZ: natural logarithm of charitable (Z known as *zakat*) disbursement
> lnθ: natural logarithm of wellbeing value (see data table for ranked computation)
> Monthly data for the period Jan 2013 – Dec 2015

Table 2.1. Statistical data and computation of estimation θ-values as ranks

	Islamic banking financing (F)	lnF	θ_F	Islamic banking mudarabah financing (M)	lnM	θ_M	Zakat distributed (Z)	lnZ	θ_Z	θ
Jan-13	149,672.38	11.9162041	7.03	12,027.11	9.39	7.65	2.16	0.77	2.19	5.620521
Feb-13	154,072.07	11.9451757	7.23	12,055.75	9.40	7.66	2.53	0.93	2.56	5.81877
Mar-13	161,080.55	11.9896599	7.56	12,101.58	9.40	7.69	2.98	1.09	3.01	6.090051
Apr-13	163,406.82	12.0039982	7.67	12,026.43	9.39	7.65	2.54	0.93	2.57	5.964319
May-13	167,259.47	12.0273016	7.85	12,168.04	9.41	7.74	2.56	0.94	2.59	6.060542
Jun-13	171,227.42	12.0507479	8.04	12,628.62	9.44	8.03	2.67	0.98	2.70	6.256648
Jul-13	174,486.36	12.0696019	8.19	13,281.33	9.49	8.44	7.19	1.97	7.28	7.972108
Aug-13	174,537.18	12.069893	8.19	13,299.10	9.50	8.46	2.92	1.07	2.96	6.535747
Sep-13	177,319.57	12.0857089	8.33	13,363.86	9.50	8.50	3.58	1.28	3.63	6.815963
Oct-13	179,283.81	12.0967254	8.42	13,663.97	9.52	8.69	6.07	1.80	6.15	7.751267
Nov-13	180,832.53	12.1053266	8.49	13,877.80	9.54	8.82	3.94	1.37	3.99	7.101494
Dec-13	184,121.93	12.1233535	8.64	13,625.27	9.52	8.66	5.23	1.65	5.30	7.534328
Jan-14	181,397.77	12.1084475	8.52	13,322.46	9.50	8.47	2.40	0.88	2.43	6.472049
Feb-14	181,772.18	12.1105094	8.53	13,299.99	9.50	8.46	2.87	1.05	2.90	6.631498
Mar-14	184,964.30	12.1279181	8.68	13,498.13	9.51	8.58	4.13	1.42	4.18	7.149841
Apr-14	187,884.80	12.1435843	8.82	13,802.15	9.53	8.78	2.30	0.83	2.33	6.642824
May-14	189,689.65	12.1531446	8.91	13,868.60	9.54	8.82	2.24	0.81	2.27	6.664078
Jun-14	193,136.03	12.1711501	9.07	14,311.67	9.57	9.10	3.68	1.30	3.73	7.298306
Jul-14	194,078.90	12.1760201	9.11	14,559.44	9.59	9.26	6.48	1.87	6.56	8.310814
Aug-14	193,983.12	12.1755264	9.11	14,276.67	9.57	9.08	2.55	0.93	2.58	6.92062
Sep-14	196,563.48	12.1887407	9.23	14,355.61	9.57	9.13	9.87	2.29	10.00	9.451841
Oct-14	196,490.58	12.1883698	9.23	14,370.71	9.57	9.14	6.12	1.81	6.20	8.18597
Nov-14	198,375.54	12.1979172	9.31	14,307.35	9.57	9.10	2.81	1.03	2.85	7.085753
Dec-14	199,329.75	12.2027158	9.36	14,354.06	9.57	9.13	1.09	0.09	1.11	6.531021
Jan-15	197,279.24	12.1923755	9.26	14,207.18	9.56	9.03	2.53	0.93	2.56	6.953005
Feb-15	197,543.17	12.1937124	9.27	14,147.49	9.56	8.99	3.43	1.23	3.48	7.248759

Month									
Mar-15	200,712.16	12.2096271	9.42	14,136.43	9.56	8.99	3.58	1.27	3.62	7.344834
Apr-15	201,526.15	12.2136744	9.46	14,388.31	9.57	9.15	5.35	1.68	5.42	8.008619
May-15	203,894.15	12.2253563	9.57	14,906.42	9.61	9.48	3.39	1.22	3.44	7.495294
Jun-15	206,056.46	12.2359055	9.67	15,667.31	9.66	9.96	3.00	1.10	3.04	7.558113
Jul-15	204,842.60	12.2299972	9.62	15,728.66	9.66	10.00	6.43	1.86	6.51	8.709581
Aug-15	205,873.62	12.2350178	9.67	15,676.15	9.66	9.97	2.98	1.09	3.02	7.551213
Sep-15	208,142.91	12.2459802	9.77	15,143.63	9.63	9.63	6.53	1.88	6.61	8.670316
Oct-15	207,767.83	12.2441765	9.75	14,924.94	9.61	9.49	3.88	1.36	3.93	7.725662
Nov-15	209,123.91	12.2506822	9.82	14,680.38	9.59	9.33	2.19	0.79	2.22	7.124398
Dec-15	212,996.47	12.2690309	10.00	14,819.94	9.60	9.42	3.30	1.20	3.35	7.589472

Sources: OJK: Otoritas Jasa Keuangan – Financial Services Authority, www.ojk.go.id/; and BAZNAS: Badan Amil Zakat Nasional – National Zakat Management Agency, http://pusat.baznas.go.id/; more precisely, the data have been collected from these websites: http://pusat.baznas.go.id/laporan-bulanan/, www.ojk.go.id/id/kanal/syariah/data-dan-statistik/statistik-perbankan-syariah/Default.aspx

Circular causation inter-variable log-linear relations to test for positive complementarities

The OLS[10] estimated equations of the circular causation relations are

$$\ln F = 0.519*\ln M - 0.132*\ln Z + 0.686* \ln\theta + 6.005 \tag{8}$$

[2.837064] [−3.934903] [3.683182]

(R² = 0.929303, Durbin-Watson = 1.053491)

$$\ln M = -0.077*\ln Z + 0.505*\ln\theta + 0.387*\ln F + 3.942 \tag{9}$$

[−2.373022] [2.968778] [2.837064]

(R² = 0.929303, Durbin Watson = 1.053491)

$$\ln Z = 5.271*\ln\theta - 2.472*\ln F - 1.940*\ln M + 39.398 \tag{10}$$

[21.90296] [−3.934903] [−2.373022]

(R² = 0.945103, Durbin-Watson = 2.017945)

Quantitative evaluation of the wellbeing function in terms of empirical knowledge-function

$$\ln\theta = 0.434*\ln F + 0.428*\ln M + 0.178*\ln Z - 7.606 \tag{11}$$

[3.683182] [2.968778] [21.90296]

(R² = 0.974572, Durbin-Watson = 2.131067)

The estimated 'θ'-values are derived from the fitted equation **(11)** over all values of the financing variables.

3.1. Interpretation of OLS statistical results

The interpretation of the estimated coefficients in terms of the variables under consideration points out that Islamic charitable spending as *zakat* (Z) is negatively related with finance (F). The estimation shows that every 1 per cent change in Z has a negative 0.132 of 1 per cent change in Islamic financing oppositely. Hence, Z and F have opposite movements. An increase in 0.00132 of F results from a diversion of 1 per cent in Z; and vice versa. Although the numerical value of the negative relationship between Z and F is small, the result shows a worrisome performance of Islamic financing that has otherwise been claiming to have a charitable impact on the social economy at large. Contrarily, Z as purely charitable social financing to alleviate poverty and deprivation does not have a positive complementary relationship with F financing. Rather, Islamic financing F and charitable Z financing ought to be integrated together to finance commerce as well as social goals to foster poverty alleviation.

The positive relationship between F financing and profit-sharing (M) is a plausible result, as M is a primary mode of Islamic financing in F. However, the impact of M on the increase (or decrease) of F is small, to the level of 0.00519 of M financing. The implication is that M, although being a primary source of Islamic financing, is losing its grounds.

Total Islamic finance still bears the highest positive relationship with the wellbeing scale (θ), at the level of F gaining 0.00686 of wellbeing (θ). This implies that Islamic wellbeing results most predominantly from the total Islamic financing aspect of the economy than should be the case of sharing in the ethico-economic order. This is an outcome that reaffirms the poor relationship between Z charitable spending and total Islamic financing F. Despite observing this result, the principle of complementarity between economic and financial effects to promote an Islamic socio-economic order aimed at integrating charitable and commercial financing activities is still lacking. The above analysis of one set of results of a circular causation equation is consistent with the other circular causation equation results and in relation to the quantitative form of the wellbeing function shown by 'θ' as a linear approximation of the conceptual wellbeing function $W(\theta)$ in terms of the non-parametric induction of the parametric variables, namely of F, M and Z.

The Islamic approach to socio-economic development in the Indonesian economy and society (to which the data of Table 2.1 refers) is still impacted mainly by the total Islamic financing activity of the Islamic economy. In such activities, the charitable role of Z has a substituting relationship with F and vice versa. The measure of this negative relationship is substantive. The negative intensifying effect is shown at the level of 2.472 of 1 per cent negative change in Z caused by a 1 per cent change of F, and 1.940 of 1 per cent negative change in Z caused by a 1 per cent change in M. The relationship between F and M as θ-induced variables is of the complementary nature. However, the complementary relationship is subdued. The estimation results of all the circular causation equations are consistent with different elasticity coefficients in the inter-variable relations. Despite the diminished and opposite impact of charitable spending Z and commercial financing F, the aggregate contribution to social wellbeing remains slightly increasing in the economy of scale. These variant effects are shown in expressions **(8)–(11)**. The total of the elasticity coefficients of each variable to social wellbeing, denoted by 'θ', being equal to 1.04 implies a 4 per cent higher contribution of the charitable and financing variables than would be the case of constant returns to scale.

Inter-variable elasticity coefficients showing their interrelated coefficients to the Islamic social financial economy

Elasticity Matrix =	F	M	Z	θ	(12)
F	1.000	0.519	−0.132	0.686	
M	0.387	1.000	−0.077	0.505	
Z	−2.472	−1.940	1.000	5.271	
θ	0.434	0.428	0.178	1.000	

3.2. The need for data-meshing to evaluate the ethical status of Islamic economics and finance

An ongoing questioning on the authenticity of the claims made by Islamic financial economic institutions and experts is widespread in the common public domain. Such over-optimistic claims need to be carefully examined. This involves the evaluation of an estimated time-series data on financial and charitable statistics, that we have interpreted through an algorithmic approach.

One way to test the Islamic reliability of the statistical results is to take the public opinion into account. This involves questionnaire survey of the common respondents regarding Islamic moral and ethical attributes impinging on financial and economic results. The statistical data and results are thus meshed with the non-parametric questionnaire results for generating the inter-meshing of data to determine the authentic state of performance of the financial economic claim of Islamic institutions.

Formalism in data inter-meshing

Data inter-meshing between time-series and cross-sectional/survey data at a given point of time is a mathematical undertaking under simplifying assumptions.

It is assumed first that survey responses to questionnaires on Islamic ethical attributes remain unchanged over the given period of time corresponding to the statistical time-series data. Second, the average value of the attribute-ranks calculated on the basis of non-parametric responses (θ^*) denotes the quantitative measure of wellbeing on the basis of the non-parametric evaluation of financial data via survey results. Third, the quantitative measure of wellbeing on the basis of time-series data denotes the average of the data-ranks estimated on the basis of the time-series data. This is denoted by 'θ'. Fourth, with the 'θ' index as quantitatively estimated wellbeing function there are the individual time-series generated 'θ_t'-values. Fifth, the numbers of attributes are devised to be the same as the number of parametric values, say by time-series. This is acceptable, for the attributes are surveyed corresponding to the specific parametric values and averaged within each such group. Sixth, Avg (θ) and Avg(θ^*) correspond to the row-specific ($\theta_{time}, \theta_{Attributes}$)-values/responses.

The following strip of the detailed table of inter-meshed data is shown below:

Parametric time-series data $\{\theta, \mathbf{x}(\theta)\}$ Non-parametric attributes data $(\theta^*, \mathbf{A}(\theta^*))$

Time $x_1 \theta_1 x_2 \theta_2 \dots x_n \theta_n$ Avg $(\theta_t) = \theta$ $A_1 \theta^*_1 \dots A_n \theta^*_n$ Avg $(\theta^*) = \theta^*$

$t = 1, 2 \dots, T$ at a point of time of questionnaire survey

We ask the statistical question: How dispersed are average values of (θ, θ^*)? In order to tally the authenticity of the wellbeing results estimated from the parametric/non-parametric sides, the smallest value of the dispersion indicator nearest to the value of zero gives the best result.

$$\text{Dispersion Indicator} = |(\theta - \theta^*)| \tag{13}$$

θ^* remains constant for the non-parametric formula.

If we take all the terms in natural logarithms, then in the coefficient form of the quantitative estimated wellbeing function expressed in natural logarithmic θ_t and θ^* values, the dispersion index is given by

$$\text{Dispersion Indicator} = \Sigma_{t=1}^{T} \alpha_t . \ln x_t - \ln \theta^* \tag{14}$$

3.3. Simulation of the wellbeing model subject to circular causation relations by the spatial domain analysis method

On the topic of desired simulation of coefficients of estimated statistical equations of evaluation (estimation followed by simulations) of the wellbeing function, subject to circular causation, the spatial domain analysis (SDA)[11] helps out. The underlying computer software method generates a vast scale of possible ranks of the coefficient values to signify better complementarities between the inter-causal variables of specific equations. Following the estimator values of the specific equations, the new simulated values of the dependent inter-causal variables and the quantitative form of the wellbeing θ-function are computed. From the estimated and the simulated results of the evaluated wellbeing function subject to circular causation relations and the quantitatively evaluated wellbeing θ-function, strategic and policy oriented results can be generated. These results lend much insight in social and financial engineering keeping in view the essential goals of ethics arising from the episteme of *tawhidi* unity of knowledge that are embedded in financial and economic variables.

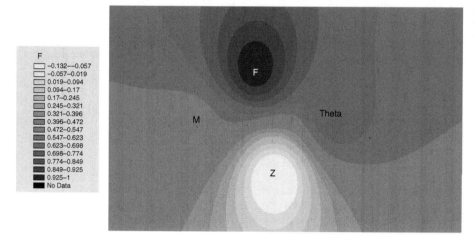

Figure 2.2. SDA interaction between F and M, Z and θ
lnF = 0.519*lnM – 0.132*lnZ + 0.686* lnθ + 6.005 (e.g. –0.132 → +0.019)

The following SDA of the social adaptation of the geographical system algorithm operation (Figure 2.2) on the evaluated quantitative form of the wellbeing function is an example of the algorithmic result. The SDA map is generated to show how simulated selection of the coefficient (bold –0.132) can be made to reduce its negative value or convert it into a small positive value. The choice of the simulated value of the coefficient is indicated by the shades of colours between the regions of lnF, lnM, lnZ in relation to lnθ. The denser region around lnF shows higher complementarities between lnθ and lnF. The same is true of the relationship between lnF and between lnZ and lnF, and lnF and lnM. All these degrees of complementarities are in respect of the direction of relationship from (lnM,lnZ,lnθ) to lnF. In this given equation any simulation will also be maintained in this direction. Such simulations can be extended to positive coefficients as well.

4. Conclusions: contribution and significance of the study

The combination of the parametric (observed) and non-parametric (ethical induction) variables provides a distinctive epistemic model of functional ontology, epistemology and phenomenology all together premised on the episteme of unity of knowledge. This attribute is explained by inter-variable complementarities caused by ethical consciousness of such pervasive interrelations in the light of the wellbeing function as objective criterion derived from the *tawhidi* framework.

The formalization of such a methodology and its empirical application is an original outcome of this chapter. In fact, only in some cases such a problem is discussed in the literature of heterodox economic thought (Lawson and Pesaran, 2009).

The emergent ethically induced epistemic model of pervasively endogenous relationship between circularly causal relations of parametric and non-parametric variables makes a significant contribution to the empirical finance literature too. No empirical work has been done in this area of ethico-financial economics with endogenous ethical embedding. Nonetheless, a contribution of this type is essential for formalizing, applying and deriving policy-theoretic implications for the greatly needed development problems at the deprived grassroots. This approach in turn contributes to the empirical ethico-financial economic policy-theoretic study of poverty alleviation, empowerment and reconstruction of entitlement out of failure at the grassroots (Sen, 1981). Shiller (2012) is a rare finance methodologist who has written on the need for ethical relevance of finance, contrary to the traditional and over-emphasized focus of ethically benign financial study of efficient capital markets (Fama, 1970). Likewise, there have not been contributions in the field of ethico-financial economics through an engineering approach that invokes endogenous epistemic questions of ethical embedding as an essential dimension of Islamic social finance. The result in relevant financial engineering would significantly examine the issue of embedding ethical issues in empirical modelling. An example in this regard certainly relates to development finance. It must be noted that both methodological issues and the consequential formalism of ethico-financial economic modelling have remained absent despite the importance that these areas could bear for the study of social inclusion.

The epistemic methodological issues (ontology of *tawhid*), the emergent formulation of the ethico-financial economic model (wellbeing function), and its operative application (Islamic ethical and social finance) have been cast in an abstracto-empirical content of this chapter. All this makes room for substantive academic and applied contribution in a domain where existing approaches in Islamic economics and finance have often failed to provide a viable alternative to conventional capitalism.

Notes

1 Note the words of A.N. Whitehead (1978, p. 48) in this regard:

> The notion of a universal is of that which can enter into the description of many particulars; whereas the notion of a particular is that it is described by universals, and does not itself enter into the description of any other particular.

2 The Statistical, Economic and Social Research Center for Islamic Countries, with its headquarter in Ankara, Turkey.

3 *Zakat* is one of the pillars of Islam and corresponds to the mandatory demand on the assets of the wealthy to provide social amelioration of the needy. The *waqf* is a well-known institute of the Islamic tradition and can be defined as 'charitable endowment'. Between *zakat* and *waqf* there is no *Shariʿah* ruling for a constant ratio to be defined.

4 Foucault (1972) defines the concept of episteme in the following words, that we accept as our understanding of the totality of functional relationship between knowledge, cognition and world-system:

> By *episteme* we mean … the total set of relations that unite, at a given period, the discursive practices that give rise to epistemological figures, sciences, and possibly formalized systems … The episteme is not a form of knowledge (*connaissance*) or type of rationality which, crossing the boundaries of the most varied sciences, manifests the sovereign unity of a subject, a spirit, or a period; it is the totality of relations that can be discovered, for a given period, between the sciences when one analyses them at the level of discursive regularities.
>
> (p. 191)

5 Q. 36:36: 'Glory to God, Who created in pairs all things that the earth produces, as well as their own kind and [other] things of which they have no knowledge.'

6 Q. 41:53 on Signs of Allah: 'Soon shall We show them Our Signs in the [furthest] regions [of the earth], and in their own souls, until it becomes manifest to them that this is the Truth. Is it not enough that thy Lord doth witness all things?'

7 **HH(θ)** as the total trajectory from the beginning to the end of the multiverse order is represented by $\Omega \to S \cup interaction \cap integration\{e(world\text{-}system)(\theta)\} \to S \to \Omega$. See expression **(1)** for definitions of symbols.

8 'Evolutionary convergence' is defined by the property of **IIE**-learning processes wherein all equilibrium points are evolutionary yet convergent in form, with only a finite number of divergences causing disequilibrium. Thus permanent disequilibrium never exists in the knowledge-induced event space under epistemic unity of knowledge. Morality and ethics pervades in the continuum of knowledge, space and time dimensions. Formally, we define evolutionary convergence as follows. Let 'θ*' denote any of the convergent values of 'θ' in the continuum of the event space. Evolutionary convergence is defined by the existence of an arbitrary positive value denoted by $\varepsilon(\theta)$, such that, $|\theta\text{-}\theta^*| < \varepsilon(\theta)$, with $\varepsilon(\theta) > 0$; $d\varepsilon(\theta)/d\theta < 0$. The same properties of evolutionary convergence are extended to all the elements of every event including the $\mathbf{x}(\theta)$-categories, and evaluative wellbeing, $W(\mathbf{x}(\theta))$ and its implicit function in terms of the positive monotonic derivation by $(\theta,\mathbf{x}(\theta))$-values continuously in time. That is, $|t(\theta)\text{-}t^*(\theta^*)| < \delta(t(\theta))$, δ being an indefinitely small arbitrary positive number, for every 'θ'-value in the neighbourhood of 'θ*'. In a pervasive evolutionary divergent form of the dialectical process none of the above properties exists. Consequently, disequilibrium as entropy is not an infinitely many continuous state of evolutionary learning universe of events governed by the *tawhidi* episteme.

9 'Formalism' – or assigning the model form for statistical valuation in terms of socio-economic variables and the corresponding 'θ' parameter.

10 I.e. Ordinary Least Square statistical method of estimating regression equations.

11 This is another analytical empirical method derived from its broader field of Geographical Information System that distributes numerical values and shapes and forms on the geographical topography. We have adapted this method to measure the numerical topography character of social space embedded by unity of knowledge, {θ}. SDA measures different topographical maps for various values of the coefficients. These are machine generated by using the estimated equation by the OLS method. The intention is to generate better scenarios of simulacra of coefficient values in terms of inter-variable complementarities.

References

Auda, J. (2008) *Maqasid al Shariʿah as Philosophy of Islamic Law: A Systems Approach.* Herndon, VA: The International Institute of Islamic Thought.

Barrow, J.D. (1991) Laws. In his *Theories of Everything: The Quest for Ultimate Explanation.* Oxford: Oxford University Press, pp. 12–30.

BAZNAS (Badan Amil Zakat Nasional – National Zakat Management Agency), http://pusat.baznas.go.id/.

Bhaskar, R. (1978, 1st ed. 1975) The logic of scientific discovery. Chapter 3 of his *A Realist Theory of Science.* Brighton, Sussex: Harvester Press.

Campbell, D.T. (1987) Evolutionary epistemology. In Radnitzky, G. and Bartley, W.W. III (eds) *Evolutionary Epistemology, Rationality, and the Sociology of Knowledge.* La Salle, IL: Open Court, pp. 47–89.

Choudhury, M.A. (2006) *Science and Epistemology in the Qur'an.* 5 volumes (different volume titles). Lewiston, NY: The Edwin Mellen Press.

Choudhury, M.A. (2007) *The Universal Paradigm and the Islamic World-System: Economics, Ethics, Science and Society.* Singapore: World Scientific Publishing.

Choudhury, M.A. (2011) On the existence of evolutionary learning equilibriums. *Sultan Qaboos University Journal for Science.* **16**, pp. 68–81.

Choudhury, M.A. (2014) *The Socio-Cybernetic Study of God and the World-System.* Philadelphia, PA: IGI Global.

Choudhury, M.A. (2016a) *The Islamic Epistemological Worldview and Empirical Study of Socioeconomic Integration in the Ummah.* Kuala Lumpur, Malaysia: International Islamic University Malaysia Press (IIUM Press).

Choudhury, M.A. (2016b) *Absolute Reality in the Qur'an.* Chapters 2 and 3. New York: Palgrave MacMillan.

Choudhury, M.A., and Hoque, M.N. (2018) *Shariʿah* and economics: a generalized system approach. *International Journal of Law and Management.* **60**(1).

Choudhury, M.A., and Rahim, H.B. (2016) An epistemic definition of Islamic economics. *ACRN Oxford Journal of Finance and Risk Perspectives.* **5**(2), pp. 106–120.

Fama, E.F. (1970) Efficient capital markets: a review of theory and empirical work. *The Journal of Finance.* **25**(2), pp. 383–417.

Foucault, M. (1972) *The Archaeology of Knowledge and the Discourse on Language* (original French ed. 1969, transl. by A.M. Sheridan Smith). London: Tavistock Publications.

Hallaq, W.B. (2009) *Shariʿa: Theory, Practice, Transformations.* Cambridge: Cambridge University Press.

Kupka, I.A.K., and Peixoto, M.M. (1993) On the enumerative geometry of geodesics. In Hirsch, M.W., Marsden, J.E. and Shub, M. (eds) *From Topology to Computation: Proceedings of the Smalefest.* New York: Springer-Verlag, pp. 243–253.

Lawson, T., and Pesaran, H. (2009, 1st ed. 1985) Methodological issues in Keynes' economics: an introduction. In Lawson, T., and Pesaran, H. (eds) *Keynes' Economics: Methodological Issues.* London: Routledge, pp. 1 6.

Lozano, J.M. (2000) *Ethics and Organization: Understanding Business Ethics as a Learning Process.* Dordrecht; London: Kluwer Academic.

Maddox, I.J. (1970) *Elements of Functional Analysis.* Cambridge: Cambridge University Press.

Modigliani, F., and Miller, M.H. (1958) The cost of capital, corporation finance, and the theory of investment. *The American Economic Review.* **48**(3), pp. 261–297.

OJK (Otoritas Jasa Keuangan – Financial Services Authority), www.ojk.go.id/.

Popper, K.R. (1965) *Conjectures and Refutations: The Growth of Scientific Knowledge.* London: Routledge.

Resnick, S.A., and Wolff, R.D. (1987) *Knowledge and Class: A Marxian Critique of Political Economy.* Chicago; London: The University of Chicago Press.

Rucker, R.v.B. (1982) Large cardinals. In his *Infinity and the Mind: The Science and Philosophy of the Infinite.* New York: Bantam Books, pp. 273–286.

Sen, A.K. (1981) *Poverty and Famines: An Essay on Entitlement and Deprivation.* Oxford: Clarendon Press.

Sen, A.K. (1987) *On Ethics and Economics.* Oxford: Basil Blackwell.

Shiller, R.J. (2012) *Finance and the Good Society.* Princeton, NJ: Princeton University Press.

Toner, P. (1999) Gunnar Myrdal (1898–1987): circular and cumulative causation as the methodology of the social sciences. Chapter 5 in his *Main Currents in Cumulative Causation, the Dynamics of Growth and Development.* Basingstoke: Palgrave MacMillan.

Vanek, J. (1971) The participatory economy in a theory of social evolution. In his *The Participatory Economy: An Evolutionary Hypothesis and a Strategy for Development.* Ithaca, NY; London: Cornell University Press, pp. 51–89.

Whitehead, A.N. (1978) *Process and Reality* (ed. Griffith, D.R. and Sherburne, D.W.). New York: The Free Press.

Wilson, E.O. (1998) *Consilience: The Unity of Knowledge.* New York: Alfred Knopf.

3 A critical appraisal of Islamic finance in the light of the *maqasid al-Shari'ah*

Atiq-ur-Rehman

1. Introduction

Unlike ordinary perception, the way of life suggested by Islam is not only the set of spiritual exercises, but it is a code of life aimed to achieve certain objectives. Within the divine orders and instructions given to mankind in the *Qur'an*, the *Qur'an* itself sometimes explicitly explains the objective, the purpose (in Arabic, *maqsad*, from which the plural *maqasid*) behind the orders; other times the underlying objectives can be found by a deeper study and interpretation of both the *Qur'an* and the *Sunnah*.

Shari'ah scholars have divided the objectives of Islamic *Shari'ah* into five broad categories. These five categories are usually referred to as the "objectives of *Shari'ah*" (in Arabic, *maqasid al-Shari'ah*), namely (1) security of faith/religion (*din*); (2) security of life (*nafs*); (3) security of intellect (*'aql*); (4) security of progeny/lineage (*nasl*); and (5) economic security, as safeguard of property and wealth (*mal*).

Looking at the list, it becomes pretty obvious that all these objectives are social in nature, since they cover various aspects of human dignity and consider economic security as one dimension of this dignity in a broad sense. On the contrary, the approaches to human welfare formulated during the nineteenth and twentieth century in the West have mainly focused on economic objectives, usually ignoring this broader social dimension of the human being. Accordingly, development policies have also followed the same direction, i.e. focusing on the economic security and considering it as the sole measure of development. Only since the late twentieth century, when people started thinking about development in a broader sense, have criteria related to social welfare been included in the measurement of development. However, the popular measures of "human prosperity" (e.g. the Human Development Index) are still far behind the achievements to be pursued according to the objectives of *Shari'ah*.

Human life in an Islamic perspective is derived from these five objectives. Therefore, the economic and financial teachings of Islam have to be understood in accordance with these purposes. This means that the *maqasid al-Shari'ah* are not driven by financial teachings: on the contrary, Islamic financial teachings are driven by the objectives of *Shariʿah*. Therefore, if one looks at the economic teachings in the *Qur'an* and the *Sunnah*, these are to be related to social outcomes embedded in the *maqasid al-Shariʿah*.

In fact, these objectives formulate very comprehensive metrics for measuring human prosperity and consist of a globally recognizable set of development indicators. Unfortunately, many scholars have confused the *target objectives* with the *recommended means to achieve the objectives*. To mention a few examples, Ali and Hasan (2014) construct an 'objectives of *Shariʿah*' index which could be measured by micro-level data where they include *zakat*, prayers, etc. among the objectives. Similarly, Amin *et al.* (undated) propose the indicators that could be used to measure the development in the light of objectives of *Shariʿah*. The indicators include soundness of faith, performing the prayers, etc. in the objectives. *Salat*, as we shall explain, is not the final objective, but a way to achieve the objective of forbidding evils. Esen (2015) lists the indicators that he thinks could be used to measure the Islamic development index. The author's prescribed indicators have only very loose relation with the objectives. For example, he mentions 'expenditure on health' among the indicators of 'security of posterity', but it is obvious that the two things have only a very weak relationship. On the other hand, some very strong indices are dropped from the construction of development index: for example, 'HIV prevalence' which indicates the occurrence of extramarital sexual relationship does not appear. Ali *et al.* (2014) attempt to develop a *Shariʿah*-based index for development; however, while doing so, their total emphasis is on economic security, badly ignoring the other objectives of *Shariʿah*.

This confusion between the *objectives* and *means* has brought about a big hurdle in the wider acceptability of the *maqasid al-Shariʿah*. In fact, as we shall show, many indicators among the *maqasid* are closely linked to the so-called Millennium Development Goals (MDGs) and Sustainable Development Goals (SDGs). In this light, an investigation into the relationship between the objectives of *Shariʿah* and Islamic finance can be taken as an analogue of the relationship between Sustainable Development Goals and social finance.

In this study, we try to analyse the inter-relation between *maqasid al-Shariʿah* and Islamic finance. The former and the latter are connected in multiple ways. First, for each of the *maqasid* there are certain provisions in Islamic finance that help to achieve the objective. Second, all the modes of finance endorsed by Islam are assumed to contribute to the fulfilment of the *maqasid al-Shariʿah*. Third, the prohibitions underlying Islamic finance (e.g. prohibition of interest) facilitate progress toward the objectives of *Shariʿah*.

These three kinds of connections are the focus of this study, as follows: in Section 2 we discuss the nature of Islamic finance and its relationship with the *maqasid al-Shariʿah*; Section 3 interprets the *maqasid* as measures of welfare; Section 4 deals with the differentiation between the *maqasid* and the means to achieve the objectives; the central part of the study, Section 5, further investigates the objectives in the light of the related financial provisions in Islam; Section 6 illustrates that the popular modes of Islamic finance help

in achieving the *maqasid* through social impact; Section 7 deals with the prohibition of *riba* (interest) in Islamic finance and its social relevance to achieve
the *maqasid al-Shari'ah*; Section 8 concludes the study.

2. The nature of Islamic finance and its relation with the *maqasid al-Shari'ah*

If one looks at the economic teachings in early Islamic traditions, one will
find that most of these teachings are related to voluntary contributions to
help each other.

'Spending in the way of Almighty Allah (*infaq fi sabilillah*)' is probably the
most emphasized economic teaching of the Holy *Qur'an*. The term *infaq* means
to spend on desirable goals, predominantly social goals, without any greed of
worldly reward and with the recompense expected from The Almighty. *Infaq*
is not about growth in personal assets, but it is about betterment in society.
The community itself becomes the top priority when it comes to economic
teaching of Islam. Even the use of one's personal property becomes imper-
missible when it conflicts with socially desirable goals. For example, nobody
is allowed to gamble even with his own money because this is harmful for all
society. Therefore, Islam has denied the absolute ownership of the economic
resources by individuals and emphasizes that absolute ownership belongs
only to Almighty Allah: men use their properties and belongings as trustees
of The Almighty. Hence, while instructing a good treatment to servants and
subordinates, the *Qur'an* (24:33) says 'Pay them from the wealth of Allah that
he has given to you.' This verse of the Holy *Qur'an* indicates that the absolute
ownership of wealth belongs to Almighty Allah and humans are authorized
to use the resources only as trustees: accordingly, human freedom in using
economic wealth terminates when there is violation of the divine orders of
The Almighty as the actual owner of any resource.

Not only voluntary contributions, but also the commercial modes of
finance endorsed by Islam have greater social inclination.

Profit-loss sharing financial arrangements (e.g. *musharakah* and *mudarabah*)
are a clear example, where the word 'sharing' automatically relates to greater
distributive justice. The *musharakah* is a business arrangement in which more
parties participate in managing capital and running an enterprise (see also
later in Section 6.1). This model has a number of social aspects: for instance,
pooling up resources to have a fruitful enterprise, and sharing the profits and
losses. This concept is the foundation of any 'company' in the modern sense.
On the contrary, in interest-based commercial loans, there is an active partner
(borrower) in the management of the business and a passive partner (lender),
where the latter earns a remuneration even if his borrower suffers severe loss,
and probably this is why interest is declared illegitimate in Islam (prohibition
of *riba*, interest).

Economic relations in the early days of Islam were social in nature and,
as we shall discuss later, they were conceived in the light of the *maqasid*

al-Shari'ah. On the other hand, contrary to the economic system of the early days of Islam, contemporary Islamic finance is less participatory, less social and more commercial. Due to this, one can argue that the industry does not truly realize (yet) an integration between the objectives of *Shari'ah* and present commercial practice. In this sense, the present study intends to highlight how a real fulfilment of the social nature of Islamic finance requires to re-assess the role of the *maqasid al-Shari'ah* as foundation of the market, and to implement these objectives as fundamental target for global welfare.

3. The *maqasid al-Shari'ah* as pillars and measures of human welfare (*falah*)

Islam seeks the welfare (*falah*) of mankind, as indicated in the Holy *Qur'an*: 'And worship your Lord and do the good deeds so that you can approach the welfare' (Q. 22:77).

The concept of welfare is well defined in Islam and covers both the society and the individual in such an integrated way that the two cannot be separated. The pursuit of *falah* stands on the *maqasid al-Shari'ah* as the pillars of human welfare. In particular, the Islamic tradition recognizes five fundamental objectives of *Shari'ah*, precisely:

a. the securing of faith (*din*);
b. the protection of life (*nafs*);
c. the safeguard of intellect (*'aql*);
d. the security of progeny (posterity, lineage) (*nasl*);
e. and economic security, with regard to wealth (*mal*).

As has been previously noted, these objectives have an intrinsically social dimension, and go far beyond mere economic indicators as commonly used in the definition of development. Differently, the definition of welfare in Islam is inherently multidimensional, including the securing of faith (hence, of freedom of religion as well), life (with health security as an essential component), intellect (thus, promotion of education) and progeny next to economic security.

From this perspective, even the most recent Human Development Index represents only a subset of the *maqasid al-Shari'ah*.

Furthermore, it is important to remark how all these objectives deeply interrelate man and society together. For instance, Islam motivates its followers to seek the bounty of Allah; however, this prosperity is at the same time integrated within the welfare of society. In fact, Islam promotes social wellbeing and the person who receives an income has to spare a compulsory share for the poor and deprived in the form of *zakat* (annual tax) and *usher* (the 10 per cent payable on agricultural income). Moreover, Islam prevents a man from consuming what is his own if this implies harm to society.

In summary, the objectives of *Shari'ah* provide a comprehensive metric to assess human prosperity (*falah*), and the *Shari'ah* itself offers appropriate tools to fulfil these objectives through numerous financial provisions (see in this regard Section 5) which actually match the criteria of social finance as recently elaborated by the Sustainable Development Goals (SDGs) of the global economy.

4. Differentiating the *maqasid al-Shari'ah* from the means to achieve the objectives

The phrase '*maqasid al-Shari'ah*' may lead to the easy misunderstanding (widespread even among Muslim scholars) that these objectives refers exclusively to Muslim believers, without any relevance for non-Muslims. The reason for such misconception is the confusion between the 'objectives' and the 'means to achieve these objectives'.

In fact, most of the 'objectives', as previously remarked, correspond to well-known sustainable development targets, that are recognized/recognizable by the entire globe. In reverse, the 'means to achieve the objectives' are specific to Muslim societies, and the non-Muslim world may not necessarily endorse them as desirable.

For example, Islam indicates *zakat* (2.5 per cent annual tax) and charity as means to reduce wealth and income inequality, 'so that it [wealth] may not [make] a circuit between the rich among you', the Holy *Qur'an* states (59:7) to condemn its concentration in few hands. Correspondingly, the reduction in the concentration of wealth and inequality is also a globally recognized objective for sustainable development. The United Nations Millennium Development Goals agenda target No. 1A aims at improving the share of the poorest quintile in aggregated income and this is consistent with the objective mentioned in the verse of the Holy *Qur'an*. Goal 10 of the Sustainable Development Goals agenda is about the reduction of inequalities between and within nations, which is also consistent with the objective stated in this verse. Therefore, there is no disagreement in the objective; however, Islam says that Muslims should pay *zakat* and offer charity as a means to achieve the purpose. The *zakat* may not be acceptable to the non-Muslim world.

Similarly, while giving the order of fasting, the *Qur'an* says: 'O ye who believe, fasting is prescribed for you, as it was prescribed for those before you, so that ye may ward-off [evil]' (Q. 2:183). This verse explains that one should fast because it will ward off evil, where the *objective* is 'to ward-off evil' and the *means* for a Muslim is 'fasting'. If we look at the objective, which is 'to ward-off evil', it is globally recognizable as valuable; differently, the means has little value for non-Muslims.

There are many other examples where the *Qur'an* explicitly explains the end objective of the divine order given to mankind. Unfortunately, there is still a confusion between 'objectives' and 'means' (even among Muslims scholars), with consequent issues. Therefore, it is very important to list the *objectives* in terms of indicators of welfare separately from the *means* to achieve the *maqasid* themselves in order to properly examine the correspondent financial provisions given by the Islamic religion for each objective, as the next section will do.

5. The objectives of *Shari'ah* and Islamic provisions regarding financing

This section explores the *maqasid al-Shari'ah* as five fundamental indicators of welfare (*falah*), and specifies which provisions regarding financial dealings Islam advances in order to fulfil these objectives. In fact, as a religion revealed for the benefit of all mankind, Islam provides clear guidelines and tools to promote individual and common welfare, hence to achieve the *maqasid*. The objectives, with their further specifications in sub-objectives, and the corresponding financial provisions are investigated in the following paragraphs of the section.

5.1. Objective 1. The securing of faith (din)

'Security of faith' is the most important objective of *Shari'ah* from a socio-religious perspective. This objective has two main sub-objectives, namely (a) adoption of Islam as religion, and (b) religious freedom. While the first one is central for Muslim proselytism, the second sub-objective has universal acceptability. To understand their meaning, we refer to some excerpts from the Holy Scriptures (*Qur'an* and *Sunnah*) which clarify their significance.

Sub-objective 1.1. People should follow Islam

According to Islamic teachings, the only religion (*din*) that will give a reward to human beings on the Day of Judgement is Islam. This is clearly stated in the Holy *Qur'an*: 'No doubt, the [true] religion with Allah is Islam' (Q. 3:19). This is probably the only sub-objective which cannot have a global acceptability.

Sub-objective 1.2. Religious freedom

Although Islam is the only (true) religion, the target of the adoption of Islam should never be achieved by enforcing anyone. In fact, *Shari'ah* also considers the choice of faith as voluntary, hence without any enforcement. Islam strongly prohibits forced religious conversion: 'There shall be no compulsion in religion; truly the Right Way has become clearly distinct from the wrong' (Q. 2:256).

So strongly does Islam advocate religious freedom that the Prophet (PBUH) is reported to have said: 'The one who kills a non-Muslim will never smell the fragrance of Heaven, even though this smell reaches a distance of 40 years' (*Ibn Majah, hadith* no. 2686).

Not only are the major offences on the basis of religion prohibited, but also the minor ones are equally condemned by the Prophet (PBUH), as mentioned in the *Sunnah*: 'Beware that if someone does unjust to a non-Muslim, or causes him a loss, or grabs something from him without his will, he will be judged as a non-Muslim on the Day of Judgment' (*Sahih Bukhari, hadith* no. 445). In other terms, in addition to the prohibition of any forced conversion, also any harm to non-Muslims is banned in Islam, to the extent that Heaven will be negated to the responsible of such a conduct. The universal acceptance of religious freedom as core social objective matches this *maqsad* of Islamic *Shari'ah*.

Provisions regarding financing for the security of faith

There are a number of financial provisions in Islam aimed at the achievement of the security of faith.

a. Emphasis is given to voluntary expenditures directed to the spreading of the Word of God. This includes expenditures on self-education and the education of others.
b. *Zakat*, which is obligatory for all Muslims, can be consumed 'to attract the hearts of those who have been inclined towards Islam', hence on religious education.
c. Ensuring religious freedom is a state's responsibility and the Prophet (PBUH) said in this regard: 'For Nijran and the people of Nijran, there is a guarantee from the Almighty Allah and His Prophet, on their blood, belonging, nation, their crosses, their trade [business], their churches, their monks and their priests' (*Subl al-Hadi wa Rashad fi Sirah Khairul-'Abad*, Vol. 6, by Muhammad bin Yusuf Al-Salhi ash-Shami).

Jihad is one of the most important duties of Muslims and there is lots of emphasis for Muslims to consume on *jihad*. *Jihad* aims at the security of Muslim state which consists of both believers and non-believers. In fact the non-Muslim deserves a priority in the security right because the holy Prophet has taken the responsibility of the protection of non-Muslims. Therefore, both Muslims and non-Muslims are the beneficiaries of the same level of this financing.

5.2. Objective 2. The protection of life (nafs)

The second most important *maqsad* in is the protection of life. This can take various forms, e.g. security against deadly diseases, killing and murders and any dangerous event.

Life in Islamic teachings is so precious that the Holy *Qur'an* states:

> For this reason, We decreed upon the Children of Israel [in the *Torah*] that whoever kills a human being – unless it be for murder or for spreading mischief in the earth –, it shall be as if he had killed all mankind. And whoever saves the life of one, it shall be as if he had saved the

life of all mankind. And certainly Our Messengers came unto them with clear proofs [of Allah's Sovereignty], yet, even after that, many of them continued to commit excesses in the earth.

(Q. 5:32)

The *ayat* tells that killing a person without justifiable reasons is like killing humanity, and saving one person's life is like saving humanity itself. Hence, even if a whole community wants to, it is not allowed to kill one person without justifiable reasons. At the same time nobody is allowed to cause any harm to society. In Islamic *Shari'ah*, creating disorder in a community is called *fitnah* and Islamic law implies strict punishment for creating *fitnah*. In this direction, Islam strictly forbids any extra judicial killings in a society and any action that may cause a threat to life: 'And do not kill the soul that Allah has forbidden [to be killed] except by [legal] right. This has He instructed you that you may use reason' (Q. 6:151).

Provisions in Islamic finance for the protection of life

Financing for the security of life can take various formats. At the beginning of Islam, health was not a commercial matter, therefore Islamic scriptures do not provide any *ayat* or *hadith* directly related to expenditures on health. However, there are several *ahadith* emphasizing the value of caring about patients. Care of patients and regular visits to them to look after their health is considered a duty for any Muslim. In fact, Abu Hurairah narrates that the Prophet (PBUH) said:

a Muslim has six duties towards other Muslims: when you meet him, you should salute him; when he invites you, accept his invitation; when he asks for your advice, give it to him; when he sneezes and praises Allah, say May Allah have mercy on you; when he is ill, visit him; and when he dies follow his funeral.

(*Sahih Bukhari, hadith* no. 1240; *Sahih Muslim, hadith* no. 2162)

Today that healthcare has become an industry, related expenditures have become an important chapter for charities and pious institutions, in order to save lives as prescribed by Islam.

One more thing to be noted is that the credit of saving a life doesn't relate to Muslim lives only; taking credit of lives of non-Muslim carries equal reward in Islamic *Shari'ah*. An example of such care of life without any distinction of religion can be found in the *Sunnah*, when there was a famine in Makkah. The people of Makkah, who were at that time strict opponents of Islam, sent their envoy to the Prophet (PBUH) for help. Despite their opposition, as the *hadith* narrates, 'the Prophet (PBUH) sent five hundred dinars to Makkah ... and ordered to pay them to Abi Sufyan ibn Harb and Safwan' (*Radd al-Mukhtar*, Vol. 2, ch. of *zakat* and *usher*).

5.3. Objective 3. The safeguard of intellect ('aql)

Intellectual capacity relates to the ability to understand the world and the *Qur'an*, in several passages, praises this understanding. Accordingly, the safeguard of intellect represents the third most important *maqsad al-Shari'ah*.

Sub-objective 3.1. Research and exploration of the creation of Allah

In relation to intellectual skills, Islam puts emphasis both on seeking knowledge and doing research about the mysteries of the universe.

In this regard, the *Qur'an* says:

> Indeed, in the creation of the heavens and the earth and the alternation of the night and the day, there are signs for those of understanding. Those who remember Allah (always, and in prayers) standing or sitting or lying down on their sides, and think deeply about the creation of the heavens and the earth, [saying]: 'Our Lord, You did not create [all] this without purpose, glory to You! [about such a thing]; then give us salvation from the punishment of the Fire'.

(Q. 3:190–191)

Sub-objective 3.2. Literacy and education

Since Islam emphasizes the seeking of knowledge, it also promotes education for every human being, men and women, the rich and the poor, the young and the old and for all nationalities and creeds. It is not by chance, in fact, that the first Revelation started with the word 'Read!', which indirectly gives evidence of the centrality of education in Islamic religion.

Financial provisions for the safeguard of intellect

The security of intellect includes promotion of education and wisdom. Consequently, a relevant target of expenditures for Islamic social finance should be addressed to this aim.

With regard to this objective, various proofs can be found in the Holy Scriptures.

The Prophet (PBUH), for instance, established a school inside Masjid-e-Nabvi in which a large number of students permanently resided to get education through charitable donations. In the *Sunnah*, it is also reported that the Messenger of Allah (PBUH) also said: 'When a man dies, his deeds come to an end except for three things: *sadaqah jjariyah* [ceaseless charity]; a knowledge which is beneficial; and a virtuous descendant who prays for him [the deceased]' (*Muslim, hadith* no.1580). Accordingly, educational institutions (*madaris*, sing. *madrasah*), either secular or religious, have been constantly promoted in the Muslim world. It is indeed important to note that education does not necessarily mean only religious knowledge, but also any other understanding that can have a social impact. Hence the Prophet (PBUH) ordered his companion Zaid bin Thabit (may Allah be pleased with him) to learn Hebrew, so that the communication with Jews could be made easier (*Musnad Ahmad*, vol. 5, *hadith* no. 182; *Tirmidhi, hadith* no. 2715).

In the Muslim world, Iraq and Spain have been two important centres for Islamic culture and several universities have been established there both for religious and secular education, many of them being financed by governments and many others financed through private funding. Today, there is a large number of religious educational institutions in Pakistan and India and some other countries under the traditional name of *madaris*. In Pakistan, about 1.3 million students get education through these institutions, without any charge and supported by charitable donations from the community.

5.4. Objective 4. The security of progeny/lineage (nasl)

The objective of the security of lineage in Islam comprises (i) the preservation of piousness by avoiding *haram* (illegitimate) sources of fulfilling sexual desire; (ii) the fulfilment of this desire in a natural way; and (iii) the securing of future generations.

Fulfilling sexual desires with the legitimate spouse realizes these purposes in compliance with Islamic religion. In relation to this, the Noble *Qur'an* prescribes: 'Do not approach any unlawful sexual intercourse. Indeed, it is a shameful, indecent thing, and an evil way [leading to individual and social corruption]' (Q. 17:32).

Provisions for the security of progeny

As stated earlier, by the preservation of progeny, Islam means security of piousness, fulfilling sexual desires in a natural way and the security of future generations. The security of progeny has been an important source of social spending in Islam throughout history.

The Prophet himself (PBUH) emphasizes the importance of marriage:

> It was narrated from Anas that there was a group of the Companions of the Prophet (PBUH), one of whom said: 'I will not marry women.' Another said: 'I will not eat meat.' Another said: 'I will not sleep on a bed.' And another: 'I will fast and not break my fast.' News of that reached the Messenger of Allah and he praised Allah and then said: 'What is the matter with people who say such and such? But I pray and I sleep, I fast and I break my fast, and I marry women. Whoever turns away from my *Sunnah* is not of me'.
>
> (*Sahih Bukhari, hadith* no. 4776)

There is also another long *hadith* reported by Ahmad (*Musnad Ahmad, hadith* no. 16330), Tarabani (*al-Mu'jam al-Kabir, hadith* no. 4445) and Hakim (*Al-Mustadrak, hadith* no. 2666) narrating the story of the Companion of Prophet (PBUH), Rabee'a Al-Aslami, to whom the Prophet (PBUH) one day asked 'Don't you want to get married?'. Rabee'a replied, 'I don't have anything that the female wants.' Then the Prophet (PBUH) sent him to an Anari tribe with the message to marry him with a particular girl. They obeyed his order, but Rabee'a didn't have anything to pay as *mahr* (i.e. the gift given to the girl at the time of marriage). The Prophet (PBUH) ordered one of his Companions to arrange some gold for him. He presented the piece of gold to the female, and came back to the Prophet (PBUH) by saying 'I have nothing for the *walimah*' (i.e. wedding reception). Hence, the Prophet (PBUH) also ordered his Companions to arrange a goat for the *walimah*, and he donated Rabee'a a piece of land for his livelihood. Similarly, when Fatima, the daughter of the Holy Prophet (PBUH) got married to Ali, Saad bin Abi Waqas took the responsibility of arranging a goat for the *walimah*. All these *ahadith* indicate the importance of marriage in Islamic culture and the relevance of all financing measures addressed to sustain the spouses in their shared life.

5.5. *Objective 5. Economic security: preservation of wealth* (mal)

The Holy *Qur'an* gives remarkable emphasis to the preservation of wealth as an objective to promote social welfare. In particular, three sub-objectives can be specified: (1) the lawful search for a sufficient income; (2) the reduction of economic inequality; and (3) poverty reduction.

Sub-objective 5.1. Legitimate income

There is a variety of words having similar meaning with regard to income and wealth in the *Qur'an* (e.g. *mal, mataa, fadhal, khayr*, etc.).

The moral acceptance for the search of legitimate benefit from the Lord (also as economic income) in Islam can be derived from the following *ayat*:

> There is no blame upon you for seeking bounty from your Lord [by trading during *hajj*, but be aware of not neglecting any of the rites]. But when you depart from 'Arafat, remember Allah at al-Mash'ar al-Haram. And remember Him, as He has guided you, for indeed, you were before among those who went astray.
>
> (Q. 2:198)

Sub-objective 5.2. Reduction in inequality

Along with giving permission to earn material resources, Islam prohibits their concentration with no benefits for others. The objective of reducing inequality is explicitly stated in the following verse of the Holy *Qur'an*:

> And what Allah restored to His Messenger ... it is for Allah and for the Messenger and for [his] near relatives and orphans and the [stranded] traveller – so that it [wealth] will not be [a benefit] going round and round among such of you as may [already] be rich.
>
> (Q. 59:7)

Islam prohibits every kind of effort and action to store wealth from one's occupation when its advantages are not widely distributed. Therefore Islam introduced the system of *zakat* and *usher* as obligatory funds disbursement which will automatically keep reducing the concentration of wealth, to expand its benefits among the needy.

In the same way, the *Qur'an* forbids any illicit accumulation of wealth, reducing the social impact that this wealth can have: 'Those who are ungenerous, and bid others to be ungenerous, and conceal whatever God has bestowed upon them out of His bounty – We have prepared for them [disbelievers] a humiliating punishment' (Q. 4:37).

Sub-objective 5.3. Reducing poverty

One of the prime sub-objectives of the economic security is the reduction in poverty and hunger. The Holy *Qur'an* advises many times that Muslims should donate (beyond the obligatory charity of *zakat* and *usher*) to the needy and the poor so that they may come out of poverty: 'Those who spend their possessions [for the sake of God] by night and by day, secretly and openly, shall have their reward with their Sustainer; and no fear need they have, and neither shall they grieve' (Q. 2:274).

The *Qur'an* urges mankind to be supportive to the deprived and poor and to bring mankind to move out of poverty: 'And We wanted to confer favour upon those who were oppressed in the land and make them leaders and inheritors' (Q. 28:5).

Financial provisions for economic security of the needy

Islam considers that the poor and deprived have their 'right' to the earnings of well-off people. Therefore, the *ayat* of the Holy *Qur'an* recommends to 'eat of [each of garden's] fruit when it yields and give its due [*zakat*] on the day of its harvest. And be not excessive. Indeed, Allah does not like those who commit excess [the wasters]' (Q. 6:141).

In order to reduce inequality and promote poverty reduction Islam invites all Muslims to be generous, both through forms of compulsory and voluntary charity. *Zakat* (2.5 per cent of income) and *usher* (a tenth of agricultural income) are the two obligatory forms of charity. However, there is much emphasis also on voluntary charity, to the extent that it is hard to differentiate it from the compulsory one. For example, as reported by Tabarani while mentioning the rights of neighbours, the Prophet said: 'A person is not a true believer if he enjoyed the meal at night whereas his neighbour remained hungry and he knew it' (*al-Mu'jam al-Kabir* by Tabarani, vol. 3, *hadith* no. 176).

Similarly, there are very strict warnings for those accumulating wealth and not using it as the *Qur'an* says: 'And there are those who bury gold and silver and spend it not in the way of Allah: announce unto them a most grievous penalty' (Q. 9:34). This verse motivates the wealthy persons to spend for the benefit of the society, with a social impact also on the needy, and not be engaged in excessive accumulation of wealth.

6. Islamic modes of finance, social impact and the objectives of *Shari'ah*

In the previous sections we have shown that for every objective the guidance of *Shari'ah* indicates one or more sources of finance. At the same time, it is also true that every mode of finance recommended by *Shari'ah* helps in achieving progress toward the *maqasid*.

As is well known, there are different contractual models that are currently in use in the Islamic financial system: *murabahah* (i.e. mark-up double sale); *ijarah* (i.e. lease of usufruct, rent agreement); *salam* (i.e. sale with advance payment); *istisna'* (contract of manufacture); *mudarabah* (silent partnership); and *musharakah* (full partnership) are the most basic forms.

This chapter does not aim at a critical perspective on the current practice of Islamic finance as regrettably oriented towards an excessive implementation of *murabahah* arrangements (hence simply focusing on trade of real assets, in line with widely accepted criteria of *Shari'ah* compliance, but in some ways replicating debt structures, instead of radically departing from them). It is also worth noting that there are a large number of modes of financing that are currently being used by the contemporary Islamic finance industry, e.g. *murabahah, musharakah mutanakisah, musawamah,* etc. These modes of financing are somehow permissible, but were never used in the earlier days of Islam as a regular mode of finance. Some of these modes, e.g. *musharakah mutanakisah,* were nonexistent at the time of the Holy Prophet in their present form. Despite their permissibility and legality in the *Shari'ah* framework, such modes of financing don't have sufficient compatibility with the objectives of *Shari'ah*. In the current section, only those modes of finance which had popularity at the time of the Holy Prophet are discussed. The discussion of these modes is outlined in the following sub-sections 6.1. and 6.2.

6.1. Musharakah *and* mudarabah

Musharakah and *mudarabah* are the two most popular modes of Islamic financing as tools of participatory profit-loss sharing in a common enterprise.

In the *musharakah* model two or more persons or entities participate in a business contributing in both capital and work services; profits and losses are to be divided between the partners in a pre-decided ratio. In the *mudarabah*, instead, one partner (*rabb al-mal*) provides capital and the other (*mudarib*) provides services; hence, the profits are distributed between them according to a predefined ratio, while the losses follow the nature of the contribution to the business (capital losses are on the *rabb al-mal*; work losses on the *mudarib*).

Since the early days of Islam, *musharakah* and *mudarabah* have been the most important modes of finance to realize the core substance of profit-loss sharing, hence promoting the social dimension of market cooperation. The Prophet (PBUH) himself did business with Khadeeja (who later became his wife) on the basis of *mudarabah*.

There is great appreciation for those participating in a *musharakah* arrangement as indicated in the following *hadith*: 'Abu Huraira reported the Holy Prophet to be saying that Allah says that when two persons participate in a business, I am third of them until they don't cheat. When anyone cheats, I get out of the arrangement' (*Abu Dawud*, hadith no. 3383).

Musharakah and *mudarabah* contribute to the achievement of the objectives of *Shari'ah* and to the realization of the social dimension of Islamic finance both by

a. *seeking bounty*
    The profit sharing arrangement provides an opportunity to pool up the resources, so that the income can be increased. As stated earlier, increasing income is one of the sub-objectives of economic security and this sub-objective brings prosperity to society.

b. *reducing inequality*
    One of the sub-objectives of economic security is reduction in income inequality, and the profit-sharing arrangement is one of the best ways to achieve this aim.

6.2. Salam *and* istisna'

Salam is a contract of future sale, in which the buyer pays the price of the commodity in advance to the seller and the seller makes a commitment to deliver the commodity on a predefined future date. *Salam* was sanctioned by Prophet Muhammad (PBUH) to facilitate farmers who were awaiting the harvest of crops. *Istisna'* (contract of manufacture) is the counterpart of *salam* used for financing the production of industrial goods, whereas *salam* is used for financing agriculture. Typically, a *salam* contract involves the following steps.

a. The financer agrees to purchase the goods produced by the recipient in a fixed amount and at a defined time.
b. The quality and quantity of the goods to be traded are specified as well.
c. The price of the good to be produced is paid by the financer in advance. In fact, full payment has to be made to the recipient at the time of the conclusion of the contract.

d. If the producer produces goods above the established quantity payable, he (the producer) is free to sell/consume this surplus as and where he wants.
e. Payment to the recipient can be made in terms of cash or in terms of commodity.

The *salam* contract (as well as *istisna'*, which can be seen as its equivalent for industrial financing, as previously remarked) has several features which make it a feasible strategy for the reduction of poverty and inequality, hence for the promotion of Islamic social finance in the light of *maqasid al-Shari'ah*.

a. The *salam* model can be seen as a cooperative in which the efficiency may increase because of the sharing of the tasks. In a conventional investment, the entrepreneur has to search for the productive skills, the capital as well as for the marketing. Many individuals who can produce fail to be good entrepreneurs because they cannot market their product in an appropriate way. However, in *salam* financing, the producer works only on the production and the financer has to market the product. This sharing of tasks may increase productivity which matches sub-objective 1 of economic security.
b. Unlike *murabahah* financing (i.e. mark-up double sale), which is the most popular mode of finance in the Islamic industry today, *salam* financing has greater harmony with the common benefit and mutual profit principles of Islamic social finance. The financer can get profit only when the producers produce, therefore this automatic checks on the income inequality. On the contrary, in the *murabahah* financing, whereas the financer sells some commodity to the businessmen on delayed payment, the financer secures his profit in advance regardless of any earning on the part of the recipients.
c. *Salam* (and correspondingly *istisna'*) is a kind of production order where the financer asks the recipient to produce certain goods for him. Accordingly, since the financer's capital is used for production, issues of credit risk and default, that in conventional finance are linked to the nominal value of money, are reduced, with limited need for collaterals or guarantees, and the possibility to nourish the social and economic growth of the community, to the advantage also of the poorest. This can help in the achievement of the second sub-objective of economic security, namely reduction in income inequality.

7. The prohibition of *riba* and its role in achieving the objectives of *Shari'ah*

A relevant aspect of the social orientation of Islamic finance with regard to the *maqasid* can also be derived from the prohibition of *riba* (usury, interest).

Charging interest on a loan in all its forms is strictly prohibited in Islam. But, unfortunately, interest has today a central place in the contemporary economy, and any monetary policy is interest centred, though *riba* pushes the economy into unemployment and brings greater inequality.

Interest, at a micro- and macro-level, leads to outcomes that are incon-sistent both with the objectives of *Shari'ah* and Sustainable Development Goals.

As just said, present monetary policies are one of the best examples of the (mis-)use of interest to achieve certain economic targets, while under-estimating its deep social impact in terms of perpetuation and increase of human inequality. However, there is a growing body of literature (e.g. Nordhaus, 1973; Easterly and Fischer, 2001; Fowler, 2005; Albanesi, 2007; Coibion *et al.*, 2012) that has indicated strong linkages between monetary policy and income inequality, which show the intrinsic contradictions of these instruments of growth and welfare, hence in opposition both to the *maqasid al-Shari'ah* and the Sustainable Development Goals (Coibion *et al.*, 2012).

This contraposition between *riba* and social interest can be shown by different examples both at a macro- and a micro-level.

Consider for instance, as first case, an economy with a rising inflation. Looking at the expected high inflation, the central bank would normally employ a 'tight' monetary policy and increase the interest rate, under the assumption that this increase shall reduce money supply, aggregate demand and ultimately inflation. But, in this process, the employment shall reduce too, and the consequences will be borne by temporary employees and daily wage workers. Unfortunately, these two groups, who are usually the most vulner-able groups in a given society, will further suffer, in an economic and social sense, due to this attempt for reduction in inflation.

Looking at the micro-level impact of interest and debt practice, this also departs from the objectives of *Shari'ah*. Suppose, for instance, that a person receives a loan to start a small enterprise and his business venture fails. This loss shall be borne only by the entrepreneur, while the obligation to repay the debt, plus interest, to the bank persists. This will lead to a negative re-distribution of income. Suppose, in reverse, that this entrepreneur earns a lot of profit on the loan: here, the profit will not be shared with the capital pro-vider, thus with a negative impact on the conception of the market as a place of social cooperation as upheld by Islam.

8. Conclusions

This chapter has dealt with the *maqasid al-Shari'ah* as a critical foundation for an Islamic social finance system (Section 2). In this regard, it has highlighted how the objectives of *Shari'ah* are not limited to the welfare (*falah*) of the Muslim community, but they relate to all human beings and their common prosperity, also in the light of the most recent criteria of sustainable develop-ment (Section 3).

The study has also clarified the distinction between the *maqasid* (general in their impact for all humanity) and the means to achieve these objectives (where a possible differentiation between Muslims and non-Muslims emerges) (Section 4).

The central part of the contribution (Section 5) has depicted the *maqasid* as core indicators of social welfare, with a link to the provisions on financing that Islamic tradition has transmitted and should be accordingly implemented today in the development of Islamic social finance. At the same time, economic security (*mal*), as one of the five fundamental objectives of *Shariʿah*, has been related to a broader social frame, comprising the securing of religion (*din*), the safeguard of life (*nafs*), the preservation of progeny (*nasl*) and of intellect (*ʿaql*). Since harmony subsists between the *maqasid* and the Sustainable Development Goals, this study can also be seen as a contribution to the worldwide debate about the future of the global economy.

In this direction, the outline of the most relevant modes of financing in Islamic finance (Section 6) has been addressed to the development of a cooperative approach to the market and its socio-economic nature. Last but not least, due to the current negative impact of interest-based economic policies, also the prohibition of *riba*, as a fundamental aspect of Islamic teachings (Section 7), has been depicted as a crucial aspect of this renovation of the market in the light of common welfare (*falah*).

References

The *ahadith* quoted in the chapter have been reported from the following collections and texts of the *Sunnah* of the Prophet: *Abu Dawud*; *Al-Mustadrak*; *Ibn Majah*; *Al-Muʿjam al-Kabir*; *Musnad Ahmad*; *Radd al-Mukhtar*; *Sahih Bukhari*; *Sahih Muslim*; *Subl al-Hadi wa Rashad fi Sirah Khairul-ʾAbad*; *Tirmidhi*.

Albanesi, S. (2007) Inflation and inequality. *Journal of Monetary Economics*. **54**(4), pp. 1088–1114.

Ali, S.S., and Hasan, H. (2014) *Towards a Maqasid al-Shariʿah Based Development Index*. IRTI Working Paper no. 1435–18.

Ali, S.S., Tohirin, A. and Ismail, A.G. (2014) *Developing a Framework for Maqasid al-Shariʿah Based Index of Socio-Economic Development.* Unpublished manuscript.

Amin, R.M., Yusof, S.A., Haneef, M.A., Muhammad, M.O. and Oziev, G. (undated) *Measuring Development from an Islamic Perspective: Construction of an Integrated Development Framework (IDF) and Index (I-Dex)*. [online]. Paper presentation available from www.irti.org/English/News/Documents/Seminars/Development%20From%20Islamic%20Perspective.pdf [Accessed 30 August 2017].

Coibion, O., Gorodnichenko, Y., Kueng, L. and Silvia, J. (2012) Innocent bystanders? Monetary policy and inequality in the US. *NBER Working Paper* no. 18170. National Bureau of Economic Research, Cambridge, MA.

Easterly, W., and Fischer, S. (2001) Inflation and the poor. *Journal of Money, Credit and Banking*. **33**(2), pp. 160–178.

Esen, M.F. (2015) A statistical framework on identification of *maqasid al-Shariah* variables for socio-economic development index. *Journal of Business Studies Quarterly*. **7**(1), pp. 107–124.

Fowler, S.J. (2005) Income inequality, monetary policy, and the business cycle. *Department of Economics and Finance Working Paper Series*. Middle Tennessee State University.

Nordhaus, W.D. (1973) The effects of inflation on the distribution of economic welfare. *Journal of Money, Credit and Banking*. **5**(1), pp. 465–504.

4 Collaborative governance, social capital and the Islamic economic organization

Charilaos Mertzanis

1. Introduction

Collaborative governance is the set of small group social interactions that, with markets and the state, determine economic outcomes. Collaborative governance has received attention from scholars and practitioners, because collaboration among public, private and local community decision-makers can achieve specific policy goals better through collective decision-making and management (Ansell and Gash, 2007). The main means to achieve complex policy goals through collaborative efforts include *inter alia* public–private partnerships, intergovernmental agreements, community-based alliances/ councils, and relational contracts of service delivery (Huxham and Vangen, 2005). The incentive for such collaboration originates more in the conscious realization of the superior outcome it can achieve in the modern complex world and less in some ideological, ethical or religious motives alone. It requires will, commitment and tolerance.

Despite the advantages of collaborative governance, inherent obstacles may impede the achievement of collective policy goals. These obstacles arise from conflicts, power imbalances, uncertainty and inadequate resource flows. Conflict and manipulative power, whether individual or group-wide, may result in poor outcomes by bringing about incongruence of goals among conflicting partners or generating powerless actors acting passively or merely in a selfish way in the collaborative process (Bryson *et al.*, 2006; Purdy, 2012). Furthermore, uncertainty in the collaborative process may prevent partners from engaging substantively in joint decision-making due to the high transaction costs in maintaining self-organizing modes of governance or shared risk and resource regimes (Ostrom and Ahn, 2003; Feiock, 2007). Risk and resource-related problems may cause collaboration to fail. Although multisector partners actively engage in search of resource optimization to achieve better policy goals, they may hesitate to commit to collaborative efforts when they confront difficulties in identifying or acquiring the resources needed or sharing unfairly large burdens of risk to accomplish their desired goals (Van de Ven, 1976; Pfeffer and Salancik, 1978).

The effectiveness of collaborative governance can be improved and barriers be reduced through the proper use of social networks, reliance on trust and local norms of behaviour (Putnam, 1993, 1995; Adler and Kwon, 2002). All of these comprise social capital. At the community level, social capital embodies important aspects of a community's beliefs, goals and willingness to cooperate. Without social capital, it would be much more difficult to pursue collaborative efforts. For instance, social capital can be instrumental in facilitating the development of network activities that strengthen the interdependence between groups through the flow of resources and information as well as risk sharing. A high level of social coherence is a crucial factor in pursuing collective goals based on mutual trust (Putnam, 1993; Fukuyama, 1995). Finally, shared norms foster collective efforts by mitigating conflict or power asymmetries due to integrating diverse values and cultures (Coleman, 1988).

In a more broad sense, social capital generally refers to trust, concern for each other, and a willingness to live by the norms of one's community and to sanction those who do not. The willingness to exit the community and to adhere to a different set of group norms and values should not be restricted or sanctioned. The question then arises as to how to effectuate collaborative governance among homogenous but differing groups in a given society or among different societies by and large. These behaviours have been recognized as essential ingredients of good governance among classical thinkers ever since Aristotle. However, in the last two hundred years, socio-economic analysis has been largely based on the concept of *homo economicus*. Accordingly, its focus has shifted to the role of competitive markets, well-defined property rights and efficient, well-intentioned states. Clear and efficient rules of the game and level playing fields have thus come to displace mutual trust and good citizenship as guiding conditions of effective governance.

This chapter argues that social capital and collaborative governance among states, markets and communities in making policy decisions addresses some common market and state failures. However, local community governance typically relies on insider-outsider distinctions that may be morally offensive and economically costly. It further argues that the individual motivations supporting collaborative governance are not captured by either selfishness or altruism at the two extremes but by harnessing the capabilities of diverse poles into an agreed upon goal, regardless of the values and ethics underlying the motives for doing so. Communities, markets and states are complements and not substitutes so, when poorly designed, markets and states weaken communities and the effectiveness of the collaborative process. In this respect, the equitable distribution of property rights and accordingly risk-sharing matter at fostering collaborative governance.

In this respect, within such a multipolar collaborative governance framework, the notion of risk-sharing inherent in the Islamic value system endows the Muslim world with a good potential to achieve an efficient economic organization and prosperity, which however could only be accomplished if

Muslim societies abide by the principles that make collaboration possible and effective. Risk-sharing-based social values and behaviour as well as specific instruments, such as those used by Islamic finance, endow its adherents with an effective potential means for engaging in effective collaborative governance within the Islamic world and between itself and the rest of the universe. Reference to historical examples and to Islamic norms and values will be used to illustrate the point.

2. Social capital and collaborative governance

The socio-economic formations that emerged in the last two centuries have advocated either laissez faire or comprehensive state intervention as the ideal form of social governance. They further defined the terms of institutional policy for much of the twentieth century.

This process, while following different paths, was observed across the globe in one or another way. However, on the one hand, driven by sentiments or constraints, varying conscience or pragmatism, daily people have adopted less dogmatic positions in order to find solutions to real social problems. On the other hand, intellectuals gave in to the fascination of comparing social and economic systems and arguing about the merits of either the market or the state. The ideological background of the former has been the spontaneous market order and that of the latter the supremacy of social engineering, both of which now seem out of fashion. The evolution of socio-economic systems and the repeated social failures and economic crises have discredited both socio-economic conceptions of social processes and the organization of economic activity. Today many have come to believe that market failures are the norm rather than the exception and that states are neither sufficiently informed nor sufficiently accountable to correct all market failures. It seems that the rising focus on the role of social capital has arisen to prominence less on its own merits and more on the defects of its alternatives.

Proponents of social intervention tend to abide by the idea of social capital because it affirms the importance of trust, generosity and collective action in social problem solving. Proponents of laissez faire tend to believe that well-defined property rights and competitive markets could successfully harness self-centred motives to public ends thereby making values of social trusting and sharing unnecessary. In the latter view, where markets fail in providing local public goods and social insurance, the solution should be sought in the private sector institutions and not the government. Proponents of social planning believe the other way around.

However, social reality has been harsh. The recurrent financial crises, the rising social and income inequalities, and the growing environmental concerns, as well as the observed limits of governmental capacity to provide solutions and proper accountability demonstrated the behavioural and irrational nature of self-interested private action and the inflexible and bureaucratic limitation of social planning. This has led to the demise of these twin illusions, thus allowing for the rise of the idea of social capital. The rise of social capital role has reflected a heightened awareness by policy-makers and academics of the importance of real people's values (rather than the empirically implausible utility functions of *homo economicus* and the ideological supremacy of the social plan), of how people interact in their daily lives, in families, neighbourhoods and work groups. People interact in many other ways, not just as buyers, sellers or passive citizens.

The term 'social capital' is a flawed one (Putnam, 1993, 1995). Capital refers to a thing that is owned. Instead, the attributes that make up social capital describe relationships among people, not ownership.

The term 'community' better captures the aspects of good governance that explain social capital's popularity, as it focuses on what groups do rather than what people own (Bowles and Gintis, 2002). A community is a network of people who interact directly, frequently and in multi-faceted ways. People who work together are usually communities in this sense, as are some neighbourhoods, groups of friends, professional and business networks, gangs and sports leagues. It is connection, not affection, which defines community. Whether one is born into a community or one entered by choice, there are normally significant costs to moving from one to another.

The term community makes it clear that understanding trust, cooperation, generosity and other behaviours emphasized in the social capital literature requires the study of the structure of social interactions, and underlines the fact that the same individuals will exhibit different levels and types of social capital depending on the social interactions in which they are engaged (Glaeser *et al.*, 2002).

However, there are considerable problems in measuring trust and thus clearly demonstrating the plausibility of the underlying behavioural assumptions of social capital. In addition to the econometric problems stressed by Durlauf (2002), commonly used survey instruments are not reliable predictors of actual behaviours. Glaeser *et al.* (2000) found that the standard questions about trust, popularized by Fukuyama (1995) and others, are uninformative about either the respondent's experimental behaviour in a trust experiment for real money or the respondent's daily behaviour (willingness to loan possessions to others, etc.).

It is also difficult to associate clearly social capital with social participation and democratic values, more so in the Islamic world. For example, Ciftci (2010) studied individual behaviour in ten Muslim countries and documented that cultural values brought about by modernity, such as gender equality and tolerance, as well as material conditions such as higher levels of education and income, are better predictors of individual support for democracy than Islamic values and religiosity.

Thus, considerable challenges remain to be addressed by those who share the conviction that policy design based on collaborative governance should recognize and enhance the complementarities among markets, states and communities (Ouchi, 1980; Hayami, 1989; Ostrom, 1998; Aoki and Hayami, 2000).

3. Communities, cooperation and risk-sharing entrepreneurship

Communities are a core element of collaborative governance because they address certain problems that cannot be solved by individuals acting alone or by markets and governments. There is considerable historical evidence that organizational innovation at the community level is essential to its survival and economic development. This is especially true with respect to the relation between risk-sharing, partnership and entrepreneurship. Drawing on the work of Max Weber (2003), Brouwer (2005) argues that the way successful societies have organized new ventures has been remarkably similar in both past and present. Organizations conducive to risk-sharing entrepreneurship prevailed in highly successful regions from the medieval Northern Italy to the late twentieth century Silicon Valley. The *commenda* organizations of medieval Italy shared many characteristics with modern start-ups financed by venture capital by using forms of profit-share contracts, limited liability and periodic evaluation. Contracts in both types of ventures were designed to absorb through risk-sharing the high level of uncertainty inherent in entrepreneurial activity. Uncertainty prohibits a unique *ex ante* ranking of investment projects and prompts investors to look for hidden social capital. Equity finance is better equipped to even out unexpected losses and gains that are inherent to uncertainty than debt finance.

Risk-sharing contracts have been especially common in Islamic economic organizations that prefer risk-sharing to risk-shifting. The Islamic values prohibit interest-based transactions but encourage business partnerships and trade. While interest transactions shift risks from the owner of capital to the entrepreneur, partnership makes the two share risks and therefore profits and losses, leading to the emergence of the Islamic community shared economy. Following an insight by Max Weber, Udovitch (1967) suggested an Islamic *mudarabah* origin for the European *commenda* based on his readings of Hanafi legal manuals dating back to the eighth century (see also Panzac, 2002; Khalilieh, 2006; Harris, 2009; Askari *et al.*, 2012). During the late twelfth century, with the help of the crusaders, the Queen of France Eleanor of Aquitaine brought the Islamic law of partnerships and the admiralty law from Jerusalem to France, which were subsequently incorporated into the *lex mercatoria*, the medieval European law of commerce. The risk-sharing *mudarabah/commenda* contract financed the large increase in trade within Europe and across the Mediterranean (Acemoglu and Robinson, 2012). Further, the Ottoman cash *waqf* and *esham* systems constituted another manifestation of the Islamic risk-sharing organization (Çizakça, 2013). Cash *awqaf* (pl. of *waqf*) were community collective investment schemes funded by private cash contributions for charitable purposes. The money was invested generating revenue to be spent for the charitable purpose of the donation. However, whilst the cash capital should be invested with *mudarabah* instruments, in practice it used *istiglal*, a risk-shifting instrument. In the *esham* system, risk-sharing was applied at the state level. The state established an investment asset, whose annual revenue was securitized into equal shares and offered for sale to the public, entitling investors a fixed share of the allocated annual revenue pro rata for as long as they lived.

Examples that are more recent illustrate the benefits of collaboration in different settings. Sampson *et al.* (1997) studied neighbourhood behaviour in Chicago, where residents speak firmly to youngsters on skipping school, avoiding disturbance or using graffiti, and intervene to maintain neighbourhood amenities such as a local fire station threatened with budget cuts. They found considerable variation in the neighbourhood levels of collective efficacy, where income, gender and race mattered. However, ethnic heterogeneity was considerably less important in predicting low collective efficacy than economic disadvantage and housing instability. Further, high levels of collective efficacy were associated with lower levels of violent crime, thus creating a positive externality. Further, Platteau and Seki (2001) showed that fishing cooperatives in the Toyama Bay in Japan, faced with variable catches and shifting skill requirements, have chosen to share income, information and training about the changing location and availability of fish. Elder members pass on their experience skills, and the more educated younger members teach others new high tech methods. The cooperative's income- and cost-pooling and sharing activities allow fishing in much riskier and higher-yield locations, and the skill- and information-sharing raises profits and reduces productivity differences among the boats. Moreover, Craig and Pencavel (1995) showed that the plywood workers who owned their firms in Oregon and Washington districts in the USA benefited from both similar peer-monitoring and risk-pooling initiatives. They elected their managers and required member ownership of the firm as a condition of employment as well as employment in the firm as a condition of ownership. For two generations these cooperatives, by expending high levels of work commitment and savings on managerial monitoring of workers, had successfully competed with conventionally organized firms in the industry. Total factor productivity was significantly higher relative to conventional corporate counterparts. When faced with cyclical downturns in the demand for plywood the cooperatives, unlike their competitors, did not fire or lay off workers, but rather chose to take cuts in either wages or hours, thus pooling the cyclical risk among all members. Other examples of community cooperation are highlighted by Ghemawat (1995), Hansen (1997), and Knez and Simester (2001).

However, risk-sharing has been effective when coupled with equal treatment of participants. For instance, the limited inequality between managers and workers in the Japanese firm is thought to be a key contributor to information-sharing between management and production workers leading to higher sustainability (Aoki, 1988). Further, members of irrigation organizations of farms in developing countries were found more likely to cooperate in making efficient use of water if status and class inequalities among them are limited (Bardhan and Dayton-Johnson, 2007). Bardhan *et al.* (2000) and Baland *et al.* (2003) highlight other similar experiences.

All these examples suggest that communities solve through risk pooling and sharing economic problems that might otherwise appear as standard market failures or state failures. These failures take the form of insufficient provision of local public goods, the absence of insurance and other risk-sharing opportunities even when these would be mutually beneficial, the exclusion of the poor from credit markets, and the excessive and ineffective monitoring of work effort.

Communities have crucial information about other members' behaviours, capacities and needs. Members use this information both to uphold norms and to make use of efficient insurance arrangements that are not plagued by the usual problems of moral hazard and adverse selection. This insider information is used in multilateral rather than centralized ways, all of which may have salience when conveyed by a neighbour or workmate.

Communities thus may make an important contribution to collaborative governance where market contracts and government approvals fail because the necessary information to design and enforce beneficial exchanges and directives cannot effectively be used by judges, government officials and other outsiders. This is particularly the case where ongoing relationships among community members support trust, mutual concern, or sometimes simply effective multilateral enforcement of group norms. Communities are one of the ways these norms are sustained (Bowles and Gintis, 1998). Interestingly, the delicate nature of trust as a basis for communal decision-making was made well aware 640 years ago by Muhammed Ibn Khaldun who held the view that:

> Now, honest traders are few. ... There will also be non-acknowledgement or denial of obligations, which may prove destructive of one's capital unless (the obligation) has been stated in writing and properly witnessed. The judiciary is of little use in this connection, since the law requires clear evidence.
>
> (*The Muqaddimah*, Ch. V, note 13)

4. Communal incentives to participate in collaborative governance

Empirical evidence and common sense suggest that different institutions handle different problems well. Markets are effective because of their ability to make use of private information. Where comprehensive contracts are written and enforced at low cost, markets are often superior to other governance structures. Further, where residual claimancy and control rights are closely aligned, market competition provides a decentralized and difficult to corrupt disciplining mechanism that punishes the inefficient and rewards the high performers.

The state is relatively effective for handling particular classes of problems. In particular, the state is attractive because it alone has the power to make and enforce the rules of the game that govern the interaction of private agents.

Therefore in cases where an economic process will be effective only if participating is mandatory (e.g. participating in a social insurance programme, or paying for national defence) governments have an advantage.

Communities may solve problems that both states and markets are ill equipped to address, especially where the nature of social interactions or of the goods and services being transacted makes contracting highly incomplete or costly. Effective community governance relies on dispersed private information often unavailable to states, employers, banks and other large formal organizations to apply rewards and punishments to members according to their conformity with or deviation from social norms. An effective community monitors the behaviour of its members, rendering them accountable for their actions. In contrast with states and markets, communities more effectively foster and utilize the incentives that people have traditionally deployed to regulate their common activity: trust, solidarity, reciprocity, reputation, personal pride, respect, vengeance and retribution, among others.

Communities have unique governance capacities. First, in a community, the probability that members who interact today will interact in the future is higher, and thus there is a strong incentive to act in socially beneficial ways now to avoid retaliation in the future. Second, the frequency of interaction among community members lowers the cost and raises the benefits associated with being acquainted with the characteristics, recent behaviour and likely future actions of other members (predictability). The more easily acquired and widely dispersed this information is, the more community members will have an incentive to act in ways that result in collectively beneficial outcomes. Third, communities overcome free-rider problems by its members directly sanctioning 'anti-social' actions of others. Monitoring and punishment by peers in work teams, credit associations, partnerships, local common situations and residential neighbourhoods is often an effective means of attenuating incentive problems that arise where individual actions affecting the well-being of others are not subject to enforceable contracts (Whyte, 1955; Tilly, 1981; Hossain, 1988; Ostrom, 1990; Dong and Dow, 1993; Sampson *et al.*, 1997).

The reasons that communities work in these ways are not to be found in individual members' self-interested behaviour and their interaction based on defection as a dominant strategy (Bowles and Gintis, 2000; Gintis, 2000; Bowles, 2003). They are rather found in the prevalent relations of altruism, affection and other non-self-regarding motives.

Many of these approaches, however, have treated the community organically without investigating whether or not its structural characteristics are consistent with conventional notions of equilibrium based on intentional action. For example, taking a focus on the Islamic world, there is a considerable literature on the syncretic and complex links between religious faith and forms of social movement and political mobilization in Islamic communities (Roy, 2004). The analytical focus has highlighted the culture of Islam, the belief systems of the faithful, and the historical and geographical trajectories of Muslim populations across the world (Modood, 2005; Ramadan 2005). However, Les Back *et al.* (2009) argue that studies of Islamic political and communal participation need to be contextualized carefully without recourse to grand generalities about a unique Islamic culture and faith. This is because both culture and faith are both structured by and in turn structuring the cultural, institutional and deliberative landscapes through which they are articulated. Similar views are echoed by Mertzanis (2016, 2017) who shows that a number of national cultures, the varying strength of family ties, and ethnic, linguistic and religious divergences affect business finance in the Islamic world: all this highlights considerable behavioural diversity among the Islamic world. Thus, like the examples in the previous section, the evidence shows that the extent to which the spiritual values underlying Islamic economic organization can be conducive to social capital enhancement should not be overstressed but instead proper contextualization, with reference to specific social and economic characteristics, is required to understand their efficacy.

5. Community failures as a collaborative governance disincentive

Like markets and states, communities also fail. The reasons can be economic, behavioural and incentive-based ones (Bowles and Gintis, 2002).

Starting from the economic ones, the personal and durable contacts that characterize communities require them to be of relatively small scale. The preference for dealing with fellow members often limits their capacity to exploit gains from trade on a wider basis. The relatively high degree of community homogeneity lowers the potential benefits of economic diversity associated with strong complementarities among differing skills and other inputs. These limitations can be overcome by sharing information, equipment and skills. Communities can exploit economies of scale unattainable by less cooperative groups, and reap benefits from the diversity of members' talents. Cooperation in the local business networks along with their associated local governments allow otherwise unviable small firms to benefit from economies of scale in marketing, research and training allowing their survival in competition with corporate giants. But compared to state bureaucracies and free markets, which specialize in dealing with anonymous actors, communities have to deal with known members thereby raising the cost of economic activity due to lower incentives for competition and transformation caused by stronger sentiments and prohibitive values. The problem is stronger in communities exposed to open environments where the competitive transformation challenges are stronger and more persistent.

Communities can fail because of behavioural reasons. Where group membership is the result of voluntary individual choice rather than enforced group decision, the composition of common value-sharing groups is likely to be more culturally and demographically homogeneous than any of the members would like. This would deprive the members of valued forms of diversity that would endow the groups as a whole with the necessary dynamism to adapt and evolve. At the presence of significant ethnic, linguistic and religious fractionalization of groups in a community, it is likely that individual members for psychological, social and economic reasons would prefer to be in the majority rather than minority fragments of the community. If individuals sort themselves among the communities along those preferences, there will be a strong tendency for all of the communities to end up perfectly isolated (Schelling, 1978). Integrated communities would make everyone better off, but they will prove unsustainable if individuals are free to move (Young, 1998; Bowles, 2003).

Moreover, like markets and states, communities often fail because of allocative inefficiency. Most individuals seek membership in a group of familiar associates and feel isolated without it. As a result, insiders enjoying solidarity and support may tend to mistreat outsiders. The problem is exacerbated by the group homogeneity resulting from the behavioural community failure described above. When insider–outsider distinctions are made on divisive and morally objectionable bases, such as race, religion, nationality or sex, community governance may contribute more to perpetuating narrow-mindedness and ethnic hostility than to addressing the failures of markets and states and therefore promote the common good. This failure becomes pronounced at the presence of large economic inequalities between the insiders and the outsiders. Communities work because they are good at enforcing norms informally, but whether this results in a good overall outcome depends on what the enforced norms are. Various forms of resistance to racial or religious or residential or other integration, both from the majorities and the minorities in a community, do not provide a good account of social capital in action (Cohen, 1998; Jung, 2001).

Thus, social capital can be enhanced if communities manage to control those economic, behavioural and incentive reasons precipitating failure. At the absence of an effective community control policy aiming at openness and diversity, cooperative transformation and qualified tolerance, shared spiritual and religious values alone may not be able to achieve the goal. Indeed, they may achieve the opposite: a condemnation of the community in a chronic economic slowdown, increasing fractionalization and xenophobia, all of which risk leading to marginalization associated with social and economic conservatism, risk, and human intolerance and social introversion. These risks may be exacerbated when the community's fear to open, collaborate, adapt and evolve leads, in search of needed moral and psychological support to maintain cohesion, to a regressive quest for 'fundamental' truths and values which, at the presence of increasing discrepancy between those and the sustainability requirements of evolving societies, can only perpetuate introversion in a vicious circle.

The progressive or regressive role of religion or culture in structuring social and economic outcomes through a more or less collaborative process has rather recently drawn proper attention. Following the insights of Weber and the analysis of North (1990), Grief (1994, 2006) showed that faith-based behaviour tends to be subsumed within cultural beliefs. Further, Baumol and Strom (2010) go as far as to state that religion is perhaps one of the strongest cultural influences on the activities of the entrepreneur throughout history. Such influences could be either positive or negative depending on the degree of flexibility of legal frameworks and behavioural norms. Kuran (2011) provided evidence that Islamic institutions, manifested in too simple, inflexible and limited contract forms, constrained long-run economic growth and accumulation in the Middle East, leading many Muslims to devise stratagems to circumvent the rules (see also Lydon, 2009).

6. Enhancing social capital and collaborative governance effectiveness

Community failures have led both conservative advocates of laissez faire and their social democratic and liberal socialist critics to view communities as anachronistic institutions that lack contract rights and are inadequate to the task of governance in a modern society. Communities have therefore been regarded as part of the problem of parochial populism or traditional fundamentalism and not the solution to the failures of markets and states. Even if both advocates reject dogmatic adherence to either social planning or free markets, they are still concerned with an optimal solution somewhere in between, but not beyond.

The advocates of social capital and collaborative governance as an important mode of policy-making and institution-building hold the belief that, in the modern information-based and complex world, states or markets and their combinations cannot be so perfected as to make local norms redundant in contributing to the solution of governance problems through adequate social policy. There are many historical and recent examples where efforts to perfect the market or assure the success of state interventions have destroyed imperfect but nonetheless workable community-based systems of governance, suggesting that non-collaborative policy paradigms confined to states and markets may be counter-productive.

There can be no blueprint for ideal social capital-based collaborative governance frameworks among states, markets and communities, as none of them has individually both the information and the inclination to offset social failures. Communities solve problems in a bewildering variety of ways with hundreds of differing membership rules, de facto property rights and decision-making procedures (Ostrom, 1990; Ostrom *et al.*, 1992; Scott, 1998). Some of the elements that are often found in well-governed communities might form part of a public policy aimed at enhancing the desirable aspects of social capital and collaborative governance. Notwithstanding the absence of blueprint frameworks, the need to abide by the principles of collaborative governance in order to achieve better social goals seems urgent.

These principles essentially imply the following.

First, the members of the community should own the fruits of their success or failure in solving the collective problems they face. The community members should own shares in the output of their cooperative and hence directly benefit from its success in a way that employees on fixed wages would not. Communities in which common business ownership and risk pooling and sharing are high exhibit higher levels of collective efficacy even after controlling for a large number of demographic and economic variables. In order to own the success of one's efforts, community members must generally own the assets with which they work, or whose value is affected by what the community does. They must also 'own' the decisions for their chosen economic organization.

Second, the unravelling of cooperation that often distresses communities can be averted if policies for mutual monitoring and punishment of non-cooperators are built into the structure of social interactions (Yamagishi, 1992). Policies to increase the visibility of the actions of peers in communities, along with policies to enhance the effectiveness of forms of multilateral sanctioning of non-cooperators may thus contribute to cooperative solutions to problems, even if many members are driven by mere self-interest. Hunter-gatherer groups that share food often practise the custom of eating in public, an effect of which is to make violations of the sharing rule evident to all. Cooperation in sizable groups is sustained by the punishment of non-cooperators in various ways. When cooperation is common, the costs incurred by civic-minded punishers is small, and they can easily persist in a population; when instead cooperation is uncommon, those who punish non-cooperators will incur heavy costs and will be likely to be eliminated by any plausible evolutionary process (Boyd *et al.*, 2001). This suggests that a heterogeneous community comprising both civic-minded members, ready to punish those who violate norms, and self-interested members, may exhibit varying degrees of cooperation depending not on the extent of the community's heterogeneity but rather on its recent history. Individuals are not uniformly selfish nor altruistic but often driven by honourable sentiments, so prudence and realism alike could recommend an alternative dictum: policy-makers should know that populations are heterogeneous and the individuals making them up are both versatile and adaptable. Thus, good policies and constitutions are those that support socially valued outcomes not only by harnessing selfish motives to socially valued ends, but also by evoking, cultivating and empowering public collaboration motives.

Third, well-working communities require a legal and governmental environment favourable to their functioning. For instance, reducing local community crime cannot be achieved if the police is not on call. Large-size cooperatives need to work within national regulatory environments that they are incentivized to complement by locally made rules, but not to violate or abuse. Effective state intervention should aim at providing a favourable institutional environment and at handling cases in which the informal community sanctions would not be adequate (Wade, 1988; Lam, 1996). Community-state synergy can be instrumental for the delivery of adequate infrastructure (Ostrom, 1996). The fact that governmental intervention has sometimes destroyed collaborative governance capacities does not support a recommendation of laissez faire. Local interactions within and between communities must be viewed as a complement to effective state government. Unfortunately, many favouring the social capital option are evidently motivated more by the fact that it would shrink government and less by the hope that it would reduce inequality and increase effectiveness. Thus, an institutional environment that complements the distinctive governance abilities of communities and a decentralized distribution of property rights that makes members the beneficiaries of community success are key aspects of policies to foster community problem-solving. However, developing a collaborative governance structure that states, markets and communities are mutually enhancing is a challenging task. For example, where the nature and distribution of property rights is ill defined whilst informal contractual enforcement is essential to mutually beneficial exchange, a policy to define property rights more precisely may reduce the multifaceted and repetitive nature of interpersonal contact on which collaborative governance is based (Bowles and Gintis, 1998). Where work effort, compliance to norms or environmental conservation is low, a policy to induce higher commitment based on the mobilization of self-interested motives with fines and sanctions may undermine reciprocity and other social motives (Fehr and Gachter, 2002).

Fourth, an active advocacy of the conventional liberal ethics of equal treatment and enforcement of conventional anti-discrimination policies needs to be incentivized and supported. Repugnant behaviours favouring 'us' against 'them' can only hamper collaborative governance, as suggested by the many examples of well-working communities that do not exhibit the ugly parochial and divisive potential of this form of governance. Communities always have to face difficult trade-offs between good governance and parochialism. Dealing with the trade-offs, community participation is required. The extent of participation is affected more by social and income inequalities than racial and ethnic diversity (Alesina and La Ferrara, 2000). Thus, policies to reduce social and income inequality would enhance participation and hence the outcome of collaborative governance. However, if successful communities prefer to be relatively homogeneous, then a heavy reliance on internalized governance would, in the absence of adequate counteracting policies, further enhance homogeneity, because the success of members and their likely longevity will depend on their homogenous integration within the group. Thus a competitive economy that includes widely worker-owned cooperatives and risk-sharing business partnerships is likely to exhibit more homogeneous business organizations than one made up of conventional business firms.

The combination of within-group homogeneity and between-group competition, while effectively promoting some desirable forms of collaborative governance, seems a recipe for generating hostile insider versus outsider sentiments. Dilemmas such as this are not likely to disappear and may manifest themselves in economic, ethnic and religious intolerance alike. Dealing with it is a major future challenge.

7. Economic evolution, collaborative governance and the Islamic economic organization

The rise of global trade and finance and the emergence of democracy cast doubt on the traditional role of communities in governance efficiency. Thinkers and policy-makers of all persuasions believed that markets and the state would extinguish the values that throughout history had sustained forms of governance based on intimate and informal relationships. Communities were perceived as carriers of parochial values that were bound to be extinguished by economic and political competition in global markets and democratic states. Such values were thought to be associated with cultural commitments that contradict those entailed by modern social institutions. As individual behaviour has been increasingly directed to individual advantage, sentiments, habits and instincts are disregarded as characteristics of communal attitudes and objectives (Hirsch, 1976).

However, global markets and democratic states evidently have not succeeded in providing adequate public goods and social insurance as well as alleviating inequalities. Markets, states and communities represent cultural environments in which some values flourish and others wither affecting their interaction and evolution. The survival, evolution and relative strength of those institutions, more so for the communities, will be determined not by the survival of 'fundamental' values and the return to eternal truths as guiding principles, but their capacity to provide successful solutions to contemporary problems of social coordination.

Thus, social capital and collaborative governance appear likely to assume more importance in the future. Based on the potential more efficient pooling and sharing of information, risk-taking and costs, as historical evidence shows, communities solve problems that governments and markets cannot. This can happen when individuals interact and transact in ways that cannot be regulated by complete contracts or by external rules, due to the complexity of the interactions or the private or unverifiable nature of the information pertaining to those transactions. These interactions arise increasingly in modern economies, as information-intensive production replaces assembly lines and other technologies traditionally handled by contract or external rules, and as intangible inputs and outputs increasingly displace tangible kilowatts and tonnes of steel. In an economy increasingly based on qualities rather than quantities, the superior capabilities of collaborative governance among states, markets and communities are likely to be manifested in increasing reliance on the kinds of multilateral monitoring and risk-pooling and risk-sharing behaviour.

In this respect, the strong risk-sharing elements of Islamic economic organization endows it with a good potential for achieving much needed efficient and effective social organization. The potential benefits of social capital and collaborative governance can be realized in Islamic societies because they traditionally share values that are more conducive to the containment of self-interest as a condition for participation and collaborative governance.

However, the capacity of communities to solve problems may be impeded by hierarchical division and economic inequality among its members as well as a reluctance to be open, tolerant and adaptable. In this respect, the record of Islamic societies is for the most part rather discouraging. Assuming that communities can indeed perform well relative to markets and states, in situations where interaction is complex, tasks are too qualitative to be captured in explicit contracts, and the conflicts of interest among members are contained, it results that largely unequal societies will be competitively disadvantaged in the future because their structures of privileged and unequal reward would limit the capacity of collaborative governance to facilitate the qualitative interactions that underpin the modern economy. This is a major future challenge for Islamic societies notwithstanding the origin of their value system and their ethnic diversity.

References

Acemoglu, D. and Robinson, J.A. (2012) *Why Nations Fail*. New York: Crown Business.

Adler, P.S. and Kwon, S.W. (2002) Social capital: prospects for a new concept. *Academy of Management Review*. **27**, pp. 17–40.

Alesina, A. and La Ferrara, E. (2000) Participation in heterogeneous communities. *Quarterly Journal of Economics*. **115**(3), pp. 847–904.

Ansell, C. and Gash, A. (2007) Collaborative governance in theory and practice. *Journal of Public Administration Research and Theory*. **18**, pp. 543–571.

Aoki, M. (1988) *Information, Incentives and Bargaining in the Japanese Economy*. Cambridge: Cambridge University Press.

Aoki, M. and Hayami, Y. (2000) Introduction. In: Aoki, M. and Hayami, Y. (eds) *Communities and Markets in Economic Development*. Oxford: Oxford University Press.

Askari, H., Iqbal, Z., Krichene, N. and Mirakhor, A. (2012) *Risk Sharing in Finance: The Islamic Finance Alternative*. Singapore: John Wiley and Sons.

Baland, J.M., Bardhan, P. and Bowles, S. (2003) *Inequality, Cooperation and Environmental Sustainability*. New York: Russell Sage.

Bardhan, P. and Dayton-Johnson, J. (2007) Inequality and the governance of water resources in Mexico and South India. In: Baland, J.M., Bardhan, P. and Bowles, S. (eds) *Inequality, Cooperation and Environmental Sustainability*. New York: Russell Sage Foundation. Princeton, NY and Oxford: Princeton University Press, pp. 97–130.

Bardhan, P., Bowles, S. and Gintis, H. (2000) Wealth inequality, credit constraints, and economic performance. In: Atkinson, A. and Bourguignon, F. (eds) *Handbook of Income Distribution*. Dordrecht: North-Holland.

Baumol, W.J. and Strom R.J. (2010) 'Useful knowledge' of entrepreneurship: some implications of the history. In: Landes, D.S., Mokyr, J. and Baumol, W.J. (eds) *The Invention of Enterprise: Entrepreneurship from Ancient Mesopotamia to Modern Times*. Princeton, NJ: Princeton University Press.

Bowles, S. (2003) *Microeconomics: Behaviour, Institutions and Evolution*. Princeton, NJ: Princeton University Press.

Bowles, S. and Gintis, H. (1998) The moral economy of community: structured populations and the evolution of prosocial norms. *Evolution and Human Behaviour*. **19**(1), pp. 3–25.

Bowles, S. and Gintis, H. (2000) Walrasian economics in retrospect. *Quarterly Journal of Economics*. **115**(4), pp. 1411–1439.

Bowles, S. and Gintis, H. (2002) Social capital and community governance. *The Economic Journal*. **112**(483), pp. 419–436.

Boyd, R., Gintis, H., Bowles, S. and Richerson, P. J. (2001) The evolution of altruistic punishment. *Proceedings of the National Academy of Science of the United States of America*. **100**(6), pp. 3531–3535.

Brouwer, M. (2005) Managing uncertainty through profit sharing contracts from medieval Italy to Silicon Valley. *Journal of Management & Governance*. **9**(3–4), pp. 237–255.

Bryson, J.M., Crosby, B.C. and Stone, M.M. (2006) The design and implementation of cross-sector collaborations: propositions from the literature. *Public Administration Review*. **66**(suppl.), pp. 44–55.

Ciftci, S. (2010) Modernization, Islam, or social capital: what explains attitudes toward democracy in the Muslim world? *Comparative Political Studies*. **43**(11), pp. 1442–1470.

Çizakça, M. (2013) Proposal for innovation in the capital markets: *Esham*. In: Dar, H. (ed.) *Global Islamic Finance Report*. London: Edbiz Consulting, pp. 91–93.

Cohen, D. (1998) Culture, social organization, and patterns of violence. *Journal of Personality and Social Psychology*. **75**(2), pp. 408–419.

Coleman, J.S. (1988) Social capital in the creation of human capital. *American Journal of Sociology*. **94**(suppl.), pp. 95–120.

Craig, B. and Pencavel, J. (1995) Participation and productivity: a comparison of worker cooperatives and conventional firms in the plywood industry. *Brookings Papers: Microeconomics*, pp. 121–174.

Dong, X. and Dow, G. (1993) Monitoring costs in Chinese agricultural teams. *Journal of Political Economy*. **101**(3), pp. 539–553.

Durlauf, S. (2002) On the empirics of social capital. *The Economic Journal*. **112**(483), pp. 459–479.

Fehr, E. and Gachter, S. (2002) Altruistic punishment in humans. *Nature*. **415**(10), pp. 137–140.

Feiock, R.C. (2007) Rational choice and regionalism. *Journal of Urban Affairs*. **29**, pp. 47–63.

Fukuyama, F. (1995) *Trust: The Social Virtues and the Creation of Prosperity*. New York: Free Press.

Ghemawat, P. (1995) Competitive advantage and internal organization: Nucor revisited. *Journal of Economic and Management Strategy*. **3**(4), pp. 685–717.

Gintis, H. (2000) *Game Theory Evolving*. Princeton, NJ: Princeton University Press.

Glaeser, E., Laibson, D. Scheinkman, J.A. and Soutter, C.L. (2000) Measuring trust. *Quarterly Journal of Economics*. **115**(3), pp. 811–846.

Glaeser, E., Laibson, D. and Sacerdote, B. (2002) The economic approach to social capital. *The Economic Journal*. **112**(8), pp. 437–458.

Grief, A. (1994) Cultural beliefs and the organization of society: historical and theoretical reflection on collectivist and individual societies. *The Journal of Political Economy*. **102**(5), pp. 912–950.

Grief, A. (2006) *Institutions and the Path to the Modern Economy*. New York and Cambridge: Cambridge University Press.

Hansen, D.G. (1997) Individual responses to a group incentive. *Industrial and Labor Relations Review*. **51**(1), pp. 37–49.

Harris, R. (2009) The institutional dynamics of early modern Eurasian trade: the *commenda* and the corporation. *Journal of Economic Behaviour and Organization*. **71**(3), pp. 606–622.

Hayami, Y. (1989) Community, market and state. In: Maunder, A. and Valdes, A. (eds), *Agriculture and Governments in an Independent World*. Amherst, MA: Gower, pp. 3–14.

Hirsch, F. (1976) *Social Limits to Growth*. Cambridge, MA: Harvard University Press.

Hossain, M. (1988) Credit for alleviation of rural poverty: the Grameen Bank in Bangladesh. *International Food Policy Research Institute Report* No. 65.

Huxham, C. and Vangen, S. (2005) *Managing to Collaborate: The Theory and Practice of Collaborative Advantage*. London: Routledge.

Ibn Khaldun, A. (1377) *The Muqaddimah* (transl. by Franz Rosenthal). Retrieved from https://asadullahali.files.wordpress.com/2012/10/ibn_khaldun-al_muqaddimah.pdf

Jung, C. (2001) *Collective Action and Trust Revisited: Evidence from a Small Case*. New School University, Department of Political Science. Unpublished manuscript.

Khalilieh, H.S. (2006) *Admiralty and Maritime Laws in the Mediterranean*. Leiden: E. J. Brill.

Knez, M. and Simester, D. (2001) Firm-wide incentives and mutual monitoring in continental airlines. *Journal of Labor Economics*. **19**(4), pp. 743–772.

Kuran, T. (2011) *The Long Divergence: How Islamic Law Held Back the Middle East*. Princeton, NJ: Princeton University Press.

Lam, W.F. (1996) Institutional design of public agencies and coproduction: a study of irrigation associations in Taiwan. *World Development*. **24**(6), pp. 1039–1054.

Les Back, Keith M., Khan A., Shukra K. and Solomos, J. (2009) Islam and the new political landscape: faith communities, political participation and social change. *Theory, Culture and Society*. **26**(4), pp. 1–23.

Lydon, G. (2009) A paper economy of faith without faith in paper: a contribution to understanding Islamic institutional history. *Journal of Economic Behaviour and Organization*. **71**(3), pp. 647–659.

Mertzanis, Ch. (2016) The absorption of financial services in an Islamic environment. *Journal of Economic Behaviour & Organization*. **132** (suppl.), pp. 216–236.

Mertzanis, Ch. (2017) Family ties and access to finance in an Islamic environment. *Journal of International Financial Markets, Institutions and Money*. **48**, pp. 1–24.

Modood, T. (2005) *Multicultural Politics: Race, Ethnicity and Muslims in Britain*. Minneapolis: University of Minnesota Press.

North, D. (1990) *Institutions, Institutional Change and Economic Performance*. Cambridge: Cambridge University Press.

Ostrom, E. (1990) *Governing the Commons: The Evolution of Institutions for Collective Action.* Cambridge: Cambridge University Press.

Ostrom, E. (1996) Crossing the great divide: coproduction, synergy, and development. *World Development.* **24**(6), pp. 1073–1087.

Ostrom, E. (1998) The comparative study of public economies. *The American Economist.* **42**(1), pp. 3–17.

Ostrom, E. and Ahn, T.K. (2003) *Foundations of Social Capital.* Cheltenham, UK: Edward Elgar.

Ostrom, E., Walker, J. and Gardner, R. (1992) Covenants with and without a sword: self-governance is possible. *American Political Science Review.* **86**(2), pp. 404–417.

Ouchi, W. (1980) Markets, bureaucracies and clans. *Administrative Sciences Quarterly.* **25**, pp. 129–141.

Panzac, D. (2002) Le contrat d'affrètement maritime en Méditerranée: droit maritime et pratique commercial entre Islam et Chrétienté (XVIIe–XVIIe siècles). *Journal of the Economic and Social History of the Orient.* **45**(3), pp. 342–362.

Pfeffer, J. and Salancik, G.R. (1978) *The External Control of Organizations: A Resource Dependence Perspective.* New York: Harper and Row.

Platteau, J.-P. and Seki, E. (2001) Community arrangements to overcome market failure: pooling groups in Japanese fisheries. In: Aoki, M. and Hayami, Y. (eds) *Communities and Markets in Economic Development.* Oxford: Oxford University Press, pp. 344–402.

Purdy, J.M. (2012) A framework for assessing power in collaborative governance processes. *Public Administration Review.* **72**, pp. 409–417.

Putnam, R. (1993) The prosperous community: social capital and public life. *The American Prospect.* **13**, pp. 35–42.

Putnam, R. (1995) Bowling alone: America's declining social capital. *Journal of Democracy.* **6**, pp. 65–78.

Ramadan, T. (2005) *Western Muslims and the Future of Islam.* Oxford: Oxford University Press.

Roy, O. (2004) *Globalized Islam: The Search for a New Ummah.* New York: Columbia University Press.

Sampson, R.J., Raudenbush, S.W. and Earls, F. (1997) Neighbourhoods and violent crime: a multilevel study of collective efficacy. *Science.* **277**(15), pp. 918–924.

Schelling, T.C. (1978) *Micromotives and Macrobehavior.* New York: W.W. Norton and Co.

Scott, J. (1998) *Seeing Like a State: How Certain Schemes to Improve the Human Condition Have Failed.* New Haven, CT: Yale University Press.

Tilly, C. (1981) Charivaris, repertoires and urban politics. In: Merriman, J.M. (ed.) *French Cities in the Nineteenth Century.* New York: Holmes and Meier, pp. 73–91.

Udovitch, A.L. (1967) At the origins of the Western *commenda*: Islam, Israel, Byzantium. *Speculum.* **37**, pp. 198–207.

Van de Ven, A.H. (1976) On the nature, formation, and maintenance of relations among organization. *Academy of Management Review.* **1**, pp. 24–36.

Wade, R. (1988) Why some Indian villages co-operate. *Economic and Political Weekly.* **33**(16), pp. 773–776.

Weber, M. (2003) *The History of Commercial Partnerships in the Medieval Ages* (trans. Lutz Kaelber; original German edition 1889). Lanham, MD: Rowman and Littlefield.

Whyte, W.F. (1955) *Money and Motivation*. New York: Harper and Row.
Yamagishi, T. (1992) Group size and the provision of a sanctioning system in a social dilemma. In: Liebrand, W.B.G., Messick, D.M. and Wilke, H.A.M. (eds) *Social Dilemmas: Theoretical Issues and Research Findings*. Oxford: Pergamon Press, pp. 267–287.
Young, H.P. (1998) *Individual Strategy and Social Structure: An Evolutionary Theory of Institutions*. Princeton, NJ: Princeton University Press.

5   *Experiences in Translation*: Islamic finance and the sharing economy

Valentino Cattelan

1. 'Translating' the sharing economy: some clues from Eco's *Experiences*

Experiences in Translation (2001) collects a number of essays that Umberto Eco originally wrote in the late 1990s as texts for conference presentations and seminars held at the universities of Toronto, Oxford and Bologna. The book maintains the tone of a conversation (as for the original purpose of the papers) where the dialogue with the reader is not about the theory of translation, but more precisely, as the title suggests, about the 'experience' of translating. Hence, Eco investigates issues related to culture, interpretation and meaning that any translator encounters in the attempt of 'saying almost the same thing' when rendering a text from an original language to a different one. Significantly, *Dire Quasi la Stessa Cosa* (2003), the exact translation of the aforementioned phrase, becomes the main title of the book in the enlarged edition for the Italian speaking readership (while, in reverse, *Esperienze di Traduzione* becomes the subtitle).

As much as introducing Umberto Eco (1932–2016) (semiotics professor, philosopher, Italian novelist best known for his masterpiece *The Name of the Rose*,[1] journalist, literary critic and, of course, translator) is nearly impossible in the space of a few lines, exploring the issues involved in the 'art of translation' represents an extremely challenging enterprise, on which thousands of volumes have been written (and sometimes themselves translated into different languages). These issues, which are well known to linguists and semioticians from a theoretical perspective, as well as to translators in their daily effort of rendering the meaning of a text into different languages are not the specific topic of this chapter.

Nevertheless, referring to semiotics offers some preliminary conceptual clues that can be of significant help, as we are going to see, when dealing with different 'languages' in economics and the change of 'meaning' of a 'text' from one to the other.[2]

As previously mentioned, *Experiences in Translation* belongs more to the field of the practice rather than the theory, and can be read as Eco's intellectual autobiography as a polyglot writer and a practising translator. But, as a semiotician himself, Eco is also engaged in philosophical reflections over the semantic variations that a certain text can experience from a language to another. Subsequently, he warns the reader that the practice of translating does not simply deal with the comparison between two languages, but necessarily implies an *experience* of (re-)interpretation, with a *shift* between *cultures* (the respective 'contexts' of the original and the receiving languages) that opens a gate to multiple (semantic) 'worlds'.

Reading Eco's *Experiences*, one can soon recognize some relevant similarities between the effort of a translator and that of a social scientist working in-between mainstream capitalism and Islamic economics and finance, when he moves from the theory to the practice in the global market.

In fact, if the comparison between the theoretical paradigms of these alternative 'economic languages' can be addressed towards aspects of distributive justice, moral economy, business ethics, law and religion, the 'experience of translating' conventional financial products into *Shari'ah*-compliant instruments involves broader dimensions of *social meaning* that impose to re-contextualize economic action, agency and relations within different semantic 'worlds' of socio-human interaction. Accordingly, moving from the 'culture' of conventional capitalism to that of Islamic economics and finance implies the (re-)interpretation of this social meaning according to *Shari'ah* rationales and objectives (*maqasid*), and strong hermeneutical concern is needed to understand how much the meaning of the 'text' of an economic product actually *changes* from one 'language' to the other, according to the systems of socio-human *values* that these languages respectively assume.

With specific regard to this change of meaning, as well-known, much dissatisfaction still affects the practice of 'translating' conventional products into the Islamic ecosystem without modifying, *de facto*, their underlying values.

This state of affairs has been described by Mahmoud El-Gamal (2006) in terms of a 'form-over-substance approach': in summary, classical sources of *fiqh* jurisprudence are employed to give the industry an 'Islamic' label (p. 2), while perpetuating a regulatory arbitrage (p. 20) that is grounded on a trade-off between market efficiency and *Shari'ah* legitimacy.[3] Hence, the majority of these resulting 'Islamic analogues', which are certainly *Shari'ah*-compliant since they adopt classical Islamic law as backbone for their 'syntax', are regrettably unable to forward the 'semantics' of *Shari'ah* in substantive terms, nor have they proved, in general, to foster a distinctive 'pragmatics' of socio-economic relation factually alternative to the values of conventional capitalism.[4]

To make a point about unsatisfactory translations (where the 'text' is replicated with scarce attention to the 'context' and the distinctive culture behind the language), Eco refers to the employ of systems of automatic translations (such as 'Babel Fish' or 'Google Translate'). Since these systems lack proper instruments of 'contextual selection' (2003, p. 29), they are of limited semantic efficacy; furthermore, as they are devoid of any 'encyclopaedia' (i.e. a whole of information beyond the text and the context, within which the text acquires its *own* specific meaning: *ibidem*, p. 31), their pragmatic value is usually rather limited.[5]

Within this introductory framework, this chapter aims at investigating a demanding 'text' that has been added very recently to the research agenda of social scientists, comparative lawyers and economists dealing both with mainstream capitalism and Islamic finance: namely the rise of the so-called 'sharing economy' in the global market.

Indeed, although employing a terminology which looks at first glance very similar to that of Islamic economics and finance (IEF) (e.g. the 'economy of sharing' as corresponding to the Islamic 'profit-, loss- and risk-sharing'), the 'sharing economy' (SE) may reveal itself a linguistic 'false friend' for the practising translator for at least three reasons.

First and foremost, if a large literature is already available on the SE, the academic study of the relation (possible overlap?) between IEF and the SE is still at an embryonic stage; furthermore, many sources reflect a market-oriented approach that responds more to the needs of entrepreneurs and businessmen, rather than to the questions of social scientists.

The second and probably most challenging reason is that when one tries to collect academic sources on the SE, one will find oneself immersed in an 'ocean of meaning' that, explicitly or implicitly, has been already 'interpreted' according to the 'semantics' spoken by the bulk of its promoters, that is to say reflecting the assumptions and the logic of conventional capitalism (the 'language' performed in the mainstream market).

Third, the existing examples of 'Islamic SE' in the present practice of the market have been developed, in Saussurian terminology, more at the level of the *parole* rather than of the *langue*:[6] in other terms, while we certainly have products and investments in the pragmatics of the Islamic market that try and are (successfully) able to integrate the 'syntax' of the SE with IEF, the 'semantics' that allows this overlap (hence the translation of this new 'text' in the *Shariʿah*-compliant ecosystem) has not been investigated yet in a satisfactory way. In a nutshell, the 'pragmatics' has run faster than the 'semantics' and, lacking a sound construction of the *langue* of the 'Islamic SE', possible misunderstandings are likely to occur in the practice of the *parole*, beyond any good intention of the promoters of this (potentially) fruitful interface.

Taking all this into consideration, the present chapter, by looking at the SE as a 'text', argues that its *meaning* radically *changes* from the 'language' of conventional capitalism to that of IEF. In particular, to support this assertion, after outlining the 'syntax' of the SE in denotative terms, the study connotes the 'semantics' of the SE in the two languages, and later advances some implications for its sound 'pragmatics' in the domain of Islamic social finance.

More precisely, the discussion proceeds as follows.

The study first examines the denotative dimensions of the technological and social drivers behind the rise of the 'sharing economy' as a new 'syntax' for market relations (Section 2).

Later on, the chapter highlights the extent to which the 'text' of the SE has been already interpreted in the global market through the 'semantics' of conventional capitalism, hence in terms of *scarcity* of resources, *division* of available property rights and *competition*. Accordingly, it shows the difficulties in 'translating' the SE into the 'language' of IEF, which assumes alternative tenets of *abundance*, *distribution* of property rights and mutual *cooperation* among economic agents in a community of shared prosperity (Section 3).

In this way, by reflecting the changing properties of what is *mine* and *yours* in conventional and Islamic economics and highlighting how IEF and the SE enjoy autonomous natures (respectively as a 'language' and a 'text'), the chapter will derive from the discussion some policy guidelines to develop a *Shariʿah*-based approach to the SE in the 'pragmatics' of Islamic social finance (Section 4).

To conclude, Section 5 will provide some final considerations on the intersection between the 'languages' of conventional capitalism and Islamic economics in the contemporary global market, and about how their *diversity* can affect the employ of the new instruments of the SE, as well as their possible impact in terms of sustainable development.

Before moving forwards, a final caveat to the contents of these pages can be useful.

As previously remarked (and also specified in endnote 2), for the purposes of this chapter a technical discussion of the terms used in semiotics and linguistics would have been superfluous, and somehow of little help to transmit the core message of the study.

To give a basic note it is sufficient to clarify here that (i) 'syntax', (ii) 'semantics' and (iii) 'pragmatics' are going to be used in the next paragraphs as referring, respectively, to

(i) the study of units of a language in a text (without the analysis of the meaning);
(ii) the investigation, in reverse, of the meaning transmitted by the text; and
(iii) the study of the relationships between the text, its meaning(s) and the users of the language in a certain context.

I trust that the distinction between 'syntax', 'semantics' and 'pragmatics' as classic tripartite formulation of semiotics (or originally advanced by Charles W. Morris in 1938)[7] will help the reader to follow my reasoning, so to recognize the substantial 'meaning' of this study.

2. The 'text' of the sharing economy as a new 'syntax' for market relations

Unpacking the 'passions' and the 'interests' underlying the SE (Codagnone *et al.*, 2016), behind the rhetoric of 'empowerment of the masses', 'democratization of finance' and of a 'peer-to-peer economy' open to everybody, represents a demanding task. An enterprise which is even more challenging when dealing with IEF, as much of this rhetoric has mainly developed according to the social meanings embedded in conventional capitalism.

To a certain extent, some emotional drivers behind these connotations of the SE can be rationally understood in the context of a persistent global financial crisis, and the 'hope' that the digital revolution can pave the way for overcoming the distortions of capitalism, hence reshaping *our* social relations (those linked to the notions of work, production, consumption and value) from a model of 'private owning' to a paradigm of 'sharing' through collaborative networks, online internet spaces, cooperatives platforms, and so on.

But the myth of a 'post-capitalism' already in action (the term has been popularized by British journalist and writer Paul Mason: see Mason, 2015a and 2015b)[8] has to be carefully judged in the light of the strong economic 'interests' that are related to the growth of information technology and business. To this objective, in particular, one should preliminarily understand the 'syntax' of the SE as a new system of *market relations*, a 'text' of *sign vehicles* (Morris, 1938, p. 3) through which social meaning is transmitted.

Which are then the 'signals' that witness the development of a new system of market relations? If information technology and the digital revolution are its fundamental enablers, three drivers can be identified for the development of the 'syntax' of this 'text' (Puschmann and Alt, 2016, pp. 93–94):

* *changing consumer behaviour*, which has shifted from a preference for ownership of goods to their temporary usage, with advantages in terms of cost reduction, flexibility, as well as ecologic sustainability;
* *social networks and electronic markets*, that have enabled easier networking among peers through online community platforms. These social networks facilitate both the sharing of resources in the business-to-business (B2B) domain (e.g. machineries for producers), as well as the interaction in the business-to-consumer (B2C) arena (e.g. car rental) and for consumer-to-consumer(C2C) transactions (e.g. online platforms for second-hand goods sale);
* *mobile devices and electronic services*. A fundamental driver for the growth of the SE has come with the global spread of mobile smart devices, such as smartphones and tablets, and the easier accessibility and provision of services through the 'app economy' in our daily life (from making a reservation for a restaurant to booking a flight, or posting an announcement to rent a spare room in our house; with regard to the rise of FinTech see also Chapter 8 of this book).

In the syntax of the SE enabled by these factors, new mechanisms of trust and reputation (e.g. rating and feedbacks) emerge in anonymous markets which often integrate transaction and payment functions. Producers and consumers of goods and services interact in 'sharing' the use of these resources without knowing directly each other, nor having any strong interest in this knowledge (apart from checking the 'reputation news' in the hosting platform). As a consequence, a new way of organizing economic activities has already substituted the traditional corporate-centred model (with its hierarchies, and its 'satellite' participants: workers, capital providers and consumers) with a horizontal 'crowd-based capitalism' (Sundararajan, 2016) where not only are the new technologies affecting today's consuming choices and commercial exchanges, but will also shape the future of work, market regulation and, in the end, our social fabric.[9]

Definitions such as 'post-capitalism' (Mason 2015a) and 'crowd-based capitalism' (Sundararajan, 2016) indirectly show the layers of 'passion' (i.e. the emotional drivers) that characterize the practice of the SE as a market in its infancy, whose potential is still far from being fulfilled. A 'passion' that reflects, as noted, expectations of a fairer economic development, larger market accessibility, and the search for new models of socio-economic interaction that may improve equality and human welfare. Interestingly, it seems to me that the rhetoric of the SE resembles in some ways that of the advocates and supporters of Islamic economics and finance (IEF) as intrinsically able to 'convert' the weaknesses of conventional capitalism into something radically different. But, as El-Gamal (2006) noted a decade ago, replicating conventional financial instruments just by adding an 'Islamic label' may render the 'hopes' of IEF promoters easy to fade within a form-over-substance rhetoric. In particular, since the 'interests' of conventional capitalism have already deeply affected the conceptualization of the SE, one should pay stronger attention when dealing with the intersection between the 'crowd' of the participants in the SE and in IEF, and the conviction that the 'syntax' of the SE (whose formulation is certainly possible both in the language of Western law and in Islamic law) immediately matches the 'semantics' of IEF.

In this light, one should preliminarily consider, for instance, that the term 'sharing economy' (*rectius*, 'sharing economies', in plural) was first mentioned in 2008 by Lawrence Lessig, professor at the Harvard Law School (pp. 143 ff.), to denote the 'collaborative consumption [or production] made [possible] by the activities of sharing, exchanging, and rental of resources without owning the goods' (as indicated by Puschmann and Alt, 2016, p. 95, with reference to Lessig). As a result, the SE 'leads to hybrid forms of economic value exchange and thus extends existing models from a micro- and macro-economic perspective' (Puschmann and Alt, 2016, p. 96) towards what these pages have defined as a new 'syntax' for market relations, whose *sign vehicles* comprise

> a wide range of digital commercial or non-profit platforms facilitating exchanges amongst a variety of players through a variety of interaction modalities (P2P [peer-to-peer], P2B [peer-to-business], B2P, B2B, G2G [government-to-government]) that all broadly enable consumption or productive activities leveraging capital assets (money, real asset property, equipment, cars, etc.) goods, skills, or just time.
>
> (Codagnone *et al.*, 2016, p. 22) (italics in the original text)

If the definition above has the merit to offer a practice-oriented, all-encompassing and denotative representation of the SE, the *designatum* ('that which the sign refers to': Morris, 1938, p. 3) linked to the socio-economic 'language' practised by the market participants connotes today the SE as a *'floating signifier* for a diverse range of activities' (Nadeem, 2015, p. 13; italics added). Some of these *signified* activities 'are genuinely collaborative and communal, while others are hotly competitive and profit-driven' to the extent that 'studying the "industry" tells us much about a culture dominated by economic imperatives but yearning for more cooperative ways of doing things' (*ibidem*).

It is in fact by moving from the 'syntax' to the 'semantics' of the SE (i.e. from the *signs* to the *meanings* that market relations have in a certain economic 'language') that essential assumptions intervene in its conceptualization in conventional capitalism, shaping its *signified*(s) according to *values* which do not correspond, as we are going to see in the next section, to the semantics of IEF. Recognizing this variation of social meaning(s) will consequently lead our discussion to claim the need for a distinctive *Shari'ah*-based SE in the 'pragmatics' of Islamic social finance (Section 4).

3. The sharing economy: from the 'semantics' of conventional capitalism to Islamic economics and finance

As already remarked, speaking of the construction of social meaning in the SE corresponds to 'a paradigmatic case of a policy-relevant issue where facts are uncertain, values disputed, and the stakes increasingly high' (Codagnone *et al.*, 2016, p. 5). Indeed, while only limited empirical evidence is available on most of the claims by the advocates of the SE, their 'discourse', if originally emerged as a 'form of social utopianism out of the broader narrative on the wisdom of the crowds and the creativity of the commons', has soon turned into 'disenchantment' (*ibidem*, p. 6). And this disillusionment has fuelled 'growing criticism' (*ibidem*) over the (neo-liberal/commercial) 'interests' that have 'poisoned' the original 'passion' (myth? dream? hope?) of 'sharing' for a more sustainable common welfare. As a result, the SE has become a space of conflicting rhetoric, public controversies and even violent protests, where 'floating signifiers' (re-)produce their own conceptual ambiguities.[10]

In the attempt to unravel the diverse connotations embedded in the SE, this section argues that (1) this rhetoric, with its conflicting dimensions, has been basically constructed till now within conventional capitalism (i.e. the syntax of SE as a new 'text' has absorbed the social meanings of the capitalist culture as the dominant 'language' of market relations); and that (2) a 'semantic shift' (in the sense of a 'paradigm shift': Kuhn, 1962) is required when 'translating' the text of the SE (as already deeply affected by the categories of conventional capitalism) into the 'language' of Islamic economics and finance.

3.1. *Conventional capitalism: 'mine' versus 'yours'*

In the midst of an exponential growth of the SE, one may wonder how much this development can tell us 'about a culture dominated by economic imperatives but yearning for more cooperative ways of doing things' (Nadeem, 2015, p. 13): in the end, about conventional capitalism itself.

The current conceptualization of the SE, in its concurrent (and somehow contradictory) narratives of economic utopianism (SE as 'collaborative' economy), optimism (a 'post-capitalism' opportunity) as well as social pessimism, certifies the embodiment of some strong underlying social meanings that are deeply rooted in mainstream market relations, as 'connoted' by conventional capitalism in terms of *scarcity* of resources, their *division* and *competition* of actors one against the other (Cattelan, 2013a, pp. 6–7). In a nutshell, one could say that the 'syntax' of the SE has already embodied the 'semantics' of capitalism as standard source of meaning for socio-economic interaction in the global economy, giving rise to an array of *designata* that have replicated that 'language' in the interpretation of the new 'text'. In other terms, the DNA of Western property rights (Cattelan, 2013a, p. 5) has been culturally embodied by the SE, shaping its contents according to corresponding rationales and objectives.

Assumptions of scarcity of resources, division and competition (what is 'mine' exists *versus* what is 'yours') can be easily revealed by looking at the available literature on the SE as further evidence of the dominant language of conventional capitalism.

Scarcity refers to the basic problem of classic economics, that is to say the gap between (practically) limited natural resources and (theoretically) limitless human desires, from which the need for an efficient allocation arises. The concept of scarcity (with all its corollaries) is so embedded in conventional capitalism that even the most basic research online (just by googling the term and reading Wikipedia) provides the following definition:

> Scarcity (also called paucity) is the fundamental economic problem of having seemingly unlimited human wants in a world of limited resources. It states that society has insufficient productive resources to fulfil all human wants and needs. Scarcity is at the core of economics, because without this concept macroeconomic and microeconomic research would be rendered meaningless.
>
> (Wikipedia, as accessed on 27 August 2017)

The transfer of the idea of scarcity to the SE (i.e. its interpretation through the 'language' of conventional capitalism, which would be meaningless (!) without that concept) is remarkably shown in the following definition given by Alex Stephany, an enthusiastic tech-entrepreneur (CEO of JustPark from December 2012 until November 2015) at the forefront of the SE: 'The sharing economy is the value in taking underutilized assets and making them accessible online to a community, leading to a reduced need for ownership of those assets' (Stephany, 2015, p. 9).

Resources are scarce, assets are (still) underutilized: their value can be (still) increased to satisfy (a little more) unlimited wants by online accessibility without ownership. Significantly, Stephany provides some further details about his idea of 'a community', which is 'more than just supply and demand', since users 'engage with each other above and beyond their transactional need. They trust each other' (Stephany, 2015, p. 11). These mechanisms of trust basically assume that competing for (scarce) resources becomes less demanding by reducing the need for ownership of the underutilized assets available online.

But, of course, this does not change (rather, it simply perpetuates) a logic of opposition between property rights as 'portions' of economic justice, where the *division* of resources among market participants (what can be called the *'mine' versus 'yours' paradigm*) is replicated online and may actually favour the 'rich' (who can pool resources thanks to dominant platform positions: should one think about Amazon?) and downgrade the 'crowd' (a crowd of 'peers' or 'poor'?) to the status of 'platform users' – hence betraying, *de facto*, the promises of the 'post-capitalistic' democratization of (limited) economic resources by simply feeding (unlimited) wants through (potentially unlimited) online access.

As a consequence, the *competition* for scarce resources at the core of conventional capitalism, absorbed in the 'text' of the SE through its dominant 'language', has already given rise to opposing perspectives over the SE in terms of economic utopia or social pessimism, while reflecting the *'mine' versus 'yours' paradigm* in its 'material' *text*-ualization.

For instance, embracing a great deal of optimism about the impact of the SE, Botsman and Rogers (2010; but also Chase, 2015, and Kramer, 2015) praise the change in market relations brought by collaborative consumption (with its four underlying principles: 'critical mass, idling capacity, belief in the commons and trust between strangers': p. xvi) as a cultural revolution, under the slogan 'what's mine is yours' (!). This revolution, in their view, supersedes the traditional notion of *value* of the ownership-based economy to the extent that

> Collaborative Consumption[11] may be consumer and community oriented, but its benefits are shared across businesses. … Also, as companies start to redefine themselves as acting as the bridge between individual users and the community, we will trust them more, and as a result interact with them in different ways. … We believe Collaborative Consumption is part of an even bigger shift from a production-oriented measurement system … to a multidimensional notion of value that also takes into consideration the well-being of current and future generations.
>
> (Botsman and Rogers, 2010, pp. 220–221)

But, at a closer look, Botsman and Rogers's utopian model of collaboration (in the persistence of parameters of *division* and *competition* of conventional capitalism) proves to be a slippery slope towards a sort of hyper-capitalism where online platforms tend to replicate the mainstream *'mine' versus 'yours'* agenda. Far from any concretization of a paradigm shift, in fact, more critical voices have contested that 'the sharing economy isn't really a "sharing" economy at all; it's an access economy' (Eckhardt and Bardhi, 2015).

> Sharing is a form of social exchange that takes place among people known to each other, without any profit. Sharing is an established practice, and dominates particular aspects of our life, such as within the family … When 'sharing' is market-oriented – when a company is an intermediary between consumers who don't know each other – it is no longer sharing at all. Rather, consumers are paying to access someone else's goods and services for a particular period of time. It is an economic exchange, and consumers are after utilitarian, rather than social, value.
>
> (*ibidem*)

Accordingly, in the 'language' of conventional capitalism, the new 'syntax' of the SE maintains social meanings whose 'semantics' is quintessentially utilitarian.

Resources are *scarce*, so efficient allocation is needed. 'Mine' is *not* (really) 'yours': rather, my profit goes *versus* yours, also when the *division* of resources is grounded in 'access' rather than in 'ownership'. Moreover, the *competition* between 'access' producers does not create social value, but is actually related to cost saving for 'access' consumers.[12]

Within this frame, if one looks at the persistence of ownership/access structures in terms of the *'mine' versus 'yours' paradigm* in the conflicting rhetoric of the SE, radical opponents have even discharged the new 'text' as a case of hyper-capitalism where 'what's yours is [actually] mine' (!) (Slee, 2016). This growing discontentment about the SE reveals a 'sense of betrayal: that what started as an appeal to community, person-to-person connections, sustainability, and sharing, has become the playground of billionaires' (*ibidem*, p. 163). Hence, from his critical perspective, Slee argues that the SE just replicates the old school of venture capitalists, extends harsh free-market and neo-liberal practices into previously protected dimensions of our private life, and, in the end, allows few people (the 'rich') to make fortunes, without 'sharing' at all this wealth with the community of their 'peers' (actually, the 'poor').

3.2. Islamic economics and finance: the 'mine' beside 'yours' of shared prosperity

The previous section referred to some sources of recent economic literature (in particular Botsman and Rogers, 2010; Eckhardt and Bardhi, 2015; Slee,

2016) where what has been defined as the *'mine' versus 'yours' paradigm* of conventional capitalism has been *text*-ualized (i.e. 'proved actual through its textual representation') in the SE.

Accordingly, the 'semantics' embedded in the parameters of *scarcity*, *division* and *competition* has affected the 'syntax' of the SE, giving rise to a narrative of praise or contestation that precisely reflects classic issues of the 'language' in use.

But what happens when we try to 'translate' the 'text' of the SE into a different 'semantics' of social meaning, and specifically into the 'language' of Islamic economics and finance (IEF), engaging with a 'paradigm shift' (Kuhn, 1962; Cattelan, 2017)?

Here the 'floating signifiers' (Nadeem, 2015, p. 13) embedded in the notion of SE navigate in an 'ocean of sense' that connotes the 'signified-s' (*designata*) of 'sharing' – beyond the denotative 'syntax' of consumer behaviour, social networks and digital devices (see Section 2) – in an alternative way from conventional capitalism. In fact, if the 'syntax' of SE can be seen as a 'system of sign vehicles', a 'text', its *meaning* changes when the agent 'speaks' the 'language' of conventional capitalism *or* that of IEF, each one transmitting its *own* system of values, rationales and objectives (i.e. its *own* 'paradigm' or 'ocean of sense').

Therefore, although they 'say almost the same thing' (Eco, 2001 and 2003) at first glance (the 'economy of sharing' as 'profit-, loss-, risk-sharing'), not only do the SE and IEF identify respectively a 'text' and a 'language', but also, since *conventional* (Section 3.1) and *Islamic* SE enjoy autonomous 'semantics', their social meanings radically differ when parameters of *scarcity*, *division* and *competition* (conventional capitalism) are replaced with assumptions of *abundance* of resources, *distribution* and *cooperation* among economic agents (IEF).

This 'paradigm shift' embraces the well-known concept of *tawhid* (see Chapter 2 of this book), where the human being, as God's agent (*khalifah*), pursues objectives of general welfare (*maqasid al-Shari'ah*: see Chapter 3), and

> far apart from the assumption of competition between economic subjects in the market which belongs to the Western model of capitalism, Islamic property rights are not conceived as 'portion' of 'divided' justice to be allocated on people … but as *shares* of a *unique justice*, in which the human beings participate by sharing economic resources.
>
> (Cattelan, 2017, p. 29) (italics in the original text)

In the *tawhidi* framework, where God is the only 'actor' of all the creation and original 'owner' of any resource, if scarcity is certainly recognized as empirical phenomenon due to the persistence of inequality and inefficient distribution, it is not assumed as a defining concept of Islamic economics (Wahbalbari *et al.*, 2015). On the contrary, since God is the 'provider' of *any* means of subsistence for everybody (*ar-Razzaq*, 'the Maintainer' is one of His ninety-nine attributes; for a link to the notion of 'risk' in Islam see Cattelan, 2014), a principle of *abundance* is embraced within a socio-economic model of 'shared prosperity'.

Of course, this abundance is not intended in terms of availability of unlimited natural resources but in the light of a balance between human desires and needs. Society has sufficient productive resources to fulfil human wants, which are not assumed unlimited (with a continuous struggle to acquire new resources), but are conceived in a balance (*mizan*) with their needs. It is this balance between human needs and desires that implies both the idea of *abundance* as reconciliation between limited natural resources and human wants, as well as the primary meaning of Islamic entrepreneurship as desirable (beneficial) commercial activity (Q. 2:275: 'Allah has permitted trade ...') that denies any undeserved profit ('... but forbidden *riba*') and pursues shared prosperity. The balance between available resources and human wants is necessarily grounded in the real economy, hence any artificial creation of nominal value (such as the practice of interest in a debt-based economy) represents a distortion in the *distribution* of property rights as *shares* of a unique justice. Accordingly, the prohibition of *riba* entails any quantitative *dis*-equilibrium (as much as those of *gharar* and *maysir* related to a qualitative imbalance: Cattelan, 2013b) between the two sides of the transaction which alters the 'unity' (*tawhid*) of justice in IEF. Indeed, when the two pans of the 'scale' are not assumed anymore as opposed one to the other (the *'mine' versus 'yours' paradigm* of conventional capitalism) but conceived as 'shares' of a unique justice, their balance exists 'by means of the centering and mediating pivot' (Smirnov, 1996, p. 347), where *'mine'* makes sense only *beside 'yours'* for a shared prosperity to be achieved.

Within the 'semantics' of an economic 'language' where a balance between resources, needs and desires is assumed, and an equilibrium among property rights is pursued, resources are not anymore the object of a division, but of *distribution*: accordingly the 'access economy' that belongs to the 'syntax' of the SE is not another place of competition for their acquisition, but a 'platform' of *cooperation* among economic agents, according to their role of *khalifah* in pursuing the general objectives (*maqasid*) of *Shari'ah*.

Criteria of cooperation, as well-known, belong to the core of IEF (from the commercial tools of *musharakah* and *mudarabah*, with their rationales of profit- and risk-sharing, to the logic underlying the obligation of *zakat* which can bring about a model of socio-humanitarian entrepreneurship: see Chapter 12 of this book) and altogether foster a *'mine' beside 'yours' paradigm* of market relations where property rights do not oppose one against the other, but are the product of a collective collaboration of personal commitments aimed at shared prosperity.

In this light, the SE, far from being the 'natural' locus for IEF (as if the logic of 'sharing' would depend on the 'syntax' rather than the 'semantics' of social meaning), has to be interpreted as a new 'text' (let's say, metaphorically, a 'boat') whose 'floating signifiers' move from a denotative to different connotative dimensions according to the 'language' applied (i.e. 'a boat that can navigate diverse oceans of sense').

The 'signified' activities, then, will tend to replicate parameters of scarcity, division and competition (i.e. a *'mine' versus 'yours' paradigm*) when the logic of conventional capitalism is perpetuated; on the contrary, assumptions of abundance, distribution and cooperation among economic agents (i.e. a *'mine' beside 'yours' paradigm*) will nourish the paradigm of the Islamic ecosystem, towards which the SE can be certainly functional.

In other terms, one should not commit the mistake to suppose that the SE *per se* immediately fulfils the potential of IEF: on the contrary, it is the 'semantics' of IEF (abundance, distribution and cooperation) that has the potential to drive this new 'text' towards outcomes of more sustainable development, where *my* welfare (only) exists *beside* (and *not* in competition, *versus*) *yours*.

Consequently, the *translation* of the market practice of the SE (whose meanings have been already *text*-ualized according to a *'mine' versus 'yours' paradigm*) requires a careful hermeneutical approach, as a challenging *experience* (Eco, 2001) of rendering the social meaning of 'sharing' into an alternative 'language'.

To conclude, it is not by opening online platforms, websites of crowdfunding, *zakat* investments or *waqf* tools (see examples in Chapters 7 and 8 of this book) (i.e. by using the 'syntax' of the SE) that the social meanings of shared prosperity of IEF will be immediately achieved at the 'semantic' level of *abundance*, *distribution* and *cooperation*. In fact, since conventional capitalism and IEF seem to 'say almost the same thing' when using the 'floating signifiers' of the SE, more attention is actually required for economic agents aiming at an alternative model of socio-economic interactions.

The 'effect on some interpreter in virtue of which the thing in question is a sign to that interpreter' (Morris, 1938, p. 3) (that is to say, the *interpretant* deriving from the application of meaning to the syntax as a sign vehicles = here, the factual outcomes of an economic paradigm through its rationales and objectives in a given social context) requires at this point to look at the ways through which a *Shari'ah*-based sharing economy (grounded in the 'semantics' of IEF) can work 'in practice' to *actualize* the 'text' of the SE in the reality of socio-economic relations. More precisely, to look at the 'pragmatics' of this alternative economic 'language' within the frame of Islamic social finance.

4. A *Shari'ah*-based sharing economy in the 'pragmatics' of Islamic social finance and shared prosperity

There is no doubt that the 'passion' behind the global spread of the SE as a new 'syntax' for market relations has recently affected also the narrative of the Islamic financial market.

In this regard, online platforms and FinTech Islamic companies (see Chapter 8 of this book) can play an easy game in their advertisement by reporting the authoritative opinion given by Sheikh Dr Ali Elgari at the World Islamic Banking Conference held in Manama (Bahrain) in 2015, when he stated that 'nothing can be closer to Islamic finance than crowdfunding' (as one of the most popular examples of the 'text' of the SE).

If one checks the reasoning followed by Dr Elgari, anyway, a more cautious perspective, with a list of caveats, was actually provided in his interview.

> Crowdfunding is a great idea … a call through the social media to participate in a project, either a charitable project or an investment project and therefore cutting the middleman, go directly to whoever you want to participate. It has grown now to what is called peer-to-peer financing. … Unfortunately it requires certain things that makes it unlikely to flourish in this area of the world [Muslim developing countries]. Firstly … very effective platform[s]. Secondly, it needs regulations, to protect the rights of the participants. And thirdly, it requires evaluators of these assets … There is an infrastructure … that is not existent right now, but if it docs, I mean nothing can be closer to Islamic finance than crowdfunding. Why? Because … it can open the door for democratization of finance, … for the revival of *waqf*, … Through crowdfunding … you will open huge potential hubs for changing the whole face of finance in Muslim countries. But legal infrastructure is not there yet.
>
> (Elgari, 2015)

Hence, paying attention to Dr Elgari's words, the enthusiastic claims that '[w]hen the crowd connects, magic happens … [and] people are empowered',[13] and that 'Islamic crowdfunding perfectly complements the Islamic finance industry, due to its focus on community and its ability to engage the masses',[14]

- if on the one side certainly mirror the global rhetoric of SE (the same that can be found in conventional capitalism),
- on the other side need to be 'translated' into the 'semantics' of IEF in order to promote a 'pragmatics' of *abundance*, *distribution* and *cooperation* as core 'interests' of an Islamic ecosystem able to promote effective social impact and shared prosperity.

But implementing the 'semantics' of IEF in the 'pragmatics' of contemporary economic exchanges does not represent an easy task for at least two reasons, that indirectly reflect the points of criticism mentioned by Dr Elgari (2015), as well as by El-Gamal (2006).

On the one side, today's IEF pragmatics (i.e. how the participants in the Islamic eco-system 'interpret' the syntax of commercial relations through the semantics of the *tawhid* and *maqasid*) does not exist in a 'separate ocean' from conventional capitalism. In fact, the practice of Islamic finance exists *next to* conventional capitalism, and *within* a global system where the emergence of the new 'text' of the SE is occurring *both* in conventional and Islamic economy *under* a global regulatory umbrella aimed at financial stability, consumer protection, transparency, with its checks-and-balances and rating criteria. This is not to mean that the global regulatory system has to apply the same rules for conventional and Islamic finance (in fact, much effort is still required to guarantee a level playing field), nor that it does not necessitate any improvement (the 2008 financial crisis has proved the opposite), but to stress the need for a strong legal infrastructure (both at the level of Muslim national jurisdictions, and according to transnational criteria of best practices) as pre-condition to make any *Shari'ah*-based tool of the SE *efficient* in the contemporary global market. To repeat Dr Elgari's advice, there is the necessity for 'an infrastructure ... that is not existent right now, but if it does, ... nothing can be closer to Islamic finance than crowdfunding'.[15]

On the other side, moving from the domain of the *efficiency* in rendering the 'syntax' of the SE to the *legitimacy* of the transmitted 'semantics' of the IEF 'language', it is clear that the *experience of translating* the SE in the actual 'pragmatics' of a *Shari'ah*-based ecosystem cannot be resolved just by adding an 'Islamic label' to the products of (conventional) SE and employing Arabic names of classical nominate contracts (e.g. *ijarah, mudarabah, qard hasan...*) or institutes of the Islamic legal tradition (e.g. *waqf, zakat*) to convince the consumers of online platforms about their *change of meaning*. On the contrary, one needs 'to understand and apply the substantive spirit of Islamic Law ... [to] pave the road for developing financial products that may be marketed more effectively to Muslims and non-Muslims alike' (El-Gamal, 2006, p. 25). In other words, one has to embrace what a classic piece of Islamic economics scholarship identifies as 'the unique Islamic concept of [an] individual's trusteeship, moral, political and economic, and the principles of social organisation' (Ahmad, 1979, p. 12; on the concept of development in Islam see recently also Askari *et al.*, 2014).

The need for a *change of semantics*, a 'paradigm shift' (Kuhn, 1962), in the translation of the 'text' of the SE from the 'language' of conventional capitalism to that of IEF is extremely important, in particular, when 'speaking' about Islamic social finance.

As previously shown (Section 3.1), in fact, the replication of the structure of Western property rights (as embedded in the *'mine' versus 'yours' paradigm*) has already interpreted the syntax of the SE through meanings of *scarcity*, *division* and *competition*: hence, a 'sense of betrayal' has soon risen among the original supporters of the SE: 'that what started as an appeal to community, person-to-person connections, sustainability, and sharing, has become the playground of billionaires' (Slee, 2016, p. 163). To a certain extent, the 'natural' development of the SE in the context of conventional capitalism could not have been different from what is occurring at the moment: the semantics of the *'mine' versus 'yours' paradigm* was already there, and has unsurprisingly been extended to the new 'text'.

But, as previously remarked, IEF assumes rationales and objectives of a *'mine' beside 'yours' paradigm*, that foster a logic of *abundance, distribution* and *cooperation* deriving from the *tawhidi* framework of the unity of the creation and the participation of the human being in this unity as economic agent (*khalifah*). Accordingly, the 'text' of the SE acquires a distinctive *Shari'ah*-based meaning when applied in the 'pragmatics' of Islamic social finance, where consumers, financers and businessmen 'share' the efforts and the outcomes of economic action as a common venture.

It is in this sense that the word 'sharing' actually 'says different things':

- it denotes a new 'syntax' for market relations, made possible by new consumer trends and the digital revolution, in the phrase 'sharing economy';
- as a 'floating signifier' (Nadeem, 2015, p. 13) this phrase is connoted through meanings of scarcity, division and competition (with all the deriving signified-s) in the 'semantics' of conventional capitalism, and its related 'pragmatics';
- it embraces, in reverse, postulates of abundance, distribution and cooperation in the language of IEF, through a socio-economic semantics that is grounded in the *tawhidi* framework and is implemented in the light of the *maqasid* and the *khalifah* role.

Therefore, in IEF the noun 'sharing' (as conceived in the risk-sharing and profit-loss sharing principles) allows to 'read' the 'text' of the SE (and equivalent synonyms: i.e. crowd- or access-based economy) through the 'semantics' of a *'mine' beside 'yours' paradigm* that proves functional to SE investments pursuing the 'pragmatics' of Islamic social finance.

Indeed, not only does this (IEF) meaning of 'sharing' define a shared commitment towards objectives of socio-inclusion (e.g. through *zakat* as a significant instrument of poverty alleviation) but it also illuminates the pragmatics of Islamic entrepreneurship (through tools of SE platforms) according to a community-based conception of the market where what is 'mine' does not exist *versus* 'yours', but thanks to my effort *beside* yours: an effort that brings about my profit *beside* yours (the well-known assumption of IEF according to which *al-kharaj bi-l-daman*, 'profit accompanies liability for loss', perfectly mirrors this logic).

To conclude, there is no doubt that the new tools of the SE can significantly contribute to 'empower people', as much as projects of micro-credit, social impact *sukuk* and the rediscovery of *waqf* can certainly be sponsored through Islamic crowdfunding, but it will not be the employ of Arabic names or the use of an 'Islamic label' to *translate* the SE from conventional capitalism into IEF.

Rather, this will be achieved through adopting, in the *governance* of Islamic financial institutions, parameters of social impact and financial inclusion that embody the semantics of abundance, distribution and cooperation in the practice of a *Shari'ah*-based sharing economy able to channel (global) crowdfunding towards (local) responsible investments in the real economy. As suggested by Dr Elgari, this governance needs also to be complemented by systems of monitoring, rating, auditing and report, in order to evaluate the actual social impact of SE initiatives.

In this context, the pragmatics of Islamic social finance will require further endeavour by the authority of *Shari'ah* scholars to foster an *experience of translation* from the conventional to the Islamic paradigm of economic relations, as well as an effort of financial education offered to the 'crowd' in order to make people responsible for 'practising' the language of IEF as *khalifah*, and for spreading its semantics among Muslims and non-Muslims, so to foster universal aims of sustainable development and human welfare.

Clearly, strategies of Islamic economy education can be nourished also through online platforms, but, as these pages have tried to underline, it is towards the *diversity* in the notion of 'sharing' and its *transforming social meaning* from conventional to Islamic economy that the bulk of energies have to be addressed, in order to avoid the (undesirable) perpetuation of a 'shared' scarcity, division and competition in the frame of the global development and move, on the contrary, towards a paradigm of 'shared' prosperity.

On the specific point of the overlap, possible contamination and conceptual diversity between the 'language uses' of conventional and Islamic economy with regard to the issue of global sustainable development, some brief considerations will be added in the conclusive section of this chapter.

5. Diversity in 'sharing' and the search for a global sustainable development

This chapter has dealt with the *meaning-s* of 'sharing' in a global market where the diverse conceptions of economic justice(-s) of conventional capitalism and IEF coexist (Cattelan, 2013c) and are currently dealing with the emergence of the 'sharing economy' as a new syntax for market relations.

To this aim valuable hermeneutical clues have been derived from Eco's *Experiences in Translations* (2001) and the tripartite notion of *semiosis* by Morris (1938).

In this light, the appearance of the SE has been denoted in terms of a new 'syntax' (a system of *sign vehicles*) for market relations (made possible by information technology and the digital revolution: Section 2), a 'text' collecting a variety of 'floating signifiers' whose *meaning* changes when either the 'language' of conventional capitalism or IEF is applied to connote the signified-s (*designata*) of economic action.

The changing properties of the concept of 'sharing', linked to alternative conceptualizations of property rights (see Von Benda-Beckmann *et al.*, 2006; Cattelan, 2013a and 2013b), have been summarized through two distinct logics: on the one side, the *'mine' versus 'yours' paradigm* of conventional capitalism, with its corollaries of scarcity of resources, division and competition; on the other side, the *'mine' beside 'yours' paradigm* of IEF, grounded in the rationales of abundance, distribution and cooperation aimed at shared prosperity. Section 3 underlined the conceptual distance that the 'text' of SE can have when *interpreted* thought the 'language' of conventional capitalism or *translated* into that of IEF.

Correspondingly, this chapter has shown how these diverse properties of 'sharing' can affect the 'pragmatics' of the SE, as performed by the interpreter either in accordance with the first or the second language. The relevance of this *diversity in sharing* has been highlighted with particular reference to Islamic social finance, as an area of market practice that can embrace the 'text' of the SE through a *Shariʿah*-based approach (Section 4).

Considering all these semantic variations, the chapter has also provided caveats to develop an *efficient* (in the light of the contemporary standards of international financial regulation) and *legitimate* (that is to say, able to embody the substantive spirit of *tawhid* and *maqasid* that belongs to Islamic law) *Shariʿah*-based sharing economy.

Towards this direction, the recognition of the 'diversity' between conventional capitalism and IEF in their own conceptualization of 'sharing' still requires energies for an Islamic economy education of the 'crowd' (in order to make people responsible for their *Shariʿah*-based practice of SE), as well as further endeavour by *Shariʿah* scholars in the process of 'translation' of the SE from conventional capitalism into IEF.

Both these efforts should be intended as a fruitful opportunity for an inter-cultural dialogue between the Western and the Muslim worlds by structuring SE products and services grounded in the Islamic legal tradition (e.g. *waqf*, Islamic crowdfunding) that can be beneficial both for Muslims and non-Muslims alike, and able to contribute in the long term to universal aims of global sustainable development, *shared* prosperity and human welfare.

Notes

1 Written in Italian in 1980 and translated into English in 1983, *The Name of the Rose* narrates the mysterious murders that take place in a medieval abbey, with a thrilling plot that matches Eco's erudition about history and philosophy. The film adaptation of 1986 starred Sean Connery as the Franciscan friar William of Baskerville, the main protagonist of the plot.

2 In a preliminary version of this chapter, the text presented a long introduction dealing with the discipline of semiotics as the 'doctrine of signs', according to the original definition given by John Locke in his *Essay Concerning Human Understanding* (1690), and the birth of the modern science of signs through two great figures, Swiss linguist Ferdinand de Saussure, with his *Cours de Linguistique Générale* (1916), and American philosopher Charles Sanders Peirce, and his *Collected Papers* (1931–1958). But, at a certain point, I realized that the complexity of all the matters involved in semiotic research would have been impossible to be summarized in an introductory paragraph, and the paragraph itself would have been of little help for the purposes of the chapter. For this reason, I decided to use many terms (such as 'text', 'language', 'translation', 'pragmatics', …) without entering any technical discussion over their meaning in semiotic studies, and without any reference to the immense literature potentially involved in the subject (for a brief outline of this debate, one can refer to the classic *Dictionnaire* by Greimas and Courtés, 1979).

I trust that this choice will not deprive the text from the accuracy of meaning that the expert in semiotics can appreciate, to the extent to which it makes its contents more readable for the layman.

3 A handy outline of El-Gamal's position can be found on the inside back cover of his volume:

> This book provides an overview of the practice of Islamic finance and the historical roots that define its modes of operation. The focus of the book is analytical and forward-looking. It shows that Islamic finance exists primarily today as a form of rent-seeking legal arbitrage. An alternative that emphasizes substance rather than form would serve religious and moral objectives better, through mutual and similar financial practices.
>
> (El-Gamal, 2006)

4 Therefore, as El-Gamal remarks,

> [t]he alternative ... is to try to understand and apply the substantive spirit of Islamic Law. This can be accomplished by understanding the economic functions served by classical legal provisions and the general principles that prompted classical jurists to pursue those functions within their economic and legal environment. This, in turn, can pave the road for developing financial products that may be marketed more effectively to Muslims and non-Muslims alike, without need for Arabic names of classical nominate contracts, and without hiding behind the 'Islamic' brand name.
>
> (El-Gamal, 2006, p. 25)

5 Eco discusses in detail the difference between 'dictionary' and 'encyclopaedia' when he deals with processes of production of meaning in real life situations (hence shifting from the semantics of a language to its pragmatics): for further references, one may look at Eco, 1984.

6 To differentiate the abstract and empirical levels of a 'language' (*langage*) as social and cultural whole of 'signs' that are shared by a given community, Ferdinand de Saussure introduced in his *Cours de Linguistique Générale* (1916) the fundamental distinction between *langue* and *parole*: *langue* being the institutionalized abstract *system* of the language (that can be conceived, and studied, on its own), and the *parole* its empirical usage as social act/fact.

7

> The process in which something functions as a sign may be called *semiosis*. This process, in a tradition which goes back to the Greeks, has commonly been regarded as involving three (or four) factors: that which acts as a sign, that which the sign refers to, and that effect on some interpreter in virtue of which the thing in question is a sign to that interpreter. These three components in semiosis may be called respectively, the *sign vehicle*, the *designatum*, and the *interpretant*; the interpreter may be included as a fourth factor.
>
> (Morris, 1938, p. 3)

From this distinction Morris derives the three levels of semiotics that correspond to syntax, semantics and pragmatics (*ibidem*, pp. 6–9): for a critical perspective, see also Sayward (1974). For a 'dictionary' on the matter, see the classic work by Greimas and Courtés (1979); for a more advanced approach, Silverstein (1972); Eco (1984); Herbert, 1996. For the distinction between 'performative' and 'constative' in pragmatics, the reference goes to the speech act theory by Austin (1962), as further developed by Searle (1969).

8

Without us noticing, we are entering the postcapitalist era. At the heart of further change to come is information technology, new ways of working and the sharing economy. The old ways will take a long while to disappear, but it's time to be utopian.

(Mason, 2015b)

9 In his review of Sundararajan's book for the LSE blog, Christopher May underlines how although

the book provides a wealth of interesting detail in accounting for the historical emergence of 'crowd-based capitalism', ... it obscures the real impact of the changes it posits on workers as well as the potential intensification of economic insecurity and inequality that may be brought by the 'sharing economy'.

(May, 2016)

10

Since 2014, the phenomenal growth of a few large commercial 'sharing' platforms, the increasing number of economic sectors affected, and conflicting interests among the stakeholders involved have made the *'sharing economy'* a domain of conflictual rhetoric and public controversies, legal disputes, and even violent protests. The various expressions used to refer to 'sharing' platforms now appropriated by practitioners and stakeholders, are 'floating signifiers' for all sorts of different activities, in what can be called the 'rhetorical politics of platformisation'. Terms and concepts are used in such confused and confusing ways that it is at times difficult to ascertain whether advocates, opponents, regulators, and policy makers are discussing the same phenomenon. There is a closed self-reproducing loop between conceptual ambiguity, rhetorical controversies, and lack of sound measurements and empirical evidence. This loop, in turn, limits the space for a rational debate about alternative policy options and contributes to the fragmented regulatory approaches which currently address the *'sharing economy'*.

(Codagnone *et al.*, 2016, p. 6)

11 I have maintained here 'Collaborative Consumption' in capital letters, as in the original text.

12

In the access economy, there will be two key elements of success: 1. Competition between companies will not hinge on which platform can provide the most social interaction and community, contrary to the current economy rhetoric ... consumers simply want to make savvy purchases, and access economy companies allow them to achieve this, by offering more convenience at a lower price. ... 2. Consumers think about access differently than they think about ownership ... Thus, trying to foster a community of consumers around an access economy brand is rarely successful ... Consumers are not looking for social value out of rental exchanges with strangers.

(Eckhardt and Bardhi, 2015)

13 Quotation taken from Umar Munshi's LinkedIn profile. Umar Munshi is the founder and CEO of EthisCrowd and founder of EthisVentures, both online platforms of Islamic crowdfunding (see Chapter 8 of this book).

14 Umar Munshi's opinion reported by Agha (2016).

15 As mentioned in the text, of course, crowdfunding is taken into consideration here as a popular case of SE, but this reasoning can be enlarged to any new tool of P2P, B2B... Chapters 7 and 8 of this book provide a broader exemplification of the current practice of Islamic FinTech and crowdfunding as emergent areas of Islamic SE.

References

Agha, S.E. (2016) Islamic finance, beyond banking system: the case of Islamic crowdfunding. *LinkedIn* [online]. Available from: www.linkedin.com/pulse/islamic-finance-beyond-banking-system-case-syed-ehsanullah-agha [Accessed 12 September 2017].

Ahmad, K. (1979) *Economic Development in an Islamic Framework.* Leicester: The Islamic Foundation.

Askari, H., Iqbal, Z., Krichene, N. and Mirakhor, A. (2014) Understanding development in an Islamic framework. *Islamic Economic Studies.* **22**(1), pp. 1–36.

Austin, J.L. (1962) *How To Do Things with Words.* Oxford: Oxford University Press.

Botsman, R., and Rogers, R. (2010) *What's Mine is Yours: How Collaborative Consumption is Changing the Way We Live.* London: Collins.

Cattelan, V. (2013a) Introduction. Babel, Islamic finance and Europe: preliminary notes on property rights pluralism. In: Cattelan, V. (ed.) *Islamic Finance in Europe: Towards a Plural Financial System.* Cheltenham, UK, and Northampton, MA: Edward Elgar, pp. 1–12.

Cattelan, V. (2013b) A glimpse through the veil of Maya: Islamic finance and its truths on property rights. In: Cattelan, V. (ed.) *Islamic Finance in Europe: Towards a Plural Financial System.* Cheltenham, UK, and Northampton, MA: Edward Elgar, pp. 32–51.

Cattelan, V. (2013c) Conclusions. Towards a plural financial system. In: Cattelan, V. (ed.) *Islamic Finance in Europe: Towards a Plural Financial System.* Cheltenham, UK, and Northampton, MA: Edward Elgar, pp. 228–234.

Cattelan, V. (2014) In the Name of God: managing risk in Islamic finance. *Eabh Working Papers Series* [online]. Paper no. 14–07. Available from: www.eabh.info/publications/eabh-papers [Accessed 20 April 2017].

Cattelan, V. (2017) Legal pluralism, property rights and the paradigm of Islamic economics. *JKAU: Islamic Economics.* **30**(1), pp. 21–36.

Chase, R. (2015) *Peers Inc.: How People and Platforms Are Inventing the Collaborative Economy and Re-Inventing Capitalism.* New York: PublicAffairs.

Codagnone, C., Biagi, F. and Abadie, F. (2016) *The Passions and the Interests: Unpacking the 'Sharing Economy'.* Institute for Prospective Technological Studies, JRC Science for Policy Report EUR 27914 EN. European Commission, European Union.

Eckardt, G.M., and Bardhi, F. (2015) The sharing economy isn't about sharing at all. *Harvard Business Review* [online]. Available from: https://hbr.org/2015/01/the-sharing-economy-isnt-about-sharing-at-all [Accessed 13 May 2017].

Eco, U. (1984) *Semiotics and Philosophy of Language.* Bloomington: Indiana University Press.

Eco, U. (2001) *Experiences in Translation* (trans. A. McEwen). Emilio Goggio Publications Series. Toronto and Buffalo: University of Toronto Press.

Eco, U. (2003) [Italian enlarged ed.] *Dire Quasi la Stessa Cosa: Esperienze di Traduzione.* Milano: Bompiani.

El-Gamal, M.A. (2006) *Islamic Finance: Law, Economics, and Practice.* Cambridge and New York: Cambridge University Press.

Elgari, A. (2015) Transcript of his interview at WIBC 2015 [online]. Available as a recorded video from: www.youtube.com/watch?v=p4qDrv0_xPU [Accessed 16 September 2017].

Greimas, A.J., and Courtés, J. (1979) *Sémiotique: Dictionnaire Raisonné de la Théorie du Langage.* Paris: Classiques Hachette.

Herbert, C.H. (1996) *Using Language*. Cambridge: Cambridge University Press.

Kramer, B.J. (2015) *Shareology: How Sharing is Powering the Human Economy*. New York: Morgan James.

Kuhn, T.S. (1962) *The Structure of Scientific Revolutions*. Chicago: Chicago University Press.

Lessig, L. (2008) *Remix: Making Art and Commerce Thrive in the Hybrid Economy*. New York: Penguin Press.

Locke, J. (1690) *An Essay Concerning Human Understanding* (ed. 1894 by A.C. Fraser). Oxford: Clarendon Press.

Mason, P. (2015a) *PostCapitalism: A Guide to Our Future*. London: Allen Lane.

Mason, P. (2015b) The end of capitalism has begun. *The Guardian*, 17 July [online]. Available from: www.theguardian.com/books/2015/jul/17/postcapitalism-end-of-capitalism-begun [Accessed 30 July 2017].

May, C. (2016) Book review. *The Sharing Economy: The End of Employment and the Rise of Crowd-Based Capitalism* by Arun Sundararajan. *LSE Review of Books* [online]. Blog entry. Available from http://eprints.lse.ac.uk/66878/ [Accessed 12 August 2017].

Morris, C.W. (1938) Foundations of a theory of signs. In: *International Encyclopedia of Unified Science*, Vol. I, no. 2 (pp. 1–59). Chicago: University of Chicago Press.

Nadeem, S. (2015) On the sharing economy. *Contexts*. **14**(1), p. 13.

Peirce, C.S. (1931–1958) *Collected Papers*. Cambridge, MA: Harvard University Press.

Puschmann, T., and Alt, R. (2016) Sharing economy. *Business & Information Systems Engineering*. **58**(1), pp. 93–99.

Saussure, F. (1916) *Cours de Linguistique Générale* (ed. 1971 by C. Bally, A. Sechehays and A. Riedlinger). Payot: Paris.

Sayward, C. (1974) The received distinction between pragmatics, semantics and syntax. *Foundations of Language*. **11**(1), pp. 97–104.

Searle, J.R. (1969) *Speech Acts: An Essay in the Philosophy of Language*. Cambridge: Cambridge University Press.

Silverstein, M. (1972) Linguistic theory: syntax, semantics, pragmatics. *Annual Review of Anthropology*. **1**, pp. 349–382.

Slee, T. (2016) *What's Yours is Mine: Against the Sharing Economy*. Toronto: Between the Lines.

Smirnov, A. (1996) Understanding justice in an Islamic context: some points of contrast with Western theories. *Philosophy East and West*. **46**(3), pp. 337–350.

Stephany, A. (2015) *The Business of Sharing: Making it in the New Sharing Economy*. Basingstoke: Palgrave Macmillan UK.

Sundararajan, A. (2016) *The Sharing Economy: The End of Employment and the Rise of Crowd-Based Capitalism*. Cambridge, MA: The MIT Press.

Von Benda-Beckmann, F., Von Benda-Beckmann, K. and Wiber, M.G. (2006) The properties of property. In: Von Benda-Beckmann, F., Von Benda-Beckmann, K. and Wiber, M.G. (eds) *Changing Properties of Property*. New York and Oxford: Berghahn Books, pp. 1–39.

Wahbalbari, A., Bahari, Z. and Mohd-Zaharim, N. (2015) The concept of scarcity and its influence on the definitions of Islamic economics: a critical perspective. *Humanomics*. **31**(2), pp. 134–159.

Wikipedia (undated) *Scarcity* [online]. Available from: https://en.wikipedia.org/wiki/Scarcity [Accessed 27 August 2017].

Part II

Social impact entrepreneurship: instruments and cases

6 A new form of global asset-backed debt market through *sukuk*

*Mohamed Ariff**

1. Introduction

This chapter aims at providing a summary discussion of an emerging debt market that saw its beginning in Malaysia in 1990, and is currently growing at a double-digit growth rate across some 18 countries, namely the market of *sukuk*.

Though mistakenly often called 'Islamic bonds', *sukuk* certificates (pl. of *sakk*) are today listed and traded in most cases in formal exchanges, but also in over-the-counter markets by a variety of private and public financial institutions. These certificates offer a completely different and new way of debt contracting in comparison with conventional bonds, as they relate to specific asset-backed funding (by contracting targeted funding of an entity instead of general funding) and embrace a set of ethical principles grounded on the Islamic teachings on financial trading.[1] The growing segment of *sukuk* has attracted attention by professionals especially because, despite the fact that the market is still young, it has chalked up an outstanding value estimated to be around USD 320 billion in 2017 (see IFSB, 2017, p. 3; for more specific data pp. 15–23) mostly in five financial centres: Malaysia, Indonesia, Saudi Arabia, United Arab Emirates and Bahrain (without considering that estimates are still unavailable for another big market centre, namely Iran). There are another 13 countries where one or more *sukuk* financial instruments are listed and traded in their respective national financial markets.[2] The London Stock Exchange listed its first *sukuk* instrument in August 2014, with the announcement made by the English Government of making London a leading centre for this form of debt contracting.[3] Furthermore, while the first convertible *sukuk* was issued in Malaysia, more such issues are currently available in different markets, amplifying the number of investors potentially interested in these instruments.

* As the author of this study, I would like to acknowledge here my students, namely Dr Meysam Safari and Dr Shamsher Mohamad, for the work we did together that enriched many ideas on this subject matter.

Given these preliminary remarks, the rest of the chapter is divided into a further six sections.

Section 2 briefly depicts the development and the essential features of Islamic finance. In the following sections, the main types of *sukuk* (Section 3), the rationale of *sukuk* for fund mobilization as asset-backed debt instruments, with their requirements and related advantages (Section 4), and the challenge for product designers and financial engineering to fully exploit the potential of *sukuk* instruments (Section 5) are explained. In particular, the text comments on the restrictive interpretation of the Islamic laws on trade in financial instruments as a straw man for the development of the market, since these restrictions are few, while the possibilities are open-ended for the useful design of contracts aimed at satisfying funding needs. Later on, Section 6 deals with some persistent issues in developing the Islamic finance debt market through *sukuk*. To conclude, Section 7 discusses the importance of *sukuk* instruments as a source of funding for governments, corporations and institutions, in relation to asset-backed investment, and their utility for emerging economies, especially as an alternative to lending interest-based financial tools, in order to avoid long-run debt issues and promote a social impact in the long-term development of local communities.

2. Islamic finance briefly

Sukuk can be seen as the latest innovation in the Islamic financial market.

At the beginning, Islamic banking was the first segment of modern Islamic finance, which started in 1963 and has since now grown to USD 1,500 billion in banking assets (IFSB, 2017, p. 3) mostly in the Gulf Region. Islamic insurance companies (*takaful*) developed soon afterwards in the 1970s, and later on Islamic mutual funds sprouted in many countries in the 1980s.[4] Since not all firms are likely to be acceptable as Islamic financial investment, attempts were made in the 1990s to identify listed companies in the stock indices that would be consistent with *Shari'ah* principles: this led to the birth of so-called *Shari'ah*-compliant stock indices.[5] As stated above, *sukuk* can be seen as the latest development of the Islamic financial market, starting at its very origin in 1990, with the first *sukuk* listed in Malaysia by a private firm.[6]

Beside all these 'market-oriented' instruments, it should also be mentioned that a vast sum of money is saved annually by Muslims who intend to perform their pilgrimage and are placed in what are called '*hajj* funds' in almost all Muslim countries. This vast sum of money has been managed as per Islamic finance principles for some 1,450 years. This is perhaps the largest amount of money (no estimates exist on how much is involved) that has been managed according to *Shari'ah*. Similarly, the institute of *waqf* is as old as Islam, and the physical assets and money given to *waqf* (i.e. foundation, or bequest for charitable purposes, religious learning and maintenance of mosques) are today managed by a myriad of committees in Muslim countries. Again, no definitive data are available, although the value of assets managed under *waqf* is likely to be one of the biggest parts of Islamic finance.

Last but not least, Muslim believers are required to pay a sum equal to 2.5 per cent of new wealth in a year to charity (*zakat*), which is a religious tithe to be disbursed voluntarily to eight categories of people in need. Payments of *zakat* are to be offset against personal and corporate taxes in several countries, to ensure a level playing field in taxation.[7]

As can be easily noted, Islamic finance is still very young compared to the two-and-a-half centuries that led modern banking institutions to reach the stage where they are today. The future path of this 50-year experiment is still uncharted, and dependent on the full realization of the potential of Islamic ethics in regulating financial transactions.[8]

Some writers have argued that funding procedures under Islamic finance are 'sticky', meaning that investors cannot exit the market quickly when a firm experiences temporary problems. Lending under Islamic finance promotes more stable banking and less volatile financial markets for securities, but also implies limits of market liquidity. Nevertheless, financial engineering in Islamic finance has led to the market acceptance of new instruments, increasing the efficiency of *Shari'ah*-compliant transactions and making *sukuk* more attractive also for non-Muslim investors. Furthermore, the International Monetary Fund (IMF) has recently underlined the intrinsic value of Islamic finance in relation to the promotion of global financial stability, against that kind of crisis brought about by easy credit and money practices promoted by conventional financial institutions. In a statement posted on the IMF online blog, dating 6 April 2015, for instance, it is claimed that Islamic finance has

> the promise of supporting financial stability, since a key tenet of Islamic finance is that lenders should share in both the risks and rewards of the projects and loans they finance. Islamic finance has an important potential to act as an engine of stability and inclusion. Since investors are required to bear losses that may arise on loans, there is therefore less leverage, and greater incentive to exercise strong risk management.
>
> (Norat *et al.*, 2015)

3. *Sukuk*: nature, development and classification

The term *sukuk* has been defined succinctly by the Islamic Financial Services Board (IFSB) in the following way: '*sukuk*, frequently referred to as "Islamic bonds", are certificates with each *sakk* representing a proportional, undivided ownership right in tangible assets or a pool of predominantly tangible assets, or a business venture'.[9] Technically speaking, *sukuk* are debt instruments whose investors own tangible assets taken as security from the borrowers during the life of the loan, for servicing the funding arrangements over the life of the project. This form of funding is mostly over a finite time period (the exception being an equity-like *musharakah sukuk*), and the transfer of ownership of assets to the borrowers provides not just security, but also incomes to service the debt. This suggests that the loan book is fully backed by the tangible assets transferred to lenders and held in a special purpose company jointly owned in the names of the lenders.

The number of countries which have initiated regulatory changes or have already passed laws to reform their financial regulations to facilitate the debut of *sukuk* markets is worth noting, including not only London, but also China, Russia, Kazakhstan, Hong Kong and Australia. Also international institutions, such as the World Bank, have raised debt using this new form of fund-raising, as have several governments and their agencies through the so-called 'sovereign *sukuk*'. Private corporations as well are keen to invest and issue *sukuk*, next to conventional bonds and bank debt instruments.[10] Hence, the rapid acceptance of this new form of debt-contracting by investors has been widely commented upon in the financial press, such as by Euromoney, *Financial Times* and Bloomberg, and in regulatory circles, such as by the IMF (see, for instance, the end of Section 2).

Speaking of the dimension of the phenomenon, the *sukuk* market is currently growing at 17–24 per cent per year in 18 countries. Compared to this, the world has seen subdued growth (in fact, declining growth during 2008–2010) in the conventional bond markets because of the deleveraging trend that has started since the global financial crisis in 2008.

There are six types of *sukuk* securities already in use both in the private sector and the public sector as issues for trading (please refer to Safari *et al.*, 2014), and namely:

 (i) *musharakah sukuk*;
(ii) *murabahah*-based *sukuk*;
(iii) *ijarah sukuk* (which are leasing contracts mostly with fixed payments; this is the most common type on offer in all markets, especially in Malaysia);
(iv) variable pay-off *mudarabah sukuk* (through a partnership between the financier and the entrepreneur; this is a pure debt contract, which forms an important type of security in most markets);
 (v) *istisna' sukuk*, to provide working capital or project financing, for an entrepreneur with experience in a certain production, with a loan without asset-backing at issue time;
(vi) *salam sukuk*, which are advance-payment contracts to facilitate a temporary arrangement to secure funds ahead of the time to sell a merchandise in the future (as in sale of agricultural produce ahead of harvest).

Figure 6.1 provides a graphical representation of these types of *sukuk*, and further possible classification of products in the market.

Another general categorization, in which the above six contract types can be easily fitted, has been proposed in a recent book (Safari *et al.*, 2014), with regard to six classes.

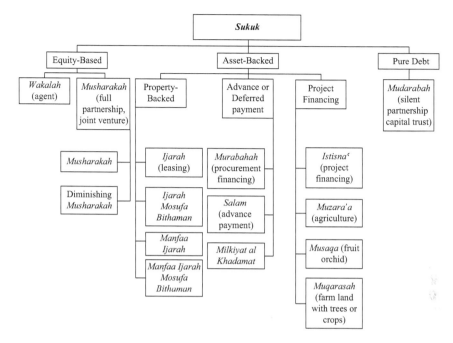

Figure 6.1. A classification of *sukuk* contracts (Safari *et al.*, 2014, p. 27)

Class I. *Musharakah sukuk* are share-like securities equity instruments, owners of which have full control of the firm either for an infinite period, in which case, risk and profit is shared; if the security has finite life, then too, there is some form of risk-sharing before profit is shared, although the profits are arranged to be paid in the lifetime of the contract or at the end.

Class II. Discount *sukuk* are when the amout to be paid back is discounted from the face value with provision normally for rewards to be paid at the end of the contract period with no servicing of the debt in the intermediate period by the special purpose company.

Class III. Fixed and constant growth payoff *sukuk* are of two types. If fixed, then the special purpose company services the investors with fixed payments at agreed regular intervals over the life of the instrument. If growing, then the periodic payments are increased at an agreed rate (say rents can go up by the amount of the inflation rate) as paid at agreed intervals by the special purpose company. This is a growing annuity paid in arrears. This class also accommodates short-term instruments over less than one-year maturities.

Class IV. Variable payoff *sukuk* have outcome-based payoff, and the outcome depends on the profits of the special purpose company, which decides on the amount based on actual cash streams. Sometimes there is a base payment to which a percentage is added as in LIBOR plus (international interest rate) or KLIBOR plus (in Malaysia).

Class V. *Istisna'* *sukuk* (as said above) are variously described as working capital funding or project funding arrangements. This type is ideal for large projects, where the assets of a firm are to be produced (some manufacturing is involved, as is clear by the Arabic word, *istisna'*) in future as in toll road construction or an energy plant construction for government.

Class VI. These are futures contracts, well suited for funding the production of items that will emerge in future, on evidence-already-in-place (for example, a blueprint, or flowers on a tree).

These six structural types are suggested as sufficient classes to accommodate the variations in each of them as the market grows. Among the earliest *sukuk* on offer are the popular lease-based contracts (*ijarah sukuk*) which will fall under Class III as a fixed payment at regular intervals based on some computation of the rental (or income-producing) value of assets being leased. One could have a variation to this basic mode by adding a growth element, say for depreciation of the assets, if the lessee is arranging for a capital lease. Such a slightly varied *ijarah* contract is called *ijarah manfaa sukuk*, which has a slight variation in the mode of payments from fixed to variable payments (see Figure 6.1). Similarly, an *istisna'* *sukuk* for leasing a farmland with trees can be arranged much as an *istisna'*. *Muqarasah* can be used just as the simple *istisna'* *sukuk* is for funding a project for the production of special furniture by a firm to be fitted in a hotel (again, Figure 6.1).

Though other classifications are in use (e.g. short- and long-term *sukuk*; or with reference to the issuer type),[11] this six-way classification is a useful way of grouping *sukuk* contracts in place in several markets and also provides enough room to include newer *sukuk* contracts. In any case, the fundamental aspect of asset-backing for *sukuk* is central for their differentiation from conventional bonds markets under which loans are based on implicit guarantee of the 'good name of the borrower' which, as recent history has proved, may unfortunately lead to widespread financial instability, in case of incapability of the issuer to repay the debt. On the contrary, under the *sukuk* model, asset-backing is defined at the conclusion of the contract through pooling the ownership of the assets within a special purpose company, with proportionate ownership of the investors in the business.

4. How and why to mobilize funds via *sukuk* contracts as asset-backed debt instruments

It used to be argued, and some scholars still do, that *sukuk* instruments are basically equity-based, and that the idea of Islamic debt instruments is not defendable. There is some merit in this argument since *sukuk* span across bills, bonds and equity-type contracting, which departs from mainstream bond instruments. Yet, this reasoning is faulty in so far as the fact goes that *sukuk* certificates are mostly based on debt-taking arrangements with the sole exclusion of *musharakah sukuk*, which are very seldom contracted as a loan agreement. Therefore, *sukuk* can be mainly described as Islamic debt market instruments, whose peculiarity relates to asset-backing (as shared ownership in an investment: see the definition at the beginning of Section 3) according to Islamic ideas of fairness, justice, society-first (i.e. social responsibility investments) and non-exploitation.

Consistent with this description, the two following sub-sections deal with the requirements for *sukuk* contracting, and the related advantages of investing in the *sukuk* market.

4.1. *Requirements for* sukuk *contracting*

There is a range of requirements and standards of *Shari'ah* compliance in order for a *sukuk* structure to be approved by *Shari'ah* scholars in Islamic financial institutions, and be subsequently offered to the public. In particular, five basic conditions can be listed.

i. Funding must embrace parameters of risk-sharing and by implication profit-sharing clauses so that reward to investors is not pre-agreed and fixed as in the normal debt contract. This fulfils a need for a two-sided arrangement to bind both parties to a common purpose of production of items useful to society, as *sukuk* are targeted investment plans under a two-sided balanced contracting.

ii. Rewards are obtained by fund providers for financing the entrepreneur with whom the financier shares the risk of business.

iii. Compliance with full disclosure is required to ensure provision of symmetric information ahead of contracting so that the investors know the exact outcomes of the contract being signed. This ensures that there are no hidden clauses, and that information that places the investment at high risk is fully understood, while gambling-type risks are not taken in financial transactions to make the funding safer.

iv. Funding can only be available for activities that promote the society's well-being. Production of intoxicants, tobacco, gambling, prostitution, weapons of mass destruction, etc., are denied funding under Islamic finance, in order to promote social growth.

v. Funding is only made if the borrower is willing to transfer part of the borrower's income-producing assets (if existing now and, if not, likely to exist in the future, when the asset becomes available through funding) to be held in the joint names of the lenders in a separate special purpose company (SPC) to service the debt out of the assets of the SPC. This is the fundamental asset-backing principle (commentators have repeatedly called for this to be the cornerstone of Islamic financing debt contracting), also emphasized in the description of *sukuk* given above. Proponents of Islamic finance insist that all lending is asset-backed and that these assets must provide incomes to service the debt. The assets could well be usufructs that have income-producing character, if these are not tangible assets.

4.2. Advantages related to sukuk *investments through asset-backing*

The nature of *sukuk* as asset-backed debt instuments implies some funda-mental advantanges for investors and the financial market as a whole.

First, asset-backing makes investors more careful about their investments, in the light of the the outcome of the entrepreneurial business. In conventional lending, investors are likely not to be interested in the outcome of the funding. On the contrary, the logic of *sukuk* not only targets funding for a particular purpose, but also ensures that the money lent is seen through the lenses of the likely success of the project. This creates an agency problem, as well as a moral hazard issue, which increases the cost of monitoring Islamic finance contracts, but at the same time this determines a better selection of funded projects.

Second, asset-backing also prevents excessive debt overhang. According to available data, the world GDP was about USD 80 trillion, but the debt overload was USD 160 trillion in 2014 (Ariff *et al.*, 2013). Under the asset-backing principle, instead, no borrower can borrow more than the total worth of assets in place. As a consequence, the optimum debt will be under 100 per cent via *sukuk* contracting. This is a desirable aspect of Islamic finance debt market instruments, in terms of financial stability and help towards developing countries to overcome the debt overhang.[12]

Third, *sukuk* are designed to borrow money for specific purposes, and not for general ones. General purpose debt-based funds can be used by top management to re-direct the funds to other projects, which increases agency problems with regard to investment strategies, especially with regard to pos-sible personal interests by the management in diverting the funds. This is avoided in *sukuk* investments, as an *istisna' sukuk* fund cannot be diverted to pay lease payments, and vice versa; a *salam sukuk* cannot be diverted to fund a building; and so on. This ensures better discipline in borrowing decision-making by encouraging more focused borrowing for specific purposes than in conventional debt markets, giving rise to what can be defined as *targeted funding* under the Islamic finance contracting model.[13]

In the light of these inherent benefits of *sukuk* debt instruments, one may argue that the economic crunch linked to financial crises (as the one the world is still experiencing from 2008) would have been prevented if Islamic finance principles had been applied. Promoting easy lending, without any asset-backing criteria, in fact, slowly leads to the explosion of a 'credit binge', and eventually a financial crisis (see Ariff *et al.*, 2012). Important scholars (see for instance, Goldsmith, as quoted in Summers *et al.*, 1991, p.137; Kindleberger, 2001; Kindleberger and Laffargue, 1982) have argued that all crises are preceded by credit binges or easy money lending policies promoting unlim-ited borrowing (Kindleberger, as quoted by Fosler, 2013).

5. *Sukuk* instruments and financial engineering

In this section, we discuss the potential of innovation in the *sukuk* market.

Professionals in the Islamic finance industry have advanced new product development through financial engineering, mainly in the major financial centres. In a recent book, an author claims that this act of engineering new products has dramatically altered the market, by extending the breadth of the Islamic finance and changing its nature (Irfan, 2014a). On the legitimacy of this product development, a persistent debate is still ongoing.

In his chapter contribution to Ariff *et al.* (2012), Iqbal (2012) offers a set of guiding principles for product engineering in Islamic finance.

i.   *Principle of ease* is a guiding principle that mandates the spirit of *Shari'ah* to make things easy for people. This means that *among the permitted options*, the practice of the Prophet was always to choose the one which is easy for people.

ii. *Doctrine of maximizing human welfare*, which means seeking benefits and repelling harm for everyone.[14]

iii. *The doctrine of general permissibility* points to the obvious fact that things/contracts that are prohibited by *Shari'ah* are very few compared to those that are permitted in one's dealing with others.

iv. *The doctrine of necessity* permits *temporary* suspension of normal laws in case of dire need. This doctrine enables innovations when *extreme* circumstances occur.

v.   *Prohibitions in Islamic finance* are enumerated as follows: no financial deals that can be described as usurious (*riba*); extreme risk-taking (*gharar* as exposing oneself or one's property to jeopardy due to asymmetric information); gambling-type risk-taking is prohibited (*maysir*). Referring to a *hadith* by the Prophet of Islam, Iqbal argues that financial products can be engineered 'unless they make something forbidden as permissible or something permissible as forbidden' (p. 31).

Though product developments have been going along for a while, it is worth noting that much of the innovation is being led by conventional finance houses trying to duplicate their products by finding new ways to comply with a given set of Islamic finance principles. That is fine since a similar process in mainstream modern finance led to the birth of so many new products that have come to stay with us. However, some commentators have remarked that there is an attempt to overstep some of the principles in the zeal to produce new Islamic finance products, especially if such products are highly profitable. An example being cited in the literature is the case of Goldman Sachs introducing an Islamic swap contract. A swap is a two-way bet on a financial situation; though it is fair game, it resembles a gamble (*maysir*) so it violates the doctrine that one should not put oneself in danger or one's property in jeopardy by taking a two-way bet.

Apart from this piece of criticism, the need for a restrictive interpretation of the Islamic laws on the trade of financial instruments is a straw man to safeguard the Islamic market, since these restrictions are actually few, while there are broad possibilities for the useful design of contracts aimed at satisfying funding needs (according to the guidelines indicated above). In fact, the Islamic financial industry is now sufficiently mature also to amend new products to render them fully *Shari'ah*-compliant. One example is that of the BAB *sukuk* in the Malaysian capital market, which until a change was made in 2013, violated some *Shari'ah* provisions as pointed out by Shaikh Taqi Usmani at that time.

6. Some important issues in developing the Islamic finance debt market

This section summarizes the major hurdles for the continued development of the *sukuk* industry. In particular, the text refers to issues of cost reduction, also considering the wide range of interpretation of *Shari'ah*; the related problem of '*fatwa* shopping'; liquidity issues; and the employ of available technology (applied software development and databases).

6.1. Cost reduction in sukuk structuring

The first issue to be mentioned is whether cost of contracting in the *sukuk* market can be brought down. Unlike the much older bond instruments, in fact, *sukuk* structures demand multiple embedded contracting, often with expensive *Shari'ah* supervision and consulting services, hence more time to be developed and implemented.

The lack of standard terms for each of *sukuk* types makes structuring time-consuming. Some solutions have been suggested. One is that, for each contract type, a standard set of rules is agreed upon; so that the time to structure contract can be reduced, and the charges limited. Another solution is to have an institution of higher learning tasked to charter Islamic finance specialists, similarly to what is available for the accounting profession worldwide.

6.2. Variance of juristic interpretations and 'fatwa shopping'

The variance of juristic interpretations by *Shari'ah* advisors and scholars has been hindering the development of the *sukuk* market.

Partly an obstacle arises from the specialization of human knowledge, and the fact that very few *Shari'ah* scholars are well trained both in theology, law and financial markets:[15] as a result, interpretations may be based on a diverse range of arguments, leading to alternative (and sometimes undesirably diversified) outcomes. But, at the same time, the reason for the diversity of opinions in Islamic finance is due to the different interpretations in the tradition of the four main schools of Islamic jurisprudence (*fiqh*), Hanafi, Maliki, Hanbali and Shafi'i.

While this problem may not be serious at country level (since country level experts will be mostly trained in the same school of thought), it becomes a major problem at an international stage. A possible solution is to identify some common framework principles, and then treat the special provision of a different school at the local level. But unfortunately today the practice of finance houses is basically to 'look for' the most appropriate juristic opinion (*fatwa*) to fit the product that has been developed, leading to the criticised phenomenon of *'fatwa* shopping'. This is certainly unsatisfactory in the long run since it undermines the confidence of investors in the *sukuk* market.

6.3. *Liquidity issues*

One study (Safari, 2013) suggests that *sukuk* certificates are traded only about 40 per cent of the time, which would mean that there is trading once every 12 trading days. This is not satisfactory, so steps are needed to be put in place to increase liquidity. Bond markets around the world suffered from this ailment for a long time. Since the 1980s, regulators have introduced reforms whereby investors can trade via internet-based portals in the bond exchanges. The liquidity in conventional bond markets has since improved because of active promotion of trading. Other measures are also needed. Designating a set of investment bankers to act as market makers would increase liquidity. This method has been widely used in stock exchanges and in recent years in bond markets to increase liquidity. Public participation in *sukuk* could also lead to liquidity improvement if closed-end *sukuk* mutual funds are established and listed for trading on stock exchanges. Closed-end mutual funds offer good returns and can be targeted to earn the average of different risk classes of *sukuk*.

6.4. *Technology (software development and databases) in the* sukuk *market*

Markets have unique differences, as do *sukuk* contracts compared with conventional bonds. Some of the software used in the industry needs to be examined *carefully* – I would say meticulously – as to whether the system incorporates the requirements of *sukuk* funds. For example, simply using the mortgage table designed for conventional bank mortgages is unlikely to give correct numbers for an Islamic finance *mudarabah* mortgage. There are important differences in the way payments must be made, and the capital to be treated, etc. This task has to be done by the regulators since leaving this to the private sector would lead to different interpretations, so the wrong application will be made.

A related issue on how to price *sukuk* is the lack/absence of pricing models for *sukuk* securities. This is important because basing investment advice on market-clearing prices is fraught with danger since markets could under- or over-price a security. In conventional markets, there are theoretical models which provide a method to estimate fair-value for securities being issued independent of the market prices. Such is possible only if the pricing models are carefully developed. This aspect requires funding research activities in higher learning institutions, and strong educational investments (see Safari, 2013).

Databases for analysis are important too to provide reliable investment advisory services. While there are many points at which data are produced and made available, it is not as easy as in conventional finance industry to have access to trading data for the *sukuk* market. Once such databases are available, the industry will develop analyst interest to provide carefully evaluated advice to investors.

7. Conclusions: asset-backed debt and economic development

The development of *sukuk* as Islamic debt market instruments has helped to complete the market landscape of the Islamic finance system (Section 2). This chapter has outlined the nature of *sukuk* (Section 3) and their fundamental principle of asset-backing, with its inherent advantages for investors, in terms of project selection and avoidance of debt overhang (Section 4). A brief discussion on *sukuk* and financial engineering (Section 5), as well as of the persistent obstacles for the further development of the *sukuk* market (from cost reduction to the lack of common juristic interpretation, software development and liquidity shortage: Section 6) have been also provided.

While debt-taking appetite is still high in the global financial economy, *sukuk* as a source of funding for governments, corporations and institutions offer an 'asset-backing' alternative that limits debt overhang. In fact, because debt via *sukuk* requires that a part of the assets of the borrower be temporarily taken to be jointly owned and controlled by the lenders in a special purpose company, borrowers cannot overload themselves with too much debt. This feature represents a first benefit linked to the *sukuk* market.

Second, the peculiar nature of *sukuk* is particularly functional to infrastructure financing (as it is grounded on real economy development), and consequently to the development of emerging economies, helping governments to raise money without too much debt-taking in relation to asset-backing.[16]

Third, as mentioned in this chapter, asset-backing makes investors more 'committed' to their investments, in the light of the outcome of the entrepreneurial business. In a certain sense, one can speak of a stronger 'stickiness' of debt via *sukuk* funding compared to mainstream debt via bonds. Since lenders have legal ownership rights on the assets of the borrowers, this makes the lenders via *sukuk* 'stick' to borrowers for a longer term, almost to the end of maturity to get their principal back. This is especially important for the success of development financing infrastructure requiring a long time to recoup the capital amount involved in large-scale projects in explorations, energy, transportation facilities, etc.

Fourth, this 'stickiness' together with risk-sharing in *sukuk* contracting promote stability in the lender-borrower relationship, so the financial market risk is reduced.

As a whole, these features – asset-backing, risk-sharing before profits and 'stickiness' – together promote stability in the financial system, and confirm the utility of *sukuk* for emerging economies, especially as an alternative to lending interest-based financial tools, in order to avoid long-run debt issues and promote a social impact in the long-term development of local communities.

Notes

1 For an outline of these ethical principles please refer to Ariff and Iqbal (2011).
2 As indicated in the text a recent report by the IFSB (2017) quotes the size of the *sukuk* market at USD 320 billion. Much of the market is over-the-counter, while the 18 jurisdictions mentioned in the main text have also listed and traded *sukuk* instruments in formalized markets. For a quick overview of the *sukuk* market, please see Figure 6.1, in this chapter; another useful reference is Vishwanath and Azmi (2009).
3

> Islamic scholars in medieval Baghdad and Cordoba developed rules and mechanisms to encourage entrepreneurship, leading to the dissemination of financial innovations along the Silk Route and into Southern Europe. Contractual structures for investment partnerships, agency and trust laws, the money transfer system, paper money, cheques and letters of credit were just some of the concepts introduced into Europe by merchants from the Islamic world. These were the roots of modern capitalism, but somehow along the way the protection of the weak became forgotten and the concept of the unfettered free market dominated.

(Irfan, 2014b)

An abridged version of the article by Irfan, from which this extract has been taken, was published in *The Guardian* (Irfan, 2014c) on 4 December 2014, and was named one of the top five stories for *Guardian Sustainable Finance*, witnessing the growing interest towards Islamic finance also in the Western economic world.
4 In 2017 there were some 600 mutual funds with a total sum under management estimated to be around USD 56 billion (IFSB, 2017, p. 3).
5 This led to the so-called 'Islamic indices' as identified in some 24 stock markets: roughly about 40 per cent of firms in such indices are deemed Islamic equities and are approved as being compliant with Islamic financing rules. The worldwide size of the listed stock markets was USD 82,000 billion in 2016. There is no way of knowing how much money has been placed in *Shariʿah*-compliant securities after these Islamic indices were established.
6 Recent writers (including Murat Çizakça) trace the use of *sukuk* from ancient times right up to the twentieth century in the Ottoman Empire. However, the idea of *sukuk* as debt instruments was advanced in modern times by a scholar in the *Journal of Islamic Economics* only in 1978.
7 The voluntary basis of *zakat* is underlined by the fact that the Prophet of Islam has consistently refrained from making this compulsorily collected by governments.

8 As is well known, these rules are interpreted by *Shari'ah* scholars, who have established a set of standards to certify permissible Islamic financial instruments. Debates are still ongoing with regard to the harmonization of criteria of *Shari'ah* compliance, with a consensus which can be reached and later challenged.

9 Safari *et al.* (2014) underlines that '*sukuk* structures are debt instruments that require the creation of assets in a separate entity, these assets being owned proportionally by lenders, the fund providers' (p. 14). This definition emphasizes the asset-backed nature as a fundamental structuring principle of this type of debt instrument.

10 About 20 per cent of the outstanding *sukuk* issues are by private firms (IFSB, 2017, p. 3), some of which are very large corporations listed in Europe, the Middle East and Southeast Asia.

11 As mentioned in the main text, popular writings in the press and in some books refer to an easier and simpler classification. All *sukuk* instruments are divided into short-term or long-term instruments. For example, a government may borrow under *mudarabah sukuk* (trust loan under silent partnership) with a special purpose company that owns government buildings for rent. The income from rents will service this loan according to either fixed or growing annuity over the life of the loan. In this case, normally it will be a long-term loan. Short-term debt arrangements are usually based on asset-backed arrangements as in this example. The long-term funding is mostly equity-backed to provide incomes to service the debt over the life of the contract. This is then short-term versus long-term with asset-backing and equity-backing classification. This is not a fully consistent classification since there are overlaps among the three types in terms of asset backing. Another favoured method of classifying *sukuk* securities is to refer to the issuer type, as has also been a common practice in the bond markets for centuries. *Sukuk* issues with a term of less than one year are called bills (if issued by the government) or papers (if issued by companies). *Sukuk* issued by government agencies are called agency *sukuk* while those issued by private companies including financial institutions are called private *sukuk* certificates. Though widely in use in the marketplaces, this method of referring to *sukuk* does not reveal the special nature of *sukuk*, which is that *sukuk* enable fund-raising for different purposes by having targeted financing.

12 The majority of Muslim countries are poor. Of the 57 such countries, 40 countries have average per capita incomes of less than USD 5,000 in 2014 (Ariff and Safari, 2014). That puts them as low-income countries. These poor nations are the ones with large debt overhang. If all their borrowing had been under Islamic finance terms, then they would have borrowed no more than what they could service, and the debt overhang of these countries would not have occurred. Iqbal (2013) points out that the nexus for debt overhang is the lack of asset-backing in conventional debt contracting. He offers the idea that *sukuk* debt contracting is a brilliant alternative to the long-run path to financially stable debt-taking, if structured in accordance with *Shari'ah* rules.

13 General purpose borrowing encourages misdirecting resources by top management: consider the leveraged buyout debacle that rocked the world's financial markets in the 1980s. So much failure in LBO-led bankruptcies would not have happened if *sukuk*-type borrowing had been in place, which through asset-backing would have limited the borrowing from exploding and then destroying so many firms (*The Economist*, 2007).

14 This is equivalent to the *greatest happiness* principle by John Stuart Mill.

15 This is a major problem in managing any organization. For instance, I had the misfortune of working under a dean, a professor of sociology, who did not understand what return on investment is. This meant that the person was simply not capable of knowing how funding decisions must be made under strict rules of cost of capital and return to capital. In a similar manner, a *Shari'ah* scholar whose education is only on theological matters and with little knowledge about finance and economics may be unable to work easily on credit and risk management.

16 This is desirable because government borrowing has doubled in the last 25 years so much so that debt servicing is reducing the abilities of governments to spend on public services. Thus, in the long run, debt cannot go beyond the ability to service the debt. That would bring stability to financial affairs of companies, institutions such as banks, and governments.

References

Ariff, M., and Iqbal, M. (eds) (2011) *The Foundations of Islamic Banking: Theory, Practice and Education*. Cheltenham, UK, and Northampton, MA: Edward Elgar Publishing.

Ariff, M., and Safari, M. (2014) A socio-economic profile of Muslim countries. In: Hassan, M.K., and Lewis, M.K. (eds) *Handbook on Islam and Economic Life*. Cheltenham, UK, and Northampton, MA: Edward Elgar Publishing, pp. 198–211.

Ariff, M., Iqbal, M. and Mohamad, S. (eds) (2012) *The Islamic Debt Market for* Sukuk *Securities: The Theory and Practice of Profit Sharing Investment*. Cheltenham, UK, and Northampton, MA: Edward Elgar Publishing.

Ariff, M., Cheng, F.-F. and Mohamad, S. (2013). *Handbook of Asian Bond Markets: Yields & Risk*. Serdang, Selangor, Malaysia: Universiti Putra Malaysia Press.

Fosler, G. (2013) Lessons from Kindleberger on the financial crisis [online]. Available from: www.gailfosler.com/lessons-from-kindleberger-on-the-financial-crisis [Accessed 24 March 2015].

IFSB (Islamic Financial Services Board) (2017) *Islamic Financial Services Industry Stability Report 2017*. Kuala Lumpur, Malaysia: Islamic Financial Services Board.

Iqbal, M. (2012) A guide to Islamic finance principles and financial engineering. In: Ariff, M., Iqbal, M. and Mohamad, S. (eds) *The Islamic Debt Market for* Sukuk *Securities: The Theory and Practice of Profit Sharing Investment*. Cheltenham, UK, and Northampton, MA: Edward Elgar Publishing, pp. 67–85.

Iqbal, M. (2013) Determining the role of debt in the economy and a new approach for solving sovereign debt crises. *International Journal of Banking and Finance*. **10**(1), pp. 94–133.

Irfan, H. (2014a) *Heaven's Bankers: Inside the Hidden World of Islamic Finance*. London: Constable Publishing.

Irfan, H. (2014b and 2014c) Could Islamic finance save capitalism? [online]. Available from https://ummahwide.com/could-islamic-finance-save-capitalism-87995fc020e0 (2014b) and www.theguardian.com/sustainable-business/2014/dec/04/could-islamic-finance-solution-capitalism (2014c) [Accessed 15 December 2016].

Kindleberger, C.P. (2001, 4th ed.; original ed. 1978) *Manias, Panics, and Crashes: A History of Financial Crises*. Basingstoke: Palgrave.

Kindleberger, C.P., and Laffargue, J.-P. (eds) (1982) *Financial Crises: Theory, History, and Policy*. New York: Cambridge University Press.

Norat, M., Pinon, M. and Zeidane, Z. (2015) The promise of Islamic finance: further inclusion with stability. *IMFBlog* [online]. Available from: https://blogs.imf.org/2015/04/06/the-promise-of-islamic-finance-further-inclusion-with-stability/ [Accessed 13 December 2016].

Safari, M. (2013) Contractual structures and payoff patterns of *sukuk* securities. *International Journal of Banking and Finance*. **10**(2), pp. 67–93.

Safari, M., Ariff, M. and Mohamad, S. (2014) *Sukuk Securities: New Ways of Debt Contracting*. Wiley Islamic Finance Series. Singapore: John Wiley & Sons.

Summers, L.H., Minsky, H.P., Samuelson, P.A., Poole, W. and Volcker, P.A. (1991) Macroeconomic consequences of financial crises. In: Feldstein, M. (ed.) *The Risk of Economic Crisis*. Chicago: Chicago University Press, pp. 135–182.

The Economist (2007) Turmoil in the markets [online]. 27 July.

Vishwanath, S.R., and Azmi, S. (2009) An overview of Islamic *sukuk* bonds. *The Journal of Structured Finance*. **14**(4), pp. 58–67.

7 Islamic entrepreneurship and the fundraising challenge

Unlocking capital via crowdfunding in the sharing economy

*Houssem eddine Bedoui and Rami Abdelkafi**

1. Introduction: private sector, social entrepreneurship and the sharing economy

With the proliferation of the impact of the financial crisis to the real economy, policies around the world have focused more on economic growth and jobs creation. Although these impacts have affected all countries, their consequences have been particularly serious in developing ones. In the MENA region, they have been compounded with the unprecedented turmoil which is still affecting the region's ability to improve its economic development.

More than ever, the role of the private sector is considered today crucial in achieving rapid economic growth. In the coming years, it is expected that the private sector will be the main provider of investment capital. The G20 Umbrella Paper (2013), for example, highlights the role of the private sector in providing long-term financing for growth and development. On the other hand, lack of private sector development has been considered as one of the major causes of the recent crisis affecting most of the developing countries. In a context of saturated public sector, the main absorber of labour force in developing nations, private sector development constitutes the ultimate solution for these countries to reduce their unemployment rates.

With this greater role assigned to the private sector, the concept of entrepreneurship has gained an increasing interest from the development community. Nallari *et al.* (2012, p. 96) define 'entrepreneurship' as a process, the means by which an individual makes use of or exploits opportunities in the marketplace for profit. Therefore, as a process, entrepreneurship is susceptible to be influenced by several factors within the social, political and economic contexts. In the current evolution of the global economy, there is no doubt that the so-called 'sharing economy', with the new technologies for fund mobilization, represents an opportunity for all the participants in the market to unlock the potential of entrepreneurship and promote the private sector, as well as social impact investments. Indeed, the overlap

---

* Disclaimer: The views and opinions expressed in this chapter are those of the authors and do not necessarily reflect the official policy or position of their institutions.

between the private market sector, social entrepreneurship and the new tools of the sharing economy constitutes a topical field of research in current times.

Given these preliminary considerations, the aim of this chapter is to discuss the potential of Islamic finance to foster social entrepreneurship by unlocking the mobilization of capital in the fundraising circle also through crowdfunding. To this objective, the study first discusses the concept of entrepreneurship and the relevance of its social dimension from an Islamic perspective (Section 2). In this regard, it highlights the incentives for individuals to be more active and to undertake the necessary steps for entrepreneurship, as well as the challenge of financing for any entrepreneur (Section 3). Later on, the chapter discusses the financing mechanisms that Islamic finance can offer as instruments for mobilizing financial resources in the fundraising circle (Section 4), with relevant cases as examples of the successful application of these instruments to nurture social entrepreneurship (Section 5). Finally, considering its relevance as a new tool of the sharing economy that can help new start-ups to take off and to develop, the chapter will focus on crowdfunding as a mechanism of fundraising that can be promoted through instruments which are compatible with Islamic finance principles (Section 6).

2. The social dimension of entrepreneurship from an Islamic perspective

One of the leading works in the domain of entrepreneurship is the contribution of the Global Entrepreneurship Monitor (GEM) based on surveys conducted on an increasing number of countries over the world.[1] To identify the factors affecting entrepreneurship during the different levels of economic development, the GEM classifies countries based on the methodology used by the World Economic Forum (WEF) Global Competitiveness Report. This Report identifies three phases of economic development based on gross domestic product (GDP) per capita and the share of exports comprising primary goods. Based on this classification, we can differentiate three phases of development: (i) factor-driven economies characterized by a dominance of agriculture and natural resources industries and an intensity of labour; (ii) efficiency-driven economies which have started their process of transition toward manufacturing; and (iii) innovation-driven economies characterized by knowledge-intensive firms and an expending service sector.

Based on this classification of countries according to their stage of development, we can distinguish two types of entrepreneurs (Acs, 2006; Nallari *et al.*, 2012): those who are entrepreneurs because of necessity and those who are opportunity entrepreneurs. With low levels of development, people have no choice other than being self-employed to generate income and assure their subsistence. However, with more advanced stages of economic development, entrepreneurship becomes an active choice by which individuals try to exploit the existing opportunities.

From an Islamic perspective, the concept of entrepreneurship has been highly affected by the low level of development of most of the Muslim countries. This has created a misunderstanding of the Islamic vision of development and the role that Islam assigns to entrepreneurship. Hassan and Hippler (2014) give an overview of the main differences between the Islamic and Western perceptions of entrepreneurship. They show that the main and most significant difference is related to the impact that economic activities may have on individuals and on the society as a whole. While Western economies put the positive financial impact of entrepreneurship on individuals as its first priority, Islam considers that societal impact of entrepreneurship should be the main objective of any economic activity.

Despite the lack of efforts provided by Muslim researchers in emphasizing the importance of entrepreneurship, it is possible to show the incentives that Islam gives to individuals in order to engage in economic activities.

The progressive alignment of *maqasid al-Shari'ah* towards the achievement of human well-being shows clearly the active role assigned by Islam to individuals in their whole life. First, Islam considers that God has the absolute ownership on everything and that man is his successor or representative on earth. Therefore, man's ownership derives from the role assigned to him by Allah in order to develop the earth. In this context, the situation of any individual is the ultimate result of his own actions. This means that the most important characteristic of Islam is the freedom given to humankind in choosing their destiny based on their proper actions. Second, unlike other economic systems, Islamic economics considers the presence of a balance between desires and resources. In this context, humans are always motivated to work and pursue the enhancement of their current situation. At the same time, any tendency to weaknesses and to apathy would not be permitted. Third, discussions related to the origins and the impacts of the recent financial crisis have highlighted the Islamic aspects of entrepreneurship in comparison with the conventional ones. As shown by Hassan and Hippler (2014), Islamic finance is always related to the impact on the real economy. Unlike debt-financing, Islamic modes of entrepreneurship financing (especially, *mudarabah* and *musharakah*) are essentially based on profit sharing. While debt financing creates a conflict of interest between the lender and the borrower, Islamic modes of financing allow for a risk sharing between the capital provider and the entrepreneur. The latter would not be pushed to undertake an excessive risk in order to pay his debt independently of the result of his investment.

Furthermore, the incentives to individuals to be responsible for their destiny can be seen in the Islamic vision of debt and its impact on society. In fact, the balance combining the incentive for wealthy people to help others and the stimulation of borrowers to be aware of the heavy commitment on their debt can avoid over-indebtedness. This balance would be maintained through two mechanisms.

The first relates to the prohibition of interest (*riba*), which limits loans to an act of charity that people undertake voluntarily, for the sole purpose of coming to help others. It therefore avoids the possibility of speculation and the willingness of some agents with surpluses to increase their capital through interest. Capital must be fructified by its participation in the economic activity through operations that are not tainted with usury and not having a perverse purpose (Tijkani, 2001). Furthermore, this fructification of capital is one of the obligations in Islam and is a part of man's mission on earth. It is, for example, one of the objectives of the obligation of *zakat*, which is one of the pillars of Islam. With charity, the prohibition of *riba* attempts ultimately to stimulate positive and participative behaviours of individuals.

The second mechanism relates to individuals' behaviour and oversees their desire and temptation to prefer the present to the future and to live beyond their capacities. Referring to the *Sunnah* of the Prophet (PBUH), we note that a large number of *hadiths* and narrated events show the seriousness that Islam gives to debt. It considers debt as a burden that overwhelms the borrower and limits his freedom. In fact, it is narrated that the Prophet (PBUH) took refuge to Allah for protecting Him from that burden of debt and its consequences in the form of submission and dependence on others.

The permissibility of credit in Islam proves that the *Shari'ah* recognizes the need for recourse to debt in certain circumstances and encourages wealthy people to put their financial surplus at the service of others. At the same time, the *Shari'ah* requires the good faith of the borrower and his intention to repay his debts. In the case of necessity and good faith, Allah will come to help borrowers. In this context, the debt repayment is an extra motivation to be more productive and independent.

Within this motivational context, Islamic finance offers a wide range of mechanisms that can enhance the entrepreneurial behaviour. In the following sections, we present some of these mechanisms after discussing the entrepreneurship financing cycle.

3. Entrepreneurship and the fundraising cycle

In general, an entrepreneur goes through different phases to establish his successful start-up. The idea and the entrepreneurial motivation for a would-be scalable product/service for a potential and sufficiently big target market are the engine of the start-up. Hence, the inception and idea phase constitutes the initial step in the entrepreneurship fundraising cycle. This phase consists in judging the different facets of the value creation of the idea. Subsequently, this idea needs to be tested and verified to prove its viability and product/market fit. This step constitutes the second phase and it is called the Prototype and Proof of Concept (PoC) phase. These two phases can be identified as the early stage financing (Dollinger, 2008). The following phase is the start-up and the launching. This is followed by the early growth stage until the business is extended (the expansion and consolidation stage).

3.1. The challenge of financing

Access to capital constitutes the most important concern for entrepreneurs. In general, debt and equity financing are the main sources of funding for new entrepreneurs. According to the Kauffman foundation (Wiens and Bell-Masterson, 2015), 40 per cent of initial start-up capital is debt originating from banks. The role of equity financing encompasses the participation in capital to include other aspects like expertise, networks and guidance (Wiens and Bell-Masterson, 2015).

For the early stage financing (Dollinger, 2008), the business idea cannot be realized without the financial support of friends and family and obviously the founder's savings. The existence of start-ups is particularly contingent upon the initial amount of cash an entrepreneur holds. At this stage, the required financial capital for new ventures is less than USD 50,000 (World Bank, 2013).

For the start-up phase, two main types of high start-up backers can empower the enterprise through their investment in equity: angel investors[2] and venture capitalists[3] (Cable, 2010). Start-ups raise money from these two types of investors mainly by selling preferred stock. Angels and venture capitalists (VCs) compete for start-ups by offering not only finance and guidance but also services.

However, the World Bank (2013) reveals a challenge of getting financed which is called the 'funding gap'. This gap occurs preceding the start-up phase where the required funding is highly superior to the one needed during the previous phase (the prototype one). This funding gap is occasionally described as the 'valley of death', a situation where numerous start-ups can experience the difficulty of raising the needed capital (Miller, 2009). According to the World Bank report, the start-up stage is closely linked to the funding gap. The financial needs for a new venture at this point might be up to USD 1 million (World Bank, 2013).

Furthermore, a bunch of challenges are faced by the entrepreneur in receiving external funding, including the entrepreneur's aptitude to plan a reliable financing proposal and the uncertainties and risks involved. These factors persist during the whole funding lifecycle. Consequently, during the early growth phase, ideas are verified, prototypes are confirmed and the client curiosity is engaged, henceforth start-ups are funded by the mainstream financing.

According to a Joint WB-IDB policy report (World Bank and Islamic Development Bank, 2015), the total funding gap for micro, small and medium-sized enterprises (MSMEs) in developing countries is estimated at USD 2.4 trillion. The IFC Financing Gap database[4] estimates a gap of about USD 1.3 trillion in the G20 countries. The value gap is even more pronounced in medium-sized enterprises in Latin America and the MENA region (IFC, 2011). Even in more developed countries, financial institutions consider SMEs as too risky due to several factors including the lack of collaterals and their insufficient credit history.

Overall, access to finance remains the main challenge that small and medium-sized enterprises are facing (World Bank and Islamic Development Bank, 2015, p. 2); according to the World Bank (2013), access to finance is among the most important hurdles to developing world enterprises growth.

4. Islamic finance and the entrepreneurial funding challenge

Within the increasing interest in Islamic finance that followed the recent financial crisis, an important share of SMEs have targeted Islamic financial sources to meet their financing needs (Makhlouf, 2017, p. 49). The demand for Islamic financial sources of funding by SMEs is particularly important in the MENA region. Some estimates show that around 32 per cent of this type of businesses remain excluded from the formal banking sector due to the lack of *Shariʿah*-compliant products. According to Makhlouf (2017), the average share of SMEs lending in the MENA banks portfolios is 8.75 per cent. In Saudi Arabia, for example, the banks' share of SMEs in total lending does not exceed 2 per cent. The increase in the demand for funding is also affected by other factors, including:

- high interest rates;
- high collateral requirements;
- cumbersome processes;
- lack of customized processes;
- financial illiteracy;
- religious beliefs.

The existing evidence shows that banks prefer lending to large firms or buying government bonds and treasury bills to financing the SMEs (Nasr and Rostom, 2013). Therefore, compared to the available supply of funding, the demand is very high (World Bank and Islamic Development Bank, 2015).

In the context of high unemployment rates affecting the MENA region, Islamic modes of financing have gained an increasing interest as instruments that can provide financial resources to new entrepreneurs. In the coming sections, we present two case studies based on Islamic finance to develop entrepreneurship initiatives.

5. Case studies of entrepreneurial funding based on Islamic finance

5.1. *Case study 1: Zitouna Tamkeen*

Unlike debt-based financing mechanisms, Zitouna Tamkeen uses an innovative approach to promote entrepreneurship among the poor and those who are in need.

Zitouna Tamkeen is the first institution in Tunisia with a genuine approach of economic empowerment through Islamic microfinance. This approach combines innovation, resourcefulness and opportunity to address critical social challenges. In its financing perception, Zitouna Tamkeen considers the poor as strategic partners to achieve equal and wide profitability and not as a burden to economic growth. To achieve this goal, it puts the poor at the heart of its approach and acts on behalf of the concerned social groups to empower them individually and collectively. The performance indicators used by Zitouna Tamkeen go beyond the financial dimension and include economic and social impacts, that are monitored via several features of the lives of the poor, and namely:

- developing economic abilities so that they can manage their daily lives;
- enabling them to participate effectively in economic projects;
- enabling them to obtain the necessary financial resources and infrastructures to operate in the market, as well as to multiply these resources so to reach an adequate income;
- support and accompaniment until the ability to independently manage administration and make appropriate economic decisions is achieved;
- obtain the minimum necessary social services.

By this approach, Zitouna Tamkeen believes that advocating a sharing economy and promoting redistribution can play a significant role in achieving a double-dividend objective consisting of ending extreme poverty and promoting prosperity (for further information, see the webpage Zitouna Tamkeen, 2017).

5.2. Case study 2: The Investment Account Platform

The Investment Account Platform (see the website IAP, 2017) is a bank-intermediated financial technology platform. It was launched by six Islamic Malaysian banking institutions.[5] On one hand, the purpose of the platform is to solve the issue of the access to finance faced by entrepreneurs and SMEs. On the other hand, it intends to reduce the initial investment costs for Islamic banking institutions embarking on a new business line. The objective is to offer access to broader *Shari'ah*-compliant investment opportunities to investors and a better funding access to ventures. The IAP provides an independent rating by a Malaysian rating agency; credit assessment and screening is completed by the banks sponsoring the platform, so to offer better and more transparent information that facilitates investors' decision-making.

6. Non- banking solutions to the entrepreneurial funding challenge: the potential of crowdfunding in the sharing economy

The difficulties faced by SMEs in accessing finance have created a non-democratized financial market at a global level. One of the solutions to this situation, through the growth of the sharing economy and the impact of new technologies, is the tool of crowdfunding.

According to the Massolution Report (2015), the crowdfunding market is estimated at USD 35 billion, while the Global Crowdfunding Market Report 2016–2020 (TechNavio, 2016) estimates a compound annual growth rate (CAGR) of 26.87 per cent during the period 2016–2020.

The concept of crowdfunding is not new and its history goes back to the nineteenth century (BBC, 2013; Simons, 2016). However, the modern vision of crowdfunding was primarily a fundraising tool for musical or arts ventures (Masters, 2013). After that, two ground-breaking platforms (Indiegogo in 2007 and Kickstarter in 2009) went viral and showed the huge opportunities related to this tool.

6.1. What is crowdfunding?

Crowdfunding is the practice of generating capital investments or funds by raising small portions for a campaign or venture from a large group of people online. It is used when a venture idea that has the potential to generate revenue requires funding to develop and become a reality.

6.2. When is crowdfunding required?

New ventures experience different endings during the 'funding gap' while collecting the required capital for the idea stage and prototyping the product/ the service.

According to the World Bank (2013, p. 16), crowdfunding can be a significant tool throughout the idea and prototype phases. The required funding during these phases is less than USD 50,000, and the business can have the support of the crowd as well as family and friends.

In general, a funding gap occurs typically following these early-stage phases (idea and prototype phases). Hence, a shortage in capital ensues while funding the prospected development steps of the venture. This gap can be usually secured through debt or can be covered by equity investment from venture capital or business angels. However, according to the World Bank (2013) the required capital varies from USD 50 thousand to 1 million and the crowdfunding could be a vital solution when the 'love money' of family and friends is no longer sufficient to go further with the venture.

Thenceforward, once this issue is bested, the start-up can be launched. However, it does have distinctive challenges when the appetite is higher in start-up investing and the funding is more than USD 1 million (World Bank, 2013, p. 16). To cover this need, the angels can play a significant role as well. According to the World Bank (*ibidem*), the help of crowdfunding ends at this stage, since mainstream financing would then play a major role, with the colossal involvement of business angels, venture capital and private equity. Lastly, through the company expansion, the capital funding would be pursued from investment banks.

To sum up, the crowdfunding would play a major role in the first stages of the ventures from inception until thrusting the idea to the market to surpass the funding gap to the launching phase. The funding spectrum varies, as said, from a small amount to USD 1 million.

6.3. Islamic crowdfunding platforms

Classifying crowdfunding business models is contingent on the funding needs of the targeted start-ups. The business model or the type of the crowdfunding platform depends on the amount needed and the fundraising life-cycle of the start-up.

First, in the early stages (i.e. idea, inception and proof of concept, prototyping) where the amount is less than USD 50,000, two types fit the need: donation-based and reward (perks)-based crowdfunding models. Both models are primarily used to fund social, charity or innovative ventures (De Buysere *et al.*, 2012). Financial returns are not envisioned for investors (backers of the project): they either obtain zero financial return (for the donation model) or a non-monetary reward of 'symbolic' value (for reward-based crowdfunding).

Second, once business ideas have evolved and have met minimum viable checks, and other crowd segments express their interest in these projects, the typical need of this crowd is clearly financial investment. Hence, debt-based and equity-based crowdfunding platforms would be more suitable for entrepreneurs' needs where the increase of capital may reach USD 1 million (World Bank, 2013).

Crowdfunding platforms can be of four types (donation-, reward-, debt-, equity-based) depending on the conditions described above.

6.3.1. Donation-based crowdfunding platform (DbCFP)

The project/idea backers' drives and incentives for such type of crowdfunding are essentially social. This inherent stimulus is commonly a suitable fundament to ensure an enduring relationship between the project and the donors, since donations unlike traditional fundraising are linked to a certain charitable project. For example, philanthropists are keener to give higher amounts because they would know exactly the project that their donations are supporting. They similarly tend to be more devoted to the project in the long-term given that they will be kept updated about the development, to ensure regular donations (De Buysere *et al.*, 2012). From a *Shari'ah* perspective, Islam recommends believers to support one another as far as the action does not violate *Shari'ah* rulings: 'Help ye one another in righteousness and piety, but help ye not one another in sin and rancour' (Q. 5:2). There are different arrangements of donations in Islam: *waqf* (endowment), *zakat* (obligatory charity), *sadaqah* (voluntary charity), *tabarru'* (voluntary donation) and *hibah* (asset distribution).

The available Islamic donation-based crowdfunding platforms present in the market are the following: 1) *tabarru'*-based crowdfunding and 2) *waqf*-based crowdfunding.

Tabarru' is a one-way transaction whereby the contributor has no right to take any benefits out of the contribution he has made.

For instance, Skolafund[6] is a Malaysian donation-based crowdfunding platform created in 2015 and designed to mobilize alternative sources of funding for tertiary education scholarships. It links philanthropists from the crowd with candidates who have been assessed to have a financial education need. Skolafund is a revenue-generating platform, which charges a 5 per cent service fee for every sponsorship, but it is looking for other ways to monetize services.

Another Malaysian platform is *waqf* based, namely WaqfWorld.[7] The idea of this type of crowdfunding was first proposed by the research centre EKONIS of UKM in a roundtable discussion organized by the Islamic Research and Training Institute of the Islamic Development Bank (IRTI-IDB), in January 2016 in Jeddah.

Waqf (pl. *awqaf*) is defined as 'an endowment made by a Muslim for a religious, educational, or other charitable cause' (Ali *et al.*, 2016, p. 209). The *waqf* is a perpetual and institutionalized donation. Once a *waqf* is formed the property may no longer be donated, bequeathed or sold in the future (Rahman and Wan Ahmad, 2011). Traditionally, the *waqf* has helped many purposes including the construction and maintenance of Islamic religious, educational, scientific and social institutions. It is highly valued today as a fundament of sustainable social entrepreneurship (Salarzehi *et al.*, 2010). More recently, the concept of cash *waqf* has emerged through online platforms, where people can establish a *waqf* 'in cash' without having any asset or property. Cash *waqf* can be a funding tool for the development of *waqf* property and for supporting the construction of schools, health centres or orphanage houses (Sadeq, 2002). It can incite individuals from different economic and social levels to donate and participate in this charity action. This contradicts the widespread misunderstanding of *waqf* according to which *waqf* is limited to the contribution of High Net Worth Individuals (HNWI) who can donate lands or properties.

The platform WaqfWorld is the *wakil* (agent) and intermediary between the fundraisers and the donors (the crowd) known as *waqif*. They can donate a minimum of 50 Singaporean Dollars per *waqf* project campaign. Each campaign in the platform is appointed to a *mutawalli* (*waqf* trustee) who is the custodian of the *waqf* property. He is responsible for its administration (preservation of property, and maximization of revenues for beneficiaries).[8] The flow of the raised *waqf* fund from the *mutawallis* to the beneficiaries depends intimately on the model adopted. First, the raised fund can remain in cash, so that the principal returns to the cycle for investment, and the proceeds from investment goes to the beneficiaries. Second, the raised fund can be transformed into a tangible asset that generates an income to buy another asset. Third, this fund may be used to acquire immovable properties (buildings or land). The appointed *mutawallis* are impelled to provide feedbacks on the social impact and the outcomes of fund utilizations.

6.3.2. Reward-based crowdfunding platform (RbCFP)

The financial contribution in such type of crowdfunding model is rather small. In return, it offers the project backers a reward (perk), grounded in a subjective link to the venture.

These perks could be the produced services/products at an earlier date, with better price which makes the participants potentially early customers, and accordingly the reward-based crowdfunding model helps in creating a market for a nascent business. Moreover, the participants to the crowd may offer to the entrepreneurs the opportunity to learn from their wisdom, which may improve and shape the suggested venture ideas (Frydrych *et al.*, 2014). Reward-based crowdfunding platforms that offer the product 'pre-selling' features are those related to novel software, hardware or other consumer products (Mollick, 2014). Although its original application occurred in 2003 (ArtistShare), the expansion of crowdfunding through this model was reached with the development of Indiegogo (2007) and Kickstarter (2009).

From an Islamic standpoint, this type of crowdfunding is compliant with *Shari'ah* values since the money is exchanged for non-financial rewards (Taha and Macias, 2014, p. 117). However, the financed venture should not be in contradiction with the principles of Islamic ethics (weapons, pornography and violent media, tobacco, alcohol, gambling, exploitation of children, environmental damage…). The Islamic reward-based crowdfunding platforms available today in the market do not stipulate that they are *Shari'ah* compliant, but highlight that they do not accept certain projects:

- Yomken[9] (Egypt): 'The products we support must also comply with our policies and terms (e.g. weapons or hazardous products cannot be featured)' (Yomken, 2012);
- Zoomaal[10] (UAE/Lebanon): 'Zoomaal does not accept projects that encourage the use of alcohol or tobacco, political or religious movements, or pornographic content' (Zoomaal, 2013);
- PitchIN[11] (Malaysia): 'There are things that are not allowed here on PitchIN which includes things like alcohol, drugs, pornography, and others. Please see the list of prohibited items/subject matters:
    - Alcohol
    - Contests (entry fees, prize money, within your project to encourage support, etc.)
    - Cosmetics
    - Drugs, drug-like substances, drug paraphernalia, tobacco, etc.
    - Financial incentives (ownership, share of profits, repayment/ loans, etc.)
    - Items not directly produced by the project or its creator (no offering things from the garage, repackaged existing products, holidays, etc.)
    - Multilevel marketing and pyramid programs
    - Offensive material (hate speech, inappropriate content, etc.)
    - Projects endorsing or opposing a political candidate
    - Pornographic material
    - Raffles, lotteries, and sweepstakes
    - Promoting or glorifying acts of violence' (PitchIN, 2012);

- FundingLab[12] (Scotland) is a Scottish Charitable Incorporated Organisation which is operating in Muslim countries. It is a rewards-based platform that launches incubators as well as fosters entrepreneurship culture in emerging markets. It doesn't emphasize that it is an Islamic platform but it mentions similar eligibility requirements: '[FundingLab] … cannot accept projects and rewards that are illegal, require local regulatory clearance (such as financial services, healthcare products etc.) and/or are deemed dangerous for backers' (FundingLab, 2017).

6.3.3. Debt-based crowdfunding platform: peer-to-peer lending (P2P lending)

Debt-based crowdfunding is also called 'peer-to-peer lending' (P2P). It occurs when an entrepreneur in need of financing and not having access to the banking system looks for a credit on a suitable platform where the crowd lends small amounts. The debt-based crowdfunding platform would be acting as a middle-man in these transactions by ensuring the repayments to the investors (lenders) (Tordera, 2012). However, some other platforms would be a match-maker of the deal and the entrepreneur and the investors will be connected when the deal is closed (De Buysere *et al.*, 2012).

The operation is basically a loan which means that the funds raised are reimbursed with an interest payment contractually agreed. This interest amount and the reimbursement period will be determined by the credit score of the debtor (entrepreneur). This score is assessed by the platform based on the due diligence on the borrower and the venture. Hence, investors will have an opportunity to diversify their risks and to create a loan portfolio to numerous entrepreneurs. The conventional way of raising funds with this model of platform is by means of *riba*, which is severely prohibited by Islamic principles. In fact, Islam allows only gratuitous loan, which is interest-free (*qard hasan*).

The conventional P2P lending platform Kiva has offered alternatives to its Muslim customer segment. Some of its field partners that assist these borrowers have designed *Shari'ah*-compliant products that are certified by their *Shari'ah* scholars.

The following debt-like contracts are recognized in Islamic finance.

First, *murabahah* is a sale contract whereby the buyer sells goods from the seller knowing the mark-up (profit margin) made. This contract is utilized now in a manner that the financier purchases goods required by the borrower and then sells them to him at a price that comprises a disclosed mark-up to be paid back (usually in instalments). There is as well another sale contract that is used as a debt-like instrument, the *musawamah*, which is a contract whereby the seller and the buyer of goods reach an agreed price. The ventures on such crowdfunding platforms can benefit from these contracts as a fixed financing rate during the funding period, which is convenient for short-term financing. In the case of default, such instrument would overcome collateral requirements by imposing the sale of goods.

Second, *salam* contract is an advance purchase of goods (generally farming crops) delivered on a future agreed date. It can be applied to provide working capital to the start-ups, which are indeed suitable for short-term funding and helpful for agricultural import and export.

GandengTangan[13] (Indonesia) is a conventional crowdfunding debt-based platform, which cooperates with an Islamic financial institution to offer some *Shari'ah*-compliant instruments through the model of *baitul maal wa tamwil* (BMT). The purpose of this platform is to help social enterprises financially by giving loans since they are struggling financially especially for the newly operating social enterprises.

The existing fully Islamic debt-based crowdfunding platforms so far are Beehive[14] (UAE), Kapitalboost[15] (Singapore) and Liwwa[16] (Jordan), which give funding to entrepreneurs using a *murabahah* financing described above. For instance, Liwwa provides investors in start-ups with different risk profiles whereby the Internal Rate of Return (IRR) starts from 6 per cent to 11 per cent. The Singaporean Islamic P2P crowdfunding Kapitalboost offers equity financing when ventures are not able to raise financing using a *murabahah* structure (see next section).

6.3.4. Equity-based crowdfunding platform (EbCFP)

Companies can have access to business angels or other private investors, however as explained above the funding gap cannot be filled only by this kind of financing. To this aim, a firm can look for other investors from the public through equity crowdfunding platforms (or 'crowdinvesting' or 'peer-to-peer (P2P) investing').

The entrepreneurs here give the investors an equity share in their business in exchange for the invested funds. On the other hand, investors have the right to share the residual income generated by the business (Fatoki, 2014). Some of these shareholders are attracted by extra financial factors: for instance, they invest in businesses that share their own values, in social engagement or in creating jobs within the investor's own community (which confirms that these equity crowdfunders are comparable to business angels).

The contracts used in this type of platforms could be *musharakah* or *mudarabah*, which are both suitable for long-term financing. *Musharakah* is a partnership agreement between two or more partners to give capital to a joint venture to share the profits and losses; hence, it is classified as a PLS (Profit and Loss Sharing) contract. *Mudarabah* is a partnership between an investor (*rabb al-mal*) and an entrepreneur acting as fund manager (*mudarib*). Profits are distributed at a pre-agreed percentage, while losses are borne only by the capital provider if there is no negligence from the *mudarib*.

The existing evidence shows that various crowdfunding platforms already operate.

One example is Shekra[17] (Egypt),which is the first Islamic investing platform. Another example is Blossom Finance[18] (Indonesia): it endorses investing in social micro businesses that engender comfortable returns for families in emerging markets. Easiup[19] operates as a French equity-based crowdfunding *Shari'ah*-compliant platform that helps entrepreneurs to raise funds. Eureeca[20] allows early-stage start-ups and SMEs in UAE raising funds through crowdfunding with equity investing. It has received regulatory approvals from the United Kingdom's Financial Conduct Authority (FCA), the Securities Commission Malaysia, the Netherlands Authority for the Financial Markets and from the Dubai Financial Services Authority. Ata-Plus[21] (Malaysia) is not only an Islamic equity crowdfunding platform but it advises investors to use *bitcoin* as an investment instrument. They accept the risk using this cryptocurrency as a medium of investment, and its fluctuation throughout the six-day cooling-off stage and until the fundraising period ends. This platform also helps the donation-based platform Skolafund (see section 6.3.1) to raise funds.

There are also other equity crowdfunding platforms with a focus on more specific type of ventures (for instance, on real estate and properties financing). Relevant examples are Yielders[22] and The Ethical Crowd[23] in the UK; EthisCrowd[24] in Singapore; and HalalSky[25] in the US.

7. Conclusions

From an Islamic perspective, two dimensions motivate entrepreneurship. The first one relates to the incentives that Islam gives to individuals to accomplish their active role on earth. The second has to do with the role that finance can play in developing social impact in the real economy beyond charity actions (such as *zakat*, *sadaqah* and *awqaf*).

Based on that, this chapter has shown how Islamic finance instruments can constitute potential mechanisms through which capital can be invested in new start-ups, nurturing the fundraising circle. These aspects have been discussed in particular with regard to the four main categories of crowdfunding that are currently evolving in the global market, and namely: (i) donation-, (ii) reward-, (iii) debt- and (iv) equity-based crowdfunding.

The extent to which the Islamic financial market will be able to take advantage of these new fundraising tools will represent one of the most important factors to guarantee the sound and comprehensive growth of the Islamic ecosystem, able to link social entrepreneurship to the new financial technologies (on the rise of FinTech see also the next chapter of this book). In this regard, unlocking capital via crowdfunding in the sharing economy can prove a winning strategy to face the challenge of fundraising by contributing at the same time to the social dimension of Islamic entrepreneurship.

Notes

1 According to the GEM website, their work includes more than 100 countries in 2016, up from 59 countries surveyed in 2010. The GEM started with 10 developed countries in 1999.

2 An angel investor, also known as a business angel (BA) or informal investor, is an individual who provides capital for a start-up, usually in exchange for debt or ownership equity.

3 Venture capital (VC) is a type of private equity, a form of financing that is provided by firms or funds to small, early-stage, emerging firms that are deemed to have high growth potential, or which have demonstrated high growth. VC firms or funds invest in these early-stage companies in exchange for equity, or an ownership stake, in the business they finance.

4 In 2010, IFC conducted a study to evaluate the number of MSMEs in 177 countries, and to assess the access to credit and the use of deposit accounts for formal and informal MSMEs.

5 Affin Islamic, Bank Islam, Bank Muamalat, Maybank Islamic, Bank Rakyat and Bank Simpanan Nasional.

6 www.skolafund.com (Skolafund, 2014).

7 www.waqfworld.org (WaqfCrowd, 2016).

8 For further explanation about the role of the *mutawalli* see The Oxford Dictionary of Islam (www.oxfordislamicstudies.com/article/opr/t125/e1666).

9 www.yomken.com (Yomken, 2012).

10 www.zoomaal.com (Zoomaal, 2013).

11 reward.pitchin.my/learn (PitchIN, 2012).

12 www.fundinglab.net/project/start#sthash.2qzlIrw7.dpuf (FundingLab, 2017).

13 www.gandengtangan.org (GandengTangan, 2017).

14 www.beehive.ae (Beehive, 2014).

15 www.kapitalboost.com (Kapital Boost, 2015).

16 www.liwwa.com (Liwwa, 2013).

17 www.shekra.com (Shekra, 2012).

18 www.blossomfinance.com (Blossom Finance, 2014).

19 www.570easi.com/easiup/ (Easi570, 2014).

20 www.eureeca.com (Eureeca, 2012).

21 www.ata-plus.com (Ata-Plus, 2015).

22 www.yielders.co.uk (Yielders, 2015).

23 www.theethicalcrowd.co.uk (The Ethical Crowd, 2017).

24 www.ethiscrowd.com (EthisCrowd, 2014).

25 www.halalsky.com (HalalSky, 2015).

References

Acs, Z. (2006) How is entrepreneurship good for economic growth? *Innovations: Technology, Governance, Globalization.* **1**(1), pp. 97–107.

Ali, S.N.M., Noor, A.H.M., Chuweni, N.N. bt, Ismail, N.R.P., Dahlan, F.M. and Shari, M.S.A. (2016) Integrating *awqaf* and *zakat*: a case study of land development for the poor in state Islamic religious councils Terengganu, Malaysia. In: Manan, S.K. Ab., Rahman, F.A. and Sahri, M. (eds) *Contemporary Issues and Development in the Global Halal Industry.* Singapore: Springer, pp. 209–217.

Ata-Plus (2015) Home page. *ata-plus.com.* [online]. Available from: http://ata-plus.com/ [Accessed 8 May 2017].

BBC (2013) The Statue of Liberty and America's crowdfunding pioneer. *BBC News.*

Beehive (2014) Faqs – peer to peer lending. [online]. Available from: www.beehive.ae/faqs/ [Accessed 8 May 2017].

Blossom Finance (2014) Crowdfunded microfinance investments. [online]. Available from: https://blossomfinance.com/#/ [Accessed 8 May 2017].

Cable, A.J.B. (2010) Fending for themselves: why securities regulations should encourage angel groups. *University of Pennsylvania Journal of Business Law*. **13**(1), pp. 107–172.

De Buysere, K., Gajda, O., Kleverlaan, R. and Marom, D. (2012) *A Framework for European Crowdfunding*. Impressum.

Dollinger, M.J. (2008) *Entrepreneurship: Strategies and Resources*. 4th edition. Upper Saddle River, NJ: Marsh Publications.

Easi570 (2014) Easi Up. [online]. Available from: https://570easi.com/easiup/ [Accessed 8 May 2017].

EthisCrowd (2014) Islamic crowdfunding. *EthisCrowd*. [online]. Available from: www.ethiscrowd.com/ [Accessed 8 May 2017].

Eureeca (2012) Welcome to Eureeca! [online]. Available from: http://eureeca.com/Crowd-funding-pages/FrontEnd/home/FAQ [Accessed 8 May 2017].

Fatoki, O. (2014) The financing options for new small and medium enterprises in South Africa. *Mediterranean Journal of Social Sciences*. **5**(20), pp. 748–755.

Frydrych, D., Bock, A.J., Kinder, T. and Koeck, B. (2014) Exploring entrepreneurial legitimacy in reward-based crowdfunding. *Venture Capital*. **16**(3), 247–269.

FundingLab (2017) FundingLab. www.fundinglab.net/. [online]. Available from: www.fundinglab.net/page/aboutus/ [Accessed 7 May 2017].

G20 Umbrella Paper (2013) *Long-Term Investment Financing for Growth and Development*.

GandengTangan (2017) BMT. [online]. Available from: https://gandengtangan.org [Accessed 8 May 2017].

HalalSky (2015) Home page. *HalalSky – Sky is the limit!* [online]. Available from: http://halalsky.com/ [Accessed 8 May 2017].

Hassan, M.K., and Hippler, W. (2014) Entrepreneurship and Islam: an overview. *Econ Journal Watch*. **11**(2), pp. 170–178.

IAP (2017) Investment Account Platform – IAP. [online]. Available from: https://iaplatform.com/ [Accessed 12 September 2017].

IFC (2011) Average value gap per enterprise by region by size | data. *World Bank Group Finances*. [online]. Available from: https://finances.worldbank.org/dataset/Average-Value-gap-per-Enterprise-by-Region-by-Size/eaau-m4v7 [Accessed 27 April 2017].

Kapital Boost (2015) Islamic crowdfunding – business finance. *Kapital Boost Crowdfunding*. [online]. Available from: www.kapitalboost.com [Accessed 7 May 2017].

Liwwa (2013) Jordan Islamic debt based crowdfunding platform. [online]. Available from: www.liwwa.com/ [Accessed 8 May 2017].

Makhlouf, M. (2017) *Islamic Banking Opportunities Across Small and Medium Enterprises in MENA: Executive Summary*. Working Paper. Washington, D.C.: The World Bank.

Massolution (2015) 2015CF. The crowdfunding industry report. [online]. Available from: https://massolutions.com/ [Accessed 23 August 2017].

Masters, T. (2013) Marillion 'understood where the internet was going early on'. *BBC News*.

Miller, B.L.K. (2009) *Financing the 'Valley of Death': An Evaluation of Incentive Schemes for Global Health Businesses*. Master Thesis. Massachusetts Institute of Technology.

Mollick, E. (2014) The dynamics of crowdfunding: an exploratory study. *Journal of Business Venturing.* **29**(1), pp. 1–16.

Nallari, R., Griffith, B., Wang, Y., Andriamananjara, S., Hiat, D.C. and Bhattacharya, R. (2012) *A Primer on Policies for Jobs.* Washington, D.C.: The World Bank.

Nasr, S., and Rostom, A.M. (2013) *SME Contributions to Employment, Job Creation, and Growth in the Arab World.* Policy Research Working Paper no. 6682. Washington, D.C.: The World Bank.

PitchIN (2012) Guidelines page. *pitchIN | Crowd Funding in Malaysia.* [online]. Available from: http://reward.pitchin.my/learn [Accessed 7 May 2017].

Rahman, A.A., and Wan Ahmad, W.M. (2011) The concept of *waqf* and its application in an Islamic insurance product: the Malaysian experience. *Arab Law Quarterly.* **25**(2), pp. 203–219.

Sadeq, A.M. (2002) *Waqf*, perpetual charity and poverty alleviation. *International Journal of Social Economics.* **29**(1/2), pp. 135–151.

Salarzehi, H., Armesh, H. and Nikbin, D. (2010) *Waqf* as a social entrepreneurship model in Islam. *International Journal of Business and Management.* **5**(7), pp. 179–186.

Shekra (2012) Shekra – how it works. [online]. Available from: http://shekra.com/en/howitworks.php#ShekraStartups [Accessed 8 May 2017].

Simons, O. (2016) Crowdfunding Comte – Positivism. [online]. Available from: http://positivists.org/blog/archives/5959 [Accessed 28 April 2017].

Skolafund (2014) Skolafund. *Financing University Education.* [online]. Available from: https://skolafund.com [Accessed 7 May 2017].

Taha, T., and Macias, I. (2014) Crowdfunding and Islamic finance: a good match? In: Atbani, F.M., and Trullols, C. (eds) *Social Impact Finance.* IE Business Publishing Series. Basingstoke, UK: Palgrave Macmillan, pp. 113–125.

TechNavio (2016) *Global Crowdfunding Market 2016–2020 – Research and Markets.* [online]. Available from: www.technavio.com/report/global-media-and-entertainment-services-crowdfunding-market [Accessed 23 August 2017].

The Ethical Crowd (2017) The Ethical Crowd. [online]. Available from: http://theethicalcrowd.co.uk/ [Accessed 8 May 2017].

The Oxford Dictionary of Islam. *Mutawalli* – Oxford Islamic Studies Online. [online]. Available from: www.oxfordislamicstudies.com/article/opr/t125/e1666 [Accessed 6 May 2017].

Tijkani, M.E.H. (2001) Législation des ventes. In: Bendijali, B. (ed.) *Les Sciences de la Chari'a pour les Economistes.* Jeddah: IRTI, Banque Islamique de Developpement, pp. 147–170.

Tordera, I. (2012) Crowdfunding business models. *European Crowdfunding Network.* [online]. Available from: http://eurocrowd.org/2012/10/26/crowdfunding-model/ [Accessed 4 May 2017].

WaqfCrowd (2016) *Waqf* for the World. [online]. Available from: https://waqfworld.org/ [Accessed 7 May 2017].

Wiens, J., and Bell-Masterson, J. (2015) How entrepreneurs access capital and get funded. *Kauffman.org* [online]. Available from: www.kauffman.org/what-we-do/resources/entrepreneurship-policy-digest/how-entrepreneurs-access-capital-and-get-funded [Accessed 23 August 2017].

World Bank (2013) *Crowdfunding's Potential for the Developing World.* Washington, D.C.: The World Bank.

World Bank and Islamic Development Bank (2015) *Leveraging Islamic Finance for Small and Medium Enterprises (SMEs)*. Joint WB-IDB Policy Report. Washington, D.C.: The World Bank.

Yielders (2015) Property crowdfunding, prefunded investments, *halal* investments. [online]. Available from: https://yielders.co.uk/about-us/ethical-sharia [Accessed 8 May 2017].

Yomken (2012) About page. [online]. Available from: www.yomken.com/about#how [Accessed 7 May 2017].

Zitouna Tamkeen (2017) Zitouna Tamkeen webpage. [online]. Available from: www.zitounatamkeen.com/ [Accessed 3 September 2017].

Zoomaal (2013) Help Center-Zoomaal: crowdfunding platform of the Arab world | support Arab creativity. [online]. Available from: www.zoomaal.com/ [Accessed 7 May 2017].

8 Islamic FinTech and the paradigm shift in the financial landscape

Fatima Z. Bensar and Gonzalo Rodríguez

1. FinTech as paradigm shift

There is nothing new about arguing that we are undergoing a change of cycle.

In fact, there seems to be a general consensus that the world is undergoing a process of transformation in many different spheres as a result of several factors. Some of these are more difficult to analyse, such as the change in the shape of the current capitalist system or the change of geopolitical influence from the West to the East, arising among other things, from the ageing of the Western population and an increasing young Asian and African population. Other factors are more evident and commonly accepted, such as the enormous impact that technological advances are having on our everyday life. These changes are significantly affecting major areas of the daily life of the majority of people living in developed or developing societies, from their way of interacting, job seeking, exercising the right to protest, seeing the doctor, travelling or looking for a partner. These technological changes are having a major impact on the entire productive model of our societies as well, with different degrees of success in their adaptation and use. The cases of South Korea and Singapore are noteworthy, as countries that have managed to anticipate these changes well in advance and to adapt their societies and productive model to this new paradigm.

A 'paradigm' can be defined as the perspective under which we perceive a reality. Accordingly, a 'paradigm shift' implies a new way of perceiving this reality, a radical innovation in the way it is understood (the concept, with regard to a fundamental change in the concepts and practices of a certain discipline, was originally coined by philosopher Thomas Kuhn in 1962). In recent years, there has been a widely held opinion that we are undergoing a paradigm shift in the reality of the financial ecosystem as a consequence of the digital revolution or the so-called fourth industrial revolution (Schwab, 2016). This revolution is characterized by bringing about radical changes at an unprecedented speed due to the convergence of technological advances in the area of artificial intelligence, big data, cloud computing and the Internet of Things (IoT).

But what key changes arising from this paradigm shift are most imminent?

Undoubtedly, one of the most interesting facts is the emergence of new players or, rather, new participants who, through innovative, technology-based business models, usually within the so-called 'sharing economy', can provide financial products and services that are traditionally offered by banks. The term normally used to identify these new players is 'FinTech', which is commonly used as an abbreviation for 'Financial Technology'.[1]

FinTech companies challenge the brokering role that banks have traditionally played among savers and investors, to offer clients financial products and services more conveniently, efficiently and cost-effectively. New start-ups and technology giants like Google, Apple, Facebook and Amazon (from which comes the acronym GAFA) have begun to participate and to some extent to take control of certain points in the value chain of traditional banking processes. New technologies have suddenly burst into the daily lives of the majority of the population and especially young people, who can be said to be digital natives in modern societies.

Telecommunication companies and social networks are of particular importance as they both have sufficient information on and direct access to a vast majority of the population. This fact, added to the potential for implementing banking services efficiently through technological media, means that these types of companies will be future players of enormous importance in the banking sector; a sector that until very recently was reserved for very specific entities, traditional banks with structures, visions and developments that had not undergone major transformations for decades, ever since the emergence of modern banking.

This situation is the proof of the paradigm shift that we have mentioned above.

Innovation in the financial system is no longer just a recommendation or a good strategy for the future, it is a necessity for survival in a hypercompetitive environment. In 10 or 15 years' time, the future clients will begin to demand more sophisticated banking products to meet their needs, i.e. mortgages, insurance, investment funds, etc. and they will simply not understand or empathize with structures that are totally foreign to the way in which they have to communicate with and understand life.

Although it is difficult to identify how and when this trend began, it is possible to say that the global financial crisis beginning in 2008 marks a turning point that has been the catalyst for the growth of the so-called FinTech 3.0 age (Arner *et al.*, 2015). Figure 8.1 shows the speed at which investments in the field of FinTech have grown in recent years.

Several factors explain the growth experienced by FinTech companies since the outbreak of the global financial crisis.

From the supply side, the reputation of some traditional financial institutions has been damaged due to their share of responsibility in the origins

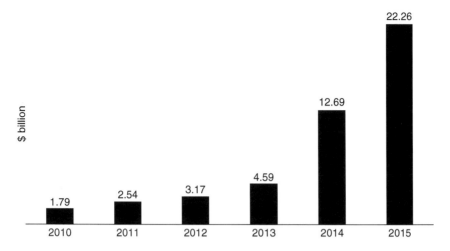

Figure 8.1. Global FinTech financing activity (2010–2015)
(Authors' graphical re-elaboration of the data presented in the report by Accenture, 2016, p. 3)

of the crisis that has reduced society's trust in them. This situation has led to consumers giving an opportunity to FinTech companies, which also usually provide a far superior user experience. In addition, the pressures stemming from low interest rates and increasing regulatory burdens have decreased the financial margins of traditional banks, implying a more cautious and stricter lending policy. As a result, those who were unable to have their financial needs covered by their usual bank were forced to resort to alternative financing options such as those offered by FinTech.

From the demand side, we are witnessing a change in the consumption patterns of a whole generation of consumers, driven mainly by the mass adoption of smartphones. The central role played by smartphones in the life of the 'millennials' (i.e. those born after 1980 and the first generation to come of age in the new millennium) is particularly significant. The habits of this generation promote the use of the mobile channel to interact with their bank, forcing all financial institutions to change in order to adapt their range of services to the demands of the new digital era.

In short, the digital revolution as a disruptive force in the financial industry has meant the beginning of a process of banking disintermediation that has led to the establishment of a new paradigm by FinTech companies. Significantly, not only has this new FinTech paradigm started to emerge in the Islamic finance industry too, but a foreseeable impact can be also evaluated in term of the promotion of a social-oriented model of financing able to address the use of new technologies towards community development.

2. Islamic FinTech experiences and their social impact

> When the crowd connects, magic happens. Ideas become real, the needy get
> helped by the rest, people are empowered.
>
> (from Umar Munshi's LinkedIn profile)[2]

The paradigm shift experienced in the conventional financial ecosystem is
beginning to become observable in the Islamic finance industry too. Islamic
banks and financial institutions must adapt to a new reality in which they
are no longer solely responsible for providing financial services in compliance with the *Shariʿah*. The digital revolution has enabled the launching of a
great number and variety of FinTech initiatives based on Islamic principles
that have recently emerged in the market with the aim to have a major social
impact in local communities, as well as at a global stage.

In particular, relevant Islamic FinTech experiences can be already found
in the fields of (section 2.1) crowdfunding platforms; (section 2.2) charitable
initiatives (*zakat* and *waqf*); (section 2.3) Islamic wealth management; (section
2.4) and blockchain technology applications (namely: smart contracts, identity authentication and cryptocurrencies). At the same time, both private and
public market actors are currently investing in Islamic FinTech to reinforce
the Islamic finance ecosystem (section 2.5).

2.1. Islamic crowdfunding and the sharing economy

The connectivity that the Internet allows today has given rise to the explosion
of new business models, commonly described under the label of the 'sharing
economy', including crowdfunding platforms,[3] which through the virtual
world are emerging with force to unite the power of the people so that it is at
the service of the community. These platforms make an efficient use of technology to give everyone the opportunity to access capital or obtain a return
from savings in an ethical, socially responsible or *Shariʿah*-compliant way.
Crowdfunding has emerged as a huge opportunity to promote Islamic finance,
especially in its equity-crowdfunding form since it involves the financiers' participation in the projects they finance, with their consequent responsibility
in the risk of both profits and losses. This opens the door to the use of the
Islamic risk-sharing contracts of *musharakah* and *mudarabah* that have been
employed very little till now by Islamic banks given their high risk. In addition, crowdfunding platforms make it possible to channel investments very
directly towards the real economy, an indispensable requirement in any investment compatible with Islamic principles. Today, there are numerous Islamic
crowdfunding platforms to meet the needs of different market segments.

The EthisVentures Islamic crowdfunding platform cluster is particularly
worthy of mention. Recently founded in 2017 and based in Singapore, it has
become the first Islamic crowdfunder signatory to the UN Global Compact

for its commitment to support its universal principles and to catalyse action to reach the broader United Nations Sustainable Development Goals (SDGs). EthisVentures consists of a set of Islamic crowdfunding platforms focused on specific niches for investments or donations with the aim of creating good through collaboration among the participants. One of its major platforms is EthisCrowd, the world's first real estate Islamic crowdfunding platform. Today, according to its website, '20,000 EthisCrowd members have supported and invested in projects to build 5,000 homes for the needy in Indonesia since 2015' with realized returns from 10 to 16 per cent. As part of EthisVentures, Kapital Boost also stands out as an Islamic P2P crowdfunding for SMEs, which raises financing for working capital needs and projects via *murabahah* (mark-up sale) and *mudarabah* (profit-sharing) structures.

Another initiative that stands out in the Islamic real estate crowdfunding area is the London-based Yielders, which in April 2017 became the UK's first *Shari'ah* FinTech company to be certified by Britain's Financial Conduct Authority. Yielders allows investments in real estate assets based in London and across the South East UK region from £100 and investors 'receive a share of the monthly rental income and benefit from capital appreciation' during the term of their investment. In addition, in the field of business project financing, Blossom Finance, with its headquarters in Indonesia, is a platform that acts as an intermediary between investors and microfinance institutions that 'invest in micro-businesses that generate liveable incomes for families in emerging markets'. In the MENA region, another example is the Egypt-based Shekra which invests through its private investor network by taking an equity stake in the projects. Outside the Muslim world, LaunchGood went live in October 2013 from the US with the aim of 'supporting Muslims launching good all over the world by helping them raise funds for their campaigns' by pairing them up with a campaign coach.

All these platforms, that are specialized in financing small entrepreneurs and SMEs, have a positive impact on society through the creation of jobs and wealth in a manner that is compatible with *Shari'ah*. In addition, they encourage the financial inclusion of both small entrepreneurs without access to formal financial services and those with savings and an interest in making them profitable according to Islamic precepts. This is important given that the problem of financial exclusion is of particular concern in Muslim-majority countries. According to a World Bank study (Demirguc-Kunt *et al.*, 2013), in fact, Muslims are significantly less likely than non-Muslims to have an account and to save at a formal financial institution. The study also found that Muslims are more likely than non-Muslims to cite religion as a barrier to account ownership, so in this respect Islamic finance would act as a catalyst for the inclusion of such individuals. However, the search by the World Bank also underlines that Muslims are more likely to cite cost, distance and documentation as barriers to account ownership. In this regard, mobile technology makes it possible to offer digital financial services in areas where bank branches are not present and the cost of offering clients digital accounts is

80–90 per cent lower than using physical branches (McKinsey & Company, 2016). In addition, this cost saving makes it possible to reach segments of the population traditionally neglected by the low or zero yield they offer.

Given the emergence of these new business models, Islamic banks have also mobilized themselves to take advantage of the efficiency and opportunities offered by technology. One of the most noteworthy achievements is the creation in 2015 of the Investment Account Platform (IAP)[4] by six Malaysian Islamic banks with the aim of 'facilitating the channelling of funds from investors to finance viable ventures and projects'.

Special mention should be also made of the platforms Muslim Women Tech and YemenAid, both belonging to EthisVentures. Founded in Malaysia in 2016, Muslim Women Tech 'is a coming together of influential or passionate Muslim Women in Tech to strategically leverage resources to promote the utilization and implementation of technology to empower Muslim Women to achieve unimagined possibilities and drive transformation'. This is a relevant step to encourage women empowerment in general, and the participation of women in the technology space in particular. YemenAid, pioneered by The Arabs' Association Singapore, is 'aimed at alleviating the difficulties faced by Yemenis in the light of recent events that have led to the deterioration of public services, crippled food security, and committed education standards'.

Another relevant area of Islamic FinTech with an inherent social impact relates to platforms that promote awareness of the importance of education. In this regard, SkolaFund, for instance, specializes in raising capital to finance university for students with financial difficulties.

2.2. *FinTech* zakat *and* waqf

FinTech initiatives that have revolutionized the way to donate *zakat*[5] and to establish a *waqf*[6] have recently emerged too.

Around May 2017, Finocracy[7] launched Human Crescent,[8] 'the world's first *zakat*-driven, humanitarian crowdfunding platform'. As they post on their website, every year Muslims give around $500 billion *zakat* but still millions of people around the world are struggling to secure their basic needs. In order to help fill this gap, Human Crescent aims to channel *zakat* donations to impactful projects that are divided into the following categories: trafficking victims; refugees/internally displaced persons; microfinance clients; education; disaster victims; poverty alleviation. As its mission states, 'Human Crescent aims to alleviate crises around the world through real-time, transparent, and impactful *zakat* donations; and create a world that is free of any humanitarian-funding deficit.'

As far as the field of *waqf* is concerned, WaqfWorld[9] is the world's first *waqf* crowdfunding platform and has emerged as a new approach to *waqf* cash fundraising with the aim of 'adding value to the Islamic economy through implementing crowdfunding technology and becoming the viable platform for *waqf* funding globally'. More specifically, WaqfWorld uses technology to make the experience of giving *waqf* cash easy, transparent and fully online and channels it to its *mutawallis* partners and charities for their campaigns, 'including Islamic microfinance, education or human capital development, humanitarian relief, social enterprise and religious activities/assets'. Other FinTech solutions for *zakat* and *waqf* management are provided by Narwi, which 'allows donors to support micro-entrepreneurs of their choice by establishing an endowment or "Narwi-*waqf*" with as little as $25'.

These examples show the tremendous effect that technology can have in enhancing the social impact of Islamic mechanisms for the redistribution of wealth through *zakat* and *waqf*. If these platforms grow and are managed properly, it will be possible to use *zakat* and *waqf* donations to finance economic or social activities for the benefit of the community that help alleviate poverty and thus contribute to a more equitable and sustainable economic development. In summary, altogether Islamic crowdfunding platforms and online *zakat* and *waqf* projects illustrate the power of technology to promote financial inclusion, entrepreneurship, the growth of SMEs, access to education and housing and, ultimately, the social progress of the communities in which they operate.

2.3. Islamic wealth management

The impact of the rise of FinTech in Islamic finance is also appearing in the field of Islamic wealth management, to support a comprehensive development of the Islamic ecosystem.

For instance, in the field of financial advice and portfolio management, Wahed Invest, the first Islamic robo-advisor, was created in New York in September 2016, with the aim of providing an efficient *Shariʿah*-compliant automated wealth advisory platform to investors across the world.[10] Wahed is configured as a platform accessible to all types of investor as it reduces the minimum investment barriers. According to its CEO, Mr Junaid Wahedna,

> sophisticated investment management services were previously only available to wealthy investors through financial advisors. We believe that the first step towards ethical investing begins with access to anyone that wants to invest ethically. By implementing a completely digital-based solution, which is informed and supervised by world-class financial expertise, Wahed democratizes access to the best financial advice for investors the world over. We are able to offer the most advanced portfolio management for investments as little as $7,500, as opposed to the usual $500,000 minimum required by most wealth management firms.
>
> (Private Banker International, 2016)

Two months after the opening of Wahed, the launch in Malaysia of Algebra, the first *Shariʿah*-compliant robo-advisor in Asia, was announced. 'Algebra brings together the sound investment principles of *Shariʿah*-compliant funds with cutting-edge investment tools', said its CEO Stuart Yeomans (Fintech Finance, 2016). It will be accessible to investors around the world from a minimum investment of $200 a month. In the asset management area another platform, Arabesque, is making use of machine learning and big data to screen companies in compliance with environmental, social and governance (ESG) parameters.

2.4. Blockchain technology applications: smart contracts, identity authentication and cryptocurrencies

Blockchain technology[11] is another great opportunity to generate new Islamic financial services or to improve the existing ones. The most immediate impact of applying this technology is cost saving, which is mainly achieved by the automation of processes, especially those that require validation, such as contracts.

In this regard, smart contracts could help simplify the complex structure of Islamic financial contracts and make it possible to execute them in a faster and more efficient manner. As an additional advantage, the possibility of committing *gharar* (by stipulating a contract affected by uncertainty in its object or consequences) would be greatly reduced, since the execution of the contract obeys clearly defined and pre-programmed requirements.

Another possibility offered by blockchain technology is the real-time monitoring of donations such as *zakat*. Since transactions are recorded publicly, it is easier to trace the source and destination of the donated funds. To this end, a platform is being developed as the result of an agreement between the University of Luxembourg, Eethiq Advisors and 570 Asset Management. This platform aims to become an open marketplace built on the blockchain protocol that enables investments through Islamic institutions' profit-sharing investment accounts.

Another potential application of blockchain technology in Islamic finance relates to identity authentication. According to the World Bank (Desai *et al.*, 2017) there are an estimated 1.1 billion people around the world, largely in Asia and Africa, who do not have an officially recognized document to prove their identity. This greatly limits their financial inclusion since the validation of identity is one of the first steps in the process of access to banking or formal financial services. Blockchain solutions can decentralize identity storage credentials on a globally distributed database and reduce the risk of identity theft (PwC, 2016). Similarly, the validation of identity through biometrics simplifies the registration process for the user and facilitates banking access to the illiterate population. It is noteworthy that, according to BBVA Research, 52 per cent of banks using biometric methods are in Asia, being particularly popular in countries like India and Indonesia (Karp, 2015).

As for the use of virtual currencies made possible by the blockchain protocol, opinions among experts and *Shari'ah* scholars still diverge. Some of them consider them inadmissible because of their intangibility and high volatility. Others argue that cryptocurrencies are totally compatible with Islamic principles and even preferable to current fiat money. Their advocates include the *Shariʿah* scholar Mufti Abdul Kadir Barkatulla, who maintains that the exchange and transfer of values with justice and through legitimate means is the main concern of *Shariʿah*, not the form or shape of the medium (Barkatulla, 2016). In the same direction, one study concludes that virtual currencies 'conform with the prohibition of *riba* (usury) – as Bitcoin does – and incorporate the principles of *maslahah* (social benefits of positive externalities) and mutual risk-sharing (as opposed to risk-shifting)' (Evans, 2015, p. 8) and that 'Bitcoin or a similar system might be a more appropriate medium of exchange in Islamic Banking and Finance than *riba*-backed, central bank fiat currency, especially among the unbanked and in small-scale, cross-border trade' (*ibidem*, p. 1).

A noteworthy fact is the existence in London of the Islamic Finance & Cryptocurrency Think Tank (IFCC), which in 2016 organized the first ever leadership summit to explore the potential applications of cryptocurrencies in relation to the Islamic banking and finance industry. Furthermore, one of the greatest breakthroughs is the creation of OneGramCoin, a gold backed digital token that has been considered *Shariʿah*-compliant by Al Maali Consulting Group.[12] It has been developed by the Islamic FinTech OneGram together with GoldGuard, a Dubai-based online gold trading platform. Each coin is backed by one gram of gold at launch and is redeemable for gold or equivalent fiat money. This achievement opens the door to cryptocurrency trading in the Islamic financial market.

2.5. *The growing community of Islamic FinTech*

As the previous paragraphs have shown, numerous FinTech initiatives have recently emerged in the Islamic financial world with a relevant impact on the industry and the Muslim community at large. However, given their young age, many of these initiatives still have to demonstrate their viability and their capacity to generate a measurable outcome on a broad scale.

As a positive point, anyway, the main players in the industry are becoming fully aware of the importance of promoting technological innovation to ensure the growth of the Islamic finance ecosystem. Today, there are several achievements that have high hopes of driving FinTech initiatives based on Islamic principles.

For instance, in April 2016 eight Islamic FinTech companies teamed up to create the Islamic FinTech Alliance[13] (IFT Alliance) with the aim of promoting a collaborative economy and FinTech ethical solutions within the framework of the Islamic economy. Also, in September 2016, Finocracy and the start-up accelerator CH9 based in Bahrain announced the creation of the first Islamic FinTech Hub with the name of Future Finance 2030. Finocracy will also collaborate with The Bahrain Institute of Banking & Finance (BIBF) in the development of training services on FinTech for Islamic finance to provide human capital with the necessary knowledge to drive the growth of industry with the aid of technological innovation. Bahrain Islamic Bank (BisB) has partnered with Flat6Labs Bahrain to introduce FinTech accelerator programmes in the kingdom.

Meanwhile, more and more initiatives are being organized to promote innovation in the Islamic financial industry through technological financial solutions. In 2016 the Ethical Finance Innovation Challenge & Awards (EFICA) was held at the initiative of Abu Dhabi Islamic Bank (ADIB) and Thomson Reuters to promote ethical and Islamic finance. In 2017 the RFI Foundation, in partnership with the Swiss Finance Technology Association, Finocracy and the Responsible Finance & Investment (RFI) Summit partners, launched the Support Disruption for Good (SDG) Challenge to find the most promising ethical, responsible or Islamic FinTech innovation and connect them to the leading institutions in the responsible finance industry. In addition, the Islamic Development Bank (IDB) together with the Saudi Spanish Center for Islamic Economics and Finance (SCIEF) have launched a competition to finance FinTech projects with a social impact. Last but not least, the Islamic Corporation for the Development of the Private Sector (ICD) plans to organize challenges to include the winning ideas in a FinTech incubator.

Within this background, not surprisingly, several countries have started a race to become the Islamic FinTech hub through institutional and governmental support.

In March 2017, the Bahrain Economic Development Board (EDB) teamed up with the Singapore FinTech Consortium to promote the development of the FinTech companies in the kingdom and attract technopreneurs.

Malaysia is the first country in the ASEAN region to regulate robo-advisors and is working on defining a robust infrastructure to accommodate the development of the FinTech ecosystem. Both countries have begun issuing regulations adapted to FinTech companies to boost their development. On another note, Malaysia was the first Muslim-majority country where a regulatory sandbox was launched in October 2016, followed by Abu Dhabi in November and Indonesia in December 2016 (IFSB, 2017).

In the light of all the aforementioned examples, there is no doubt that all the financial solutions resulting from recent technology initiatives have high hopes in contributing to the social agenda of Islamic finance.

Directly or indirectly, in fact, their underlying purpose is to employ new technological tools to facilitate Muslim (and non-Muslim) people to unite and cooperate in order to achieve a change in their local communities, as well as the global society, through projects with tangible and productive results. Although they can only be appreciated on a small scale given their recent creation, each of these small FinTech start-ups is making its contribution to moving towards a more just and equitable society through the democratization of access to finance. In addition, they are all promoting financial innovation through technology, hence placing the Islamic financial industry at the forefront of the FinTech sector.

3. Islamic FinTech: potential, open issues and the future of Islamic banking and finance

The Islamic finance industry is relatively young. Its initial development has been driven mainly by the surpluses generated by the oil boom in the Gulf countries since the 1970s. Islamic banks, which constitute the largest segment in the industry, have developed following a rather traditional pattern of being based on branches offering *Shari'ah*-compliant products very similar to what their clients were familiar with, i.e. current and savings accounts, mortgages or investment funds. However, innovation has been present throughout the developmental process of the industry to respond to the same financial needs through different products and services.

In the era of the digital revolution, technological innovation is a key element for ensuring the ongoing growth experienced so far. As we have seen throughout the chapter, there is already a large number and variety of FinTech start-ups that are based on Islamic principles. Although most of them are of recent creation, an important fact is that there are various public and private initiatives to promote the FinTech ecosystem in the industry and to make technological innovation a driver for its growth.

There are different elements that are relevant to understand the potential of Islamic FinTech.

The first aspect to take into consideration is the efficiency that arises from the implementation of these new innovative technologies. Greater efficiency results in lower costs for both the users and the financial service providers. This can greatly improve the competitiveness of the industry and contribute to its expansion, as it makes it possible to serve large niches of potential clients yet to be discovered. Second, it is essential to mention the enormous possibilities of generating social impact through new technologies applied under the criteria of Islamic finance, as this chapter has highlighted. FinTech companies can have a profound social impact on communities that have not been adequately served until now, that is to say on large sectors of the population with no access to banking or with basic financial needs that are not adequately addressed. The economic opportunities that arise from having access to credit, a home or education through the aforementioned crowdfunding platforms and *zakat* and *waqf* initiatives have enormous potential for social transformation.

In order to foster this potential, it is also essential to consider several existing factors that currently affect the development of Islamic FinTech.

As mentioned, financial exclusion is higher in Muslim-majority countries than in other parts of the world. These same countries, which obviously represent the natural market of the Islamic finance industry, have a very young and therefore highly technologically savvy population, that is to say, with a great capacity for absorbing changes and new ideas. In addition, the use of mobile phones is high[14] and this is a key factor, as the social impact of FinTech companies is magnified through mobile technology.

All these elements offer a clear opportunity for Islamic finance to find new market niches by applying innovative solutions using technology. For instance, one can think about creating means of payment or sending money through efficient analogue telephones for rural areas with few banking services; as well as Islamic microcredit solutions, crowdfunding platforms for micro-entrepreneurs; or about connecting capital with young people with innovative ideas.

However, all this is far from being straightforward. There are in fact some obvious challenges: those which are typical of Islamic banking, in addition to those arising from FinTech companies themselves.

One of the most notable issues is still the lack of homogenization in the criteria for considering a product or service *Shari'ah*-compliant. This is a constant debate in the industry itself, recurring in all its literature and certainly representing a weakness for its development. Let us consider cryptocurrencies, for example. In this respect, some very interesting and well-formed analyses are already available for or against their possible acceptance as a *Shari'ah*-compliant product, but, to go directly to the point, what may happen if a successful financial product is accepted today by one important scholar but not by another one? Uncertainties about the *Shari'ah* compliance of instruments or techniques that spread rapidly in conventional finance may become effective obstacles for an upgrade of Islamic finance in many areas where FinTech has replaced traditional practices and has driven conventional finance to higher efficiency and consumer satisfaction (IFSB, 2017).

Another relevant point is the possible existence of limitations arising from the labelling of such products as 'Islamic'. Could this fact be a glass ceiling for their development in the West? Is it really important to present them as such? If a successful product were to be released in non-Muslim societies such as in Latin America, would it have to change its 'market name' without using the label 'Islamic'?

There are also other aspects of the technological revolution that present some doubts, such as those related to consumer protection, data protection and intellectual property; aspects which, while not exclusive to the Islamic FinTech companies, also represent a constant concern that can only be resolved over time through adequate regulation at the global level.

Last but not least, it is important to note that according to many reports there is still a clear imbalance in access to technology between men and women in developing countries. This fact should somehow be taken into account when dealing with the development of Islamic finance in these countries. According to GSMA (online source: see list of references), 'a significant gender gap in mobile phone ownership and usage in low- and middle-income countries is hindering growth for the mobile industry and means women are missing out'. In addition, the study adds that 'successfully targeting women not only advances women's digital and financial inclusion but also unlocks significant growth potential for the mobile industry'.

The Islamic financial segment, given its young age, is in an exceptional situation for adapting successfully to the new FinTech paradigm.

In fact, being open to change and innovation from its inception, the Islamic finance industry should have the competitive advantage of knowing how to anticipate, adapt to and even lead this new stage. At the same time, this pioneering sector has high hopes of democratizing the use of technology, facilitating access to the most basic services for those who still suffer today from a situation of financial exclusion and building a fairer world in accordance with the principles of Islam.

Very diverse experiences in different regions, from the success of some ethical banks in Europe to the widespread use of digital payments in Africa, is convincing about the fact that the target market of Islamic banking is fully open to accepting new tools. In fact, these instruments and services are welcome as they offer a more ethical option, in accordance with *Shari'ah* values and principles; but, at the same time, they must be efficient, professional and useful for community development and empowerment. In other terms, it is not sufficient to offer a *Shari'ah*-compliant service if your conventional competitor has a much better solution in technical terms: offering both an ethical and technology-advanced product, on the contrary, can make the outcome unquestionably more appealing for financial consumers. Indeed, one should not forget that before being a good Islamic banker (hence embracing the ethical dimension of *Shari'ah*), one has to be able to manage well the banking business (i.e. being able to recognize the opportunities offered by the new technologies and the digital revolution).

From a complementary perspective, if many communities have still financial needs that have not been covered sufficiently in Muslim majority countries (where Islamic finance has its natural market), these needs may be met in the future through FinTech instruments. Therefore, also in the light of a social impact outcome (in terms of financial access and economic development), Islamic finance should fully embrace the technological paradigm shift, discovering what the main demands of its potential clients are and fostering the Islamic FinTech ecosystem to the benefit of both local communities and the global economy.

Notes

1 It should be noted that the term 'FinTech' refers not only to technology-based start-ups offering financial products and services but also, more generally, to the application of technology in finance, either by financial or non-financial institutions.
2 Umar Munshi is the founder and CEO of EthisCrowd and founder of EthisVentures.
3 In accordance with a recent study carried out by the Islamic Financial Services Board (IFSB, 2017) based on Crowdsurfer database, there are 80 distinct crowdfunding platforms with a primary location in an OIC member state, from which profiles only 4 can be identified as Islamic.
4 According to its website,

   IAP is a wholly-owned subsidiary of Raeed Holdings Sdn Bhd (Raeed), which
   is a consortium of four Islamic Banks in Malaysia; namely Affin Islamic Bank
   Berhad, Bank Islam Malaysia Berhad, Bank Muamalat Malaysia Berhad and
   Maybank Islamic Berhad. The consortium was later joined by Bank Kerjasama
   Rakyat Malaysia Berhad and Bank Simpanan Nasional.

5 As is well known, *zakat* or *zakah* is an annual 2.5 per cent tithe that is mandatory
   on Muslims who have a minimum amount of wealth. There is no definitive stat-
   istic for annual global *zakat* donations and estimates range from $200 billion to
   $500 billion.

6 *Waqf* refers to a religious endowment, i.e. a voluntary and irrevocable dedication of one's wealth or a portion of it – in cash or kind, and its disbursement for
   Shariʿah-compliant projects (MIFC, 2015).

7 Finocracy is a company with a focus on Islamic FinTech development. It offers
   a wide variety of services that range from advisory, executive training, business
   development consultancy to global accelerator programmes.

8 Partners: World Congress of Muslim Philanthropists, Islamic Development Bank,
   United Nations Development Programme, World Humanitarian Summit.

9 According to its website, WaqfWorld (part of EthisVentures) is still a work in progress, and it will continue to build on its initial concept.

10 According to a press release published on the firm's website, Wahed Invest is
   accessible in the United States but it is going to be available in more than 100
   countries by 2017–2018.

11 According to Blockchain Technologies' website (see reference list) a blockchain is
   a type of distributed ledger, comprised of unchangeable, digitally recorded data
   in packages called blocks. These digitally recorded 'blocks' of data are stored in
   a linear chain. Each block in the chain contains data (e.g. bitcoin transaction)
   which is cryptographically hashed. The blocks of hashed data draw upon the previous block (which came before it) in the chain, ensuring all data in the overall
   'blockchain' have not been tampered with and remain unchanged.

12 For further details, please consult the *Sharia Whitepaper* referred to by
   OneGramCoin for permissibility from a *Shariʿah* point of view. Available at the
   OneGramCoin website (OneGram.org).

13 The eight founding members are Blossom Finance (USA/Indonesia), EasiUp
   (France), EthisCrowd (Singapore), Narwi (Qatar), FundingLab (Scotland/Palestine),
   KapitalBoost (Singapore), Launchgood (USA) and SkolaFund (Malaysia).

14 According to McKinsey & Company (2016), nearly 80 per cent of adults in emerging economies have mobile subscriptions.

References

Accenture (2016) *Fintech and the Evolving Landscape: Landing Points for the Industry*.
   [online]. Available from: www.accenture.com/us-en/insight-fintech-evolving-landscape
   [Accessed 27 August 2017].

Arner, D., Barberis, J. and Buckley, R. (2015) *The Evolution of FinTech: A New
   Post-Crisis Paradigm?* University of Hong Kong Faculty of Law Research Paper
   no. 2015/047. [online]. Available from: www.ssrn.com [Accessed 6 August 2017].

Barkatulla, A.K. (2016) *How Does Sharia View Crypto-Currencies and Finance?*.
   [online]. Available from: https://ebrahimcollege.org.uk/how-does-sharia-view-crypto-
   currencies/ [Accessed 13 August 2017].

Blockchain Technologies website. [online]. Available from: www.blockchaintechno logies.com/blockchain-definition [Accessed 29 August 2017].

Demirguc-Kunt, A., Klapper, L. and Randall, D. (2013) *Islamic Finance and Financial Inclusion: Measuring the Use of and Demand for Formal Financial Services among Muslim Adults.* The World Bank Development Research Group, Finance and Private Sector Development Team. Policy Research Working Paper 6642.

Desai, V., Witt, M., Chandra, K. and Marskell, J. (2017) Counting the uncounted: 1.1 billion people without IDs. *The World Bank Group Blog.* [online]. Available from: http://blogs.worldbank.org/ic4d/counting-uncounted-11-billion-people-without-ids [Accessed 27 August 2017].

Evans, C.W. (2015) Bitcoins in Islamic banking and finance. *Journal of Islamic Banking and Finance.* **3**(1), pp. 1–11.

Fintech Finance (2016) Algebra, Asia's first *Shariah*-compliant robo-advisor, set to launch. [online]. Available from www.fintech.finance/01-news/algebra-asias-first-shariah-compliant-robo-advisor-set-to-launch/ [Accessed 27 August 2017].

GSMA (undated) *Connected Women Programme. Accelerating Digital and Financial Inclusion for Women.* [online]. Available from: www.gsma.com/mobilefordevelopment/programmes/connected-women [Accessed 27 August 2017].

IFSB (Islamic Financial Services Board) (2017) *Islamic Financial Services Industry Stability Report 2017.* Kuala Lumpur: Islamic Financial Services Board.

Karp, N. (2015) *Biometrics: the Future of Mobile Payments.* [online]. BBVA Research, U.S. Economic Watch. Available from: www.bbvaresearch.com/wpcontent/uploads/2015/07/150720_US_EW_Biometrics.pdf [Accessed 27 August 2017].

Kuhn, T.S. (1962) *The Structure of Scientific Revolutions.* Chicago: Chicago University Press.

McKinsey & Company (2016) *Digital Finance for All: Powering Inclusive Growth in Emerging Economies.* McKinsey Global Institute.

MIFC (Malaysia International Islamic Financial Centre) (2015) *Waqf: realising the social role of Islamic finance* (10 June 2015).

OneGram.org (undated), *Shariah Whitepaper.* [online]. Available from: https://onegram.org/whitepaper/ [Accessed 11 September 2017].

Private Banker International (2016) Wahed Invest rolls out Islamic robo advisor. [online]. 27 September 2016. Available from: www.privatebankerinternational.com/news/wahed-invest-rolls-out-islamic-robo-advisor-270916-5016932/ [Accessed 27 August 2017].

PwC (2016) *DeNovo Q2 2016 FinTech ReCap and Funding ReView.* [online]. Available online from: www.strategyand.pwc.com/media/file/DeNovo-Quarterly-Q1-2016.pdf [Accessed 8 August 2017].

Schwab, K. (2016) *The Fourth Industrial Revolution: What It Means, How To Respond.* [online]. Available from the World Economic Forum website: www.weforum.org/agenda/2016/01/the-fourth-industrial-revolution-what-it-means-and-how-to-respond [Accessed 4 August 2017].

9 Islamic green finance

A new path to environmental protection and sustainable development

*Marianella Piratti and Valentino Cattelan**

1. Introduction: religion, sustainability and Islamic green finance

Officiating the 'International Conference on Religion and Civilizational Sustainability' held in Kuala Lumpur on 20–21 February 2017,[1] Prime Minister of Malaysia Dato' Sri Najib Tun Razak[2] addressed the topical issue of sustainable development from the distinctive angle of its relevance as a religious obligation. In his view, beyond the persuasive arguments of environmentalists, 'we have even more compelling reasons for making sustainability an integral part of our lives, our Government and our International relations. For religion demands that we do' (Razak, 2017). Although Najib Razak refers in many passages of his discourse to sustainability as a matter of inter-faith dialogue, his attention, in a Muslim majority country like Malaysia, goes mainly to Islamic teachings.

> Let me give you the example of a well known *hadith*, in which the Prophet Muhammad said that even if the Hour of Judgment Day is about to occur, plant a tree. He also prohibited poisoning wells and cutting trees for no reason. What greater evidence can we summon to demonstrate that Islam insists that we humans are responsible for caring for all that sustains earthy life? This *hadith* teaches us that we are to do this not only until the end of our individual lives, but also till the Last Day – the end of our collective existence on earth. ... And just as God and the Prophet teach us that God created and continues to sustain the world, as God's *khalifahs*, we too have to discharge our role in sustaining life on earth.
>
> (Razak, 2017)

Prime Minister Razak also relates the concept of *khalifah* (the human being as God's 'agent on earth', His 'steward', 'representative') to that of *maqasid al-Shari'ah*, the 'objectives of Islamic law', thus referring to rationales of commitment, endeavour and responsibility towards the (local/global) community that belongs to the core of Islam.

---

* Although this chapter is the result of a sharing of thoughts and mutual cooperation, Part One can be attributed to Marianella Piratti and Part Two to Valentino Cattelan.

Taking this link between religion and sustainability in Islam as a starting point of discussion, this chapter aims at investigating one of the most innovative segments in the Islamic financial market, namely that of 'green' investments. In particular, the chapter intends to show how 'Islamic green finance' (as the result of the intersection between Islamic finance and the green economy) successfully realizes social impact objectives by protecting the environment, and has to be subsequently considered as a positive innovation in the market both in the light of *Shariʿah* standards and the widespread concern about environmental sustainability that has been emerging in the global economy.

To this objective, the study is divided into two main parts.

Part One provides an outline of the Islamic doctrine on environment protection, its principles and fundamental precepts. In particular, it contextualizes the rise of Islamic environmentalism from the 1980s onwards within the emerging of a global ecological movement in the second half of the twentieth century. By comparing on a temporal perspective the birth of modern Islamic economics and the revitalization of the Islamic thought on environment protection, Part One highlights the intrinsic ecological dimension of an Islamic model of development, as grounded on the reconciliation between individual and community needs, as well as those of the entire creation (Section 2). This system finds its roots in the religious principles of the Islamic legal tradition, that nurture an ethical balance among the individual, the community and the entire nature as God's creation, through the core concepts of *fitrah*, *tawhid*, *mizan* and *khalifah* (Section 3).

Moving from the Islamic tradition on environment protection to the contemporary realm of Islamic economics and finance, Part Two evaluates the theory and practice of the latter as a distinctive *locus* for the implementation of this *Shariʿah*-based ecological consciousness in the global economy. In particular, Section 4 critically comments on some persistent shortcomings in the Islamic economics literature with regard to issues related to environmental protection and sustainable development. To make up for this weakness, Part Two suggests that the field of 'Islamic environmental/ecological economics' should undertake a dialogical comparison with conventional environmental economics to reinforce its own paradigm. Given this suggestion as a tool to improve the research agenda of Islamic economics, Section 5 provides an overview of 'Islamic green finance' and the most innovative financial tools (such as green *sukuk* and *awqaf*) that are currently fostering a *Shariʿah*-based eco-friendly market. Moreover, it also proposes that specific *Shariʿah*-compliance criteria should be implemented in the light of green economy objectives.

To conclude (Section 6), final considerations will remark the inherent social impact of Islamic green finance investments, both towards local recipient communities and the global society as a whole, hence defining Islamic green finance as a core operative dimension for the social finance sector.

PART ONE – ECOLOGY, DEVELOPMENT AND THE ISLAMIC TRADITION

2. The global environmental concern and the Islamic answer

If the first examples of modern Islamic finance date back to the 1960s–1970s, the revitalization of a specific Islamic thought on environmental protection started basically ten years later, in the 1980s, following the rise of a global environmental concern that took its first steps in the West, together with the demand for a new model of development respectful of nature (Erdur, 1997, pp. 152–154). The increasing awareness of the need to preserve the environment has led since that time to enact rules both at a national and international level aimed to cope with the environmental crises.[3] The Islamic world has been certainly involved in this process as well but, as remarked by Llewellyn,

> virtually all environmental legislation in Muslim countries is borrowed from the industrialized West, in spite of the many principles, policies, and precedents of Islamic law governing the protection and conservation of the environment and the use of natural resources. Much of this legislation remains inadequate and unenforced.
>
> (Llewellyn, 2003, p. 186)

This observation, pointing out the link between the cultural background and the effectiveness of norms, recalls what historian White wrote in 1967 ('What people do about their ecology depends on what they think about themselves in relation to things around them. Human ecology is deeply conditioned by beliefs about our nature and destiny – that is, by religion': White, 1967, p. 1205), as well as what one of the first studies expressly devoted to the Islamic conception of the environment (apart from the pioneering work by Seyyed Hossein Nasr, published in 1964) underlines: '[t]he implementation of environmental management depends on the existence of appropriate legislation, and legislation becomes more effective and useful when it emanates from a nation's creed and when it represents its cultural and intellectual heritage' (Ba Kader *et al.*, 1983, p. 9).

Despite these statements of principle, as remarked by Mekouar in 1983 in an essay about Islam and environment (to be found in a volume by the same author published in 1988), the issue of the Islamic conception of the environment – *mutatis mutandis* the environmental conception emanating from the 'nation's creed' – was at the time not fully addressed by Muslim scholars (p. 33). While since then significant improvements have occurred, as lastly testified by the adoption on 18 August 2015 of *The Islamic Climate Change Declaration*[4] – it is still worth reminding the time delay between the development of Islamic economics (as a discipline) and the re-discovery of Islamic environmental law. In fact,

[m]uch as the discipline of Islamic economics has been formulated and developed in recent decades, that of environmental law can be derived from the objectives, principles, precepts, and instruments of Islamic jurisprudence, as well as the myriad substantive rulings of the *Shariʿah* that pertain to environment.

(Llewellyn, 2003, p. 186)

Beside the time delay that Llewellyn briefly sketches in the previous extract, he nevertheless remarks on a convergence between Islamic economics and environmental law that is significant at least on two levels: a core of common values based on *Shariʿah*, regardless of the secular laws in force in the different states; the economic implications connected with the concept of sustainable development. This last one, formally internationally enshrined in the well-known *Rio Declaration on Environment and Development* of 1992,[5] is indeed a constant in the Islamic discourse on environment, that maintains an inter-generational perspective. For instance, Bagader *et al.* (1994) remark how

[a]ll of the resources upon which life depends have been created by God as a trust in our hands. … Hence, man should take every precaution to ensure the interests and rights of all others since they are equal partners on earth. Similarly, he should not regard such use as restricted to one generation above all other generations. It is rather a joint usufruct in which each generation uses and makes the best use of nature, according to its need, without disrupting or adversely affecting the interests of future generations. Therefore, man should not abuse, misuse, or distort the natural resources as each generation is entitled to benefit from them but is not entitled to 'own' them in an absolute sense.

(pp. 2–3)

Significantly, the same principles were already delineated from an economic perspective by Sid Ahmed in 1982, when the reflection of the Islamic doctrine on environment was still at a very early stage:

[o]n voit donc qu'il n'existe guère de différends entre les principes de l'Islam et les objectifs fondamentaux du capitalisme (profits résultant de l'activité commerciale, rendements financiers d'investissements à risque, propriété privée, etc.). L'Islam cependant n'accepte les pratiques capitalistes que dans la mesure où elles ne nuisent pas au bien-être social. Les préférences de l'Islam vont donc à un capitalisme relativement égalitaire; l'État étant habilité à prendre des mesures en ce sens. Pour l'Islam enfin, il existe des limites à l'appropriation des ressources naturelles par l'homme et à l'exercice au plan général du droit de propriété.

(p. 882)[6]

This reflection, that encloses an embryonic conceptualization of Islamic green finance, witnesses an early development of the Islamic doctrine on environment that would have proceeded in the following decades along two main complementary lines of thought.

The first one is structured in a discourse that, even though maintaining a universal aim, proceeds as a whole within the framework of the Islamic precepts based on the *Qur'an* and the *Sunnah*, that are assumed as the general background to assert the spirit of solidarity that human beings are asked to manifest both among them and towards the whole of the creation. Within this frame, where it is argued that human salvation relates to the respect of the nature and to community solidarity as concurrent religious obligations, 'each individual Muslim as well as the Muslim community must honestly strive toward the welfare of the whole' (Bagader *et al.* 1994, p. 17; see also Bakhashab, 1988, p. 289).[7]

The second approach focuses more on Islamic environmental prescriptions as guidelines for sustainable development. Within this line of argumentation (though maintaining the religious and universally oriented tone of the perspective mentioned above) a stronger attention goes towards aspects of political economy, with an explicit criticism of the Western capitalistic model of growth that, for this point of view, is held the most accountable for the current global environmental crisis. As a clear example of this second tendency in the literature, we can mention Abdul Aziz Said and Nathan C. Funk (2003), according to whom 'Islam prescribes a strong sense of community and solidarity of people; it postulates a collaborative concept of freedom; and it demystifies the Western myth of triumphant material progress' (p. 177). In brief, here the Islamic tradition challenges the Western model of development, while re-affirming the centrality of the principle of sustainability in the Islamic eco-system.[8]

Within this background one of the most authoritative voices of the Islamic doctrine on environment is that of Seyyed Hossein Nasr (1964, 1990) who, starting from an ethical concern and the cosmic dimension of the *Qur'an*, moves towards a critique of the dominant economic system grounded on Western capitalism. Nasr criticizes the West for having placed man at the centre of the world in a secular perspective, thus removing the spiritual foundations of environmental protection. According to him, the gradual de-sacralization of the cosmos that has occurred since the Renaissance and continued with the Enlightenment, with its scientific revolution, has also led the West to a blind faith in technological progress. Hence, the belief that creation is placed at the exclusive service of man, has implied an uncontrolled exploitation of natural resources and a global environmental crisis for which the industrialized world has to be considered responsible. Furthermore, not only was the colonial domination over the Muslim world addressed towards economic exploitation, but it also favoured the introduction of secular laws that have determined the departure of the population from the teachings on the responsibility toward environmental resources emanating from the sacred *Shari'ah*. In front of the global environmental crisis, only the re-discovery of the sacred Law of Islam can offer the opportunity of building a new relationship between the human being and the environment, based on the sustainability of resources. In summary, according to Nasr, only the revival of religion and spiritual values can allow mankind to escape from the environmental catastrophe, an exhortation that he also addresses to Christianity (Nasr, 1990, p. 229).[9]

Following Nasr, some Muslim scholars have criticized the Western economic and financial system as responsible for the global environmental crises. According to these voices, assuming the principles of Islamic economics as the framework for sustainable development represents the alternative to Western capitalism and its dogmas of an infinite growth (in contrast with the finite availability of natural resources) and the creation of money 'out of nothing', made possible by a system based on interest (*riba*). A change of direction may hence arise adopting a financial system based on the principles of the *Shari'ah* that, as well known, permits trade but forbids usury (*riba*) (Q. 2:275), with the consequent promotion of trade in real economy instead of *riba*, the avoidance of excessive risk (*gharar*) and speculation (*maysir*) (on these prohibitions, see Saleh, 1992, and Saeed, 1996). The adoption of such an economic perspective would allow fulfilment of the obligations of Islamic ethics regarding environmental protection (Vadillo and Khalid, 1992, pp. 77–78, 83–85; Khalid, 2002; Dutton, 2003, pp. 331–337; Khalid, 2003, pp. 307–314) operating a welding between green and financial Islamic principles.

Within this frame, it is important to bear in mind that even if the West is considered the most responsible for the environmental crisis, there is a collective obligation to cope with it that affects Muslims as well. The obligation to care about environmental protection affects in fact the promotion of a sound Islamic eco-system in the light of the five essential objectives of the *Shari'ah* (religion, life, intellect, progeny and property: Shah Haneef, 2002, pp. 253–254), as well as of the general duty to do what is right and avoid what is wrong as a constitutive element of the *ummah* (Q. 3:104; 3:110). This duty burdens equally individuals and the whole Muslim community and falls within the socio-economic duty of solidarity, together with the obligation of helping others and supporting certain categories of persons (Izzi Dien, 1992, pp. 30–33; Aldeeb Abu-Sahlieh, 2008, pp. 585–588).

On the matter of environmental protection a cardinal principle enunciated by the Holy Book is that of not bringing corruption on the earth (Q. 2:11–12; 4:119; 7:56; 30:41). From the duty of solidarity as a general duty to do what is right, it is hence possible to derive an obligation not only towards humans, but also towards the natural world – not to cause corruption on the earth. This principle, formulated in negative terms, has indeed an equivalent positive expression, because if human beings are obliged to abstain from taking actions that might harm the environment, it follows that they must also adopt a behaviour aimed at protecting it from any danger that can threaten it. In this sense, the duty to care about environmental protection comprises both the avoidance of any harm to nature, as well as the prevention of its occurrence and the remedy of any consequence derived from this damage: in other terms, not only is it a duty to abstain, but also a duty to act to preserve (Mekouar, 1988, p. 41).

As already mentioned, the concern about the state of the environment affects nowadays both individuals and institutions, that should act in a responsible way for the protection and preservation of the natural world. In this sense a significant role in contrasting the environmental crisis can be played by all the different stakeholders involved in the economic process, given the inherent economic dimension of the concept of sustainable development. The principles of Islamic ethics for environmental protection seen until now constitute a precious guide for an (individual and collective) economic action inspired by a spirit of solidarity, caring for the community and for a balanced and inclusive development that meets the rationales of an ethical market. As we are going to see in the next section, the guiding principle should be the comprehensive responsibility for the creation that the human being holds as God's vice-regent on earth (*khalifah*) and that defines in the Islamic legal tradition the relation that humankind must have with the natural world.

3. The Islamic tradition on environment: principles and institutes

It is often quoted that Abu Bakr, the first of the 'Rightly Guided' Caliphs of Islam, proscribed to his armies the destruction of palms, fruit-bearing trees and the unnecessary killing of animals. Although this view later on was not held by all the Muslim jurists dealing with the rules of the conduct of war, it testifies how the preservation and protection of the natural elements have been a major concern since the very early stage of Islamic history (Mahmassani, 1966, pp. 309–310; Sonbol, 2009, p. 274; Afsaruddin, 2013, p. 51), a time in which the Islamic legal system was not yet finalized. Once the construction of this system was achieved we do not find anyway a *corpus iuris* expressly dedicated to environment but an array of principles, rules and institutions that are meant to preserve the creation in the frame of the objectives of the *Shari'ah* (on the *maqasid al-Shari'ah* see Kamali, 1999). The research by contemporary scholars on the sources of Islamic law is aimed to collect all these teachings in a coherent system that, from the basic principles to the rules related to the different subject areas, can provide a comprehensive environmental ethic to face today's global environmental crises that, as an unprecedented situation, challenges contemporary Islamic legal hermeneutics to develop a new jurisprudence. To this aim, as well-known, if the revealed sources of the *Shari'ah*, namely the Holy *Qur'an* and the *Sunnah*, are the principal sources of the sacred Law of Islam, the *usul al-fiqh*, i.e. the science of methodology, also employs other tools to make up legal shortcomings (Kamali, 1997), such as *qiyas* (analogy), *maslahah* (public good) and *ijtihad* (exercise of personal reason). Furthermore, an increasing attention is given today to *maqasid al-Shari'ah* (Llewellyn, 2003, p. 193) and to the closely related *qawa'id al-fiqhiyah* (general principles of law or legal maxims) (Heinrichs, 2002) in the definition of the principles governing the Islamic ethics of the environment.

Through this hermeneutical endeavour the contemporary doctrine has defined, by drawing from the long-established Islamic legal tradition, a range of general principles and institutes that by adopting a more pragmatic attitude, can be effectively applied to foster sustainable development,[10] as this chapter will show with regard to Islamic finance (see here Part Two, in particular Section 5).

The Islamic reflection on the environment is grounded on the way in which Islam conceives the universe, the natural elements and the relation between humankind and 'nature'. In this context the world 'nature' must be understood according to the concept of *fitrah* as revealed in the *Qur'an*:

> So set your face towards the [true] religion, in pure worship, Allah's *fitrah* with which He has created mankind. There can be no alteration in the Nature made by Allah. This is the right and true faith, but most people do not know.
>
> (Q. 30:30)

Accordingly *fitrah* is to be understood as 'state of nature', primigenial state, primordial nature of creation, original state of man as God's creature, hence defining the identity 'state of nature'–'natural religion'–'Islam' (Mohamed, 1996; Chishti, 2003; Özdemir, 2003, pp. 16–19). As for the meaning of 'nature' in the sense of 'environment', the closest word in Arabic is *bi'a*.[11]

The principle of *fitrah* is essential to the holistic Islamic conception of the universe, where there is no sharp demarcation between the sacred and the secular and between humankind and the natural world. It derives from the *Shari'ah*, the sacred Law embracing the whole reality and whose cardinal principle is the unity and oneness of God (*tawhid*), the foundation of Islamic monotheism. *Tawhid* 'plays a unifying role which binds the community together and constitutes its source of equality, solidarity and freedom' (Kamali, 1989, p. 218).[12] In the contemporary Islamic environmental thought the principle of *tawhid* is extended to the whole creation (Shah Haneef, 2002, p. 245), because as there is a unity in God, there is a unity in His creation: 'And to Allah belongs all that is in the heavens and all that is in the earth. And Allah is Ever Encompassing all things' (Q. 4:126; see also Q. 2:115; 2:255; 2:107; 24:42).

Humankind belongs then to the natural order like the other elements of the creation that all are interconnected. Such an holistic approach poses a sacred nexus between human beings and the natural world, as they participate in the same cosmic order established by God. Human beings are part of the nature and, as natural entities, they are subject to the natural laws like any other entity of the creation: accordingly, they are an integral part of the global ecological balance (*mizan*) that exists in the vastness of the cosmos, a balance that they are asked to maintain (Q. 55: 5–8; Nomanul Haq, 2003, pp. 132 and 136). The balance principle concurs to form the ideological frame-work of the Islamic view on the natural world where every single element of creation is subject to a command (*'amr*), that is 'the specific principle of being of each thing in *relation to that of all other things*, inhering in it according to the command it uniquely receives from God' (Nomanul Haq, 2003, p. 137; Q. 24:43–45).

In this order, however, the human being is 'a distinct part of the universe and has a special position among the other parts of the universe' (Ba Kader *et al.*, 1983, p. 13). God breathed into him His spirit (Q. 32:9; Ben Achour, 2011, pp. 44–45, 75–76) and has invested him with a special responsibility by giving him the role of *khalifah* ('stewardship') (Q. 2:30–31). The relationship between human beings and creation follows nevertheless the relationship that is first established between God and the creation. The human being is not the owner of the natural world and in his role of *khalifah* he is not entitled to exploit it according to his mere will, but he can use the natural resources (see *inter alia* Q. 16:65–69; 36:61–62) according to the purposes set by the Creator. The role of *khalifah* implies therefore that the human being is in charge of caring and guarding the creation that has been entrusted to him and, as the responsibility towards creation is voluntarily accepted (Q. 33:72), the human being will have to account for his behaviour (Q. 99: 4–8) (Shah Haneef, 2002, pp. 243–244; Llewellyn, 2003, pp. 190–191).

From the core principles listed above (namely the concepts of *fitrah; tawhid; mizan; khalifah*) the contemporary Islamic doctrine has then elaborated the norms governing the use of the various natural elements (water, air, land and soil, plants and animals) and has shown how some traditional institutes can be re-discovered and be functional to environmental protection and sustain-able development (Bakhashab, 1988, pp. 291–297; Bagader *et al.*, 1994, pp. 6–12; Llewellyn, 1992, pp. 92–97; and 2003, pp. 207–221). These institutes, in particular, are

- *ihya*: acquisition of un-owned land through reclamation, to make it pro-ductive (hence, bringing life to the land);
- *iqta'*: land granted by the state to farmers;
- *ijarah*: leasing of the land to cultivators;
- *harim*: the institution of protected zones;
- *hima*: the reserve of land established for public purposes and for preser-vation of natural habitat;
- *waqf*: endowment established for charitable purposes;
- *hisbah*: the traditional office of the public inspector to ensure that public and private land, resources and property are used correctly (Llewellyn, 1992, p. 92).

It is not the aim of this study to outline in detail the practical applications that the Islamic environmental principles by subject area and the traditional institutes can have in today's modern economy, in order to promote a more responsible use of natural resources (more in-depth analysis can be found in the references mentioned above). What is important to remark here is that the fundamental principles explained in this section constitute a common conceptual background that is the basis of the contemporary application of Islamic ecological thought in the realm of Islamic economics as well.

Part Two of this chapter is expressly dedicated to highlighting how this connection is fostering today the pioneering segment of 'Islamic green finance'.

PART TWO – ISLAMIC ECONOMICS, GREEN FINANCE AND SUSTAINABLE DEVELOPMENT

As much as Warde describes Islamic finance as 'a young industry rooted in a very old tradition' (2012, p. 2), Islamic ecology can be conceived as a recent movement grounded in the long-lasting principles of Muslim religion and ethics. In this light, Part One has shown how, although a specific Islamic discourse on contemporary environmental issues started only in the 1980s, its arguments derive from the fundamental tenets of Islam on *fitrah* (the natural state of Islamic monotheism), the unity (*tawhid*) and balance (*mizan*) of the creation, and the duty of care of the human being as *khalifah* towards natural resources.

Part Two of this chapter has two major objectives. First, to evaluate from a critical perspective some persistent shortcomings in Islamic economics literature with regard to the topics of environmental protection and sustainable development. Second, to look at the emergent market of 'Islamic green finance' as a tool through which the Islamic financial market can actively contribute to the pursuit of sustainable development policies.

4. Reviewing the research agenda of Islamic economics: environmental protection and sustainable development as neglected subjects, and the way forward

Considering the strong connection between ecology and economy for global sustainability, one may wonder to which extent environmental issues have been taken into consideration by Islamic economics literature from its inception. In this regard, a desolate yet honest reply was already given 20 years ago by Akhtar in recognizing how

> [t]he Muslim economists have so far made relatively insignificant contribution to the subject of environment. Most of them have only discussed the moral aspect of the subject in general terms. In fact, there are very few studies which have approached the problem systematically. Even those few studies have not worked out the practical ways and means for ensuring environmental security.
>
> (Akhtar, 1996, p. 58)

In more detail Akhtar refers to the studies by Husaini (1980), Llewellyn (1984), Nasr (1990), Akbar (1992) and Chapra (1993). But apart from these works, where ecological issues are considered from an axiomatic perspective, it is only from the start of the twenty-first century that environmental protection and sustainable development have become specific subjects of discussion in Islamic economics (IE).

This chronological delay suggests that 'Islamic environmental/ecological economics' (IE/EE) scholarship should be first considered in comparison to the 'older' conventional green economics in the West (see Section 4.1) and later contextualized within the evolution of the paradigm of IE as an autonomous discipline and an alternative to Western capitalism. As we are going to see, in fact, to the extent to which IE/EE scholarship certainly represents a positive step forward in the advance of the IE paradigm, it can also offer a privileged viewpoint to assess the 'story' of IE (Section 4.2) as well as some constructive criticism to incorporate the ecological discourse within its *tawhidi* framework (Section 4.3).

4.1. Environmental and ecological economics

With regard to the aforementioned notion of 'Islamic environmental/ecological economics' (IE/EE), used to describe the ecological advance in IE scholarship, some learned readers may actually remark that environmental[13] and ecological economics, whose origins date back respectively to the 1970s and 1980s,[14] are already considered distinct fields by their respective specialists, each one with its own assumptions, methodology and (somehow) values.

In fact, although both of them take as their core principle the notion of 'sustainable development' (from the Latin *sustinere*, 'to hold up', 'to support', 'to endure', hence the *ability* to *sustain* a 'development that meets the needs of the present without compromising the ability of future generations to meet their own needs', according to the famous definition by the Brundtland Commission: United Nations, 1987),[15]

- most environmental economists have been trained as (neo-classical) economists and tend to analyse environmental issues in terms of market failures, cost allocation, externalities and the governance of common and public goods;[16] differently, ecological economists have been trained as ecologists, have expanded their work into (human) economic actions, and hence look at 'economy' as a subfield of 'ecology';
- the former are more 'pragmatic' in their policy-making, while the latter are considered more 'idealistic', on the grounds of a holistic analysis of human actions as part of a global eco-system, hence referring to the general goal of a human-ecosystem equilibrium (homeostasis) for a functioning long-term sustainable development; and so on.

More in general, a comprehensive list of these differences (somehow reflecting alternative philosophical foundations of economic science) can be found in the article by Van den Bergh (2001), who emphasizes, for instance,

- how environmental economics assumes criteria of (a) optimal allocation and maximization of utility, (b) priority of market efficiency (with sustainability as abstract value), (c) cost-benefit analysis, (d) isolated individuals acting in a global market, and (e) functionalism;
- on the contrary, ecological economics embraces principles of (a) optimal scale and balancing, (b) priority of sustainability (in its empirical realization), (c) multi-dimensional evaluation, (d) persons acting in local communities, and (e) environmental ethics as guiding value (Van den Bergh, 2001, pp. 15–17).

If one looks at the methodological differentiation between environmental and ecological economics, the terminology in use in the emerging IE/EE scholarship does not seem to make a formal distinction between the two areas (see, for instance, Hassan, 2005; Naiya, 2007; Shaikh, 2013). At the same time, the holistic perspective of *tawhid*, the attention to community development, optimal balance (*mizan*) rather than optimal allocation make the paradigm of IE more adherent to ecological rather than environmental economics, offering some preliminary guidelines for the future evolution of IE/EE as well.

4.2. IE/EE: from the story of IE scholarship...

After a preliminary reference to conventional environmental and ecological economics, two considerations can be advanced on the nature of IE/EE as an emerging subfield in IE theory.

[First consideration] From a descriptive perspective, this work has already mentioned the delay of IE in considering environmental protection and sustainable development issues as core subjects of research. This delay can find an explanation in relation to the 'story' of the construction of IE as an alternative paradigm to conventional capitalism, through the convergence of different elements, such as: (i) the re-affirmation of the ethical nature of the human being as religious agent (*homo islamicus*), in opposition to the assumption of the pure secular rationality of the *homo oeconomicus*; (ii) the consequent normative differentiation of this religious agent from the conventional actor, hence the reference to the prohibitions of *riba*, speculation, gambling and *fiqh* rules in economic analysis; (iii) the attempt to define a political economy model based on the morality of Islam; and so on.

But, while this dialectical approach could be justified in the past due to the need for 'marking' the distinct identity of IE, its perpetuation today as an antithetical construction to (any aspect of) Western economics can be self-defeating for IE for at least two reasons.

First, because it can be indirect evidence of the lack of maturity of IE research policies as autonomous paradigm. Second, because it can paradoxically lead to a logical default in the long term, due to a 'universal-particular' narrative that 'implicitly *re*-affirms the validity of the … [conventional paradigm], locating *Shari'ah* economics … in an *ana*-logical relationship with it, where Islamic values *rectify*, but do not substitute, … [its] rationales' (Cattelan, 2013, p. 3). On the contrary, it is by embracing a '*dia*-logical relation' (where Islamic economics does not affirm its *own* identity by merely denying its conventional counterpart, but engages in a conversation with it through the understanding of God's Will) that 'the *theoretical* distance between conventional and *Shari'ah* economics as *autonomous* paradigm can be *practically* reconciled in the ethical agency of the Muslim believer' (*ibidem*, p. 9).

4.3. … to a reinforced IE paradigm

[Second consideration] Moving from a descriptive to a normative dimension, the research agenda of IE/EE can be seen as a promising field for a dialogical relation aimed at reinforcing the IE paradigm, as described in the previous section.

As Part One of this chapter has shown, in fact, it is undeniable that the ethical discourse and the natural order depicted in Islam (*fitrah*), embodying principles of unity (*tawhid*) of the creation, balance (*mizan*) and responsibility of the man as God's vice-regent (*khalifah*) – in a relationship between the Creator, humankind and the creation – looks at the rationales of environmental protection and sustainability as fundamental guidelines for human economic action. Recognizing this interrelation, the fruitful dialogue between Islamic and conventional scholarship on the problem of environmental sustainability was already implicitly recognized by Hasan more than a decade ago.

> One need not shy away from accepting that Islam does not deal with development issues as they are being spelled out today … To do otherwise may involve the risk of being apologetic or stretchy in argument. But the statement does not negate the fact that *Shari'ah* contains many unmistakable, even if generic, warnings that the world is likely to be overwhelmed by the development problems of the sort it is now facing if men do not resist selfishness, greed and rapacious exploitation of natural resources. On a more important side, the way of life Islam prescribes offers ample possibilities of extracting a whole blue print of instruction which, if put into operation, would not only help resolve current problems but may usher in positive improvement in the situation. *Maqasid-al-Shari'ah* – the objectives of the Islamic law – … provide the broad framework for such a blue print.
>
> (Hasan, 2006, p. 5)

Section 4.2 remarked how, while the deficiencies of IE on environmental sustainability could be bearable in the past, they risk today representing a serious weakness for IE scholarship.[17] This delay, in fact, apart from dismissing the clear *Shariʿah* warnings mentioned by Hasan, does not appear reconcilable anymore neither with

- the recent United Nations Resolution (25 September 2015) on *Sustainable Development Goals* (SDGs), listing 17 goals with 169 targets for the global economy;[18]
- nor with the current emergence of 'Islamic green finance' as an innovative segment in the financial market (see Section 5), for which stronger theoretical elaboration is needed to look at the implementation of SDGs through a distinctive *Shariʿah*-based perspective.

In the attempt to make up for these deficiencies, one primary guideline and two research policy options can be advanced to enhance the research agenda of IE.

The principal guideline consists in the promotion of a stronger *dialogical* relation between IE and conventional environmental and ecological economics. An example of this methodological approach can be found in Hasan's article with reference to the United Nations Commission's definition of sustainable development: '[t]he definition must also be welcome from an Islamic angle to the extent that it seeks a balance between economy, society, and environment' (Hasan, 2006, p. 7); '[i]nterestingly, the approach of the Commission is largely in consonance with the *maqasid* or objectives of the *Shariʿah*' (*ibidem*, p. 8).

Hasan also reproduces in his work the 'three circles' model on the interaction between economy, society and environment (2006, p. 7) which is commonly used in sustainable development theory (see for instance Adams, 2006, p. 2; Scott Cato, 2009, p. 37). In particular, he maintains an external interaction which does not imply the complete overlapping of the three domains (Figure 9.1 (a)). At any rate, a more suitable representation of their mutual interdependence should employ concentric circles, where, as highlighted by Scott Cato, 'economy operates within social relationships and the whole of society is embedded within the natural world' (2009, p. 37) (Figure 9.1 (b))[19] – in accordance as well with the *tawhidi* paradigm underlying the rationales of IE.

As far as the two research policy options are concerned, they can be seen as a direct corollary of this dialogical approach and complementary pathways to enhance the research agenda of IE as an autonomous discipline and an alternative to Western capitalism.

From the side of sustainable development literature, an important improvement has been recently made through adding to the layers of economy, ecology and politics (hence, the 'environment' and the 'society' circles), a fourth domain about 'cultural sustainability'. The resulting four-dimensional 'circles of sustainability' method (with the cultural domain comprising practices, elements of identity, belief and meaning, memory and general wellbeing) is already being used by organizations such as the United

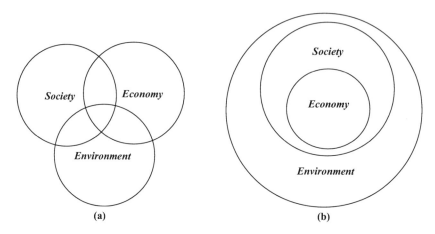

Figure 9.1. Sustainable development and the relation between economy, society and environment: from external interaction (a) to embedded interdependence (b)

Nations City Programme and Metropolis (World Association of Major Metropolises) and can become an important instrument for fieldworks focused on the intersection between environmental and development economics (on the new field of 'envirodevonomics' see Greenstone and Jack, 2015; on the link between culture, ecology and development, see also the reflections by Llewellyn, White and Ba Kader *et al.*, mentioned in Section 2). This intersection, in particular, can be of significant relevance for the economies of Muslim developing countries, especially in relation to urban politics and planning (James, 2015).

From the side of Islamic economics, some contributions to the paradigm shift towards sustainable development have appeared in recent years (see for instance, Orhan Aström, 2011; Sarkawi and Abdullah, 2015; Sarkawi *et al.*, 2016). In their paper, Sarkawi and Abdullah (2015, p. 1254) present a conceptual model of what they define as the 'Islamic built environment' where the environment appears as a sub-system of a broader religious approach to the conceptualization of the reality (in the light of the *maqasid*), and society and economy overlap as sub-systems that are internal to the environment, thus recognizing the priority of ecological issues as a religious duty. Figure 9.2 provides a graphical representation of this model.

The diagram has the merit to suggest that societal and economic needs should be fulfilled in an Islamic eco-system through the pursuit of an environmental balance (as their interaction occurs *within*, and not outside, the environment), which is itself embodied within the unity (*tawhid*) of the creation, hence incorporating the primary role of *khalifah*. It is in the light of this general scheme, which locates the interdependence between society, economy

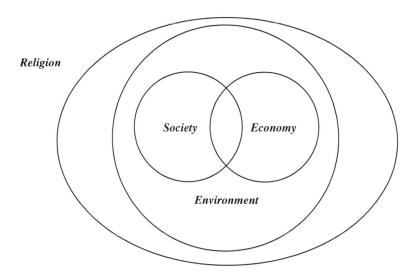

Figure 9.2. A conceptual model for an Islamic approach to sustainable development

and environment in the *tawhidi* paradigm, that the research agenda of IE can actually provide a theoretical support to Islamic green finance as an emergent market combining the objectives of the green economy with *Shari'ah* values.

5. The current practice of Islamic green finance: *sukuk*, *awqaf* and *Sharī'ah*-compliance criteria

If Section 4 underlined how a 'green approach' in the discipline of IE is still at a formative stage, the practice of the market has already registered examples of 'Islamic green finance', where *Shari'ah* values match the growing concern about environmental protection in the global economy. Generally speaking, the appearance in the global market of 'green *sukuk*' and 'green *awqaf*' as new tools to promote environmental sustainability can be inserted in a more general trend recognizing the social impact of Islamic finance beyond the borders of Islamic economics, as witnessed by a recent policy paper by the World Bank Group (Ahmed *et al.*, 2015).

With the Millennium Development Goals (MDGs) having expired at the end of 2015, the world is preparing for the global development agenda to succeed them. The proposed 17 Sustainable Development Goals (SDGs)[20] are more ambitious and holistic than their predecessors, and countries will require commensurately ambitious financing to implement them, with a paradigm shift towards sustainability. Islamic finance has a potential to play a transformative role in supporting the implementation of the post-2015 agenda (Ahmed *et al.*, 2015, p. 2). But, while this potential certainly exists, there is also a dramatic need for further investments, as '[s]everal studies find that the

Islamic financial sector's role in addressing environmental and social goals is either small or non-existent' (*ibidem*, p. 24).

Considering this, the current emergence of green *sukuk* (Section 5.1) and *awqaf* (Section 5.2) should be read in a context where environmental sustainability has not been fully incorporated yet in the *Shari'ah* screening of Islamic financial institutions (Section 5.3). In other terms, the few green *sukuk* and *awqaf* already available in the market should be seen as pioneering examples of a new trend in Islamic finance, re-affirming the Islamic tradition about environmental protection (Part One) within a broader attention towards green investments that is spreading in the global economy. Notwithstanding, as we will see, major interventions are still required for a 'greener' Islamic finance to be fostered worldwide.

5.1. The global appeal of green sukuk

The global trend recognizing the potential of Islamic finance to foster environmental sustainability finds probably the best example today in the market of 'green *sukuk*'.

'Green *sukuk* are *Shari'ah* compliant investment vehicles that fund environmentally friendly projects such as solar parks, bio-gas plants and wind farms' (Alam *et al.*, 2016, p. 167).

While, structurally speaking, green *sukuk* replicate traditional *sukuk* (that is to say, for instance, the well-known structures of *ijarah* or *mudarabah sukuk*), they also address, from a functional perspective, specific *Shari'ah* concerns for environmental protection, combining in this way the nature of conventional green bonds with *Shari'ah* values (on the topic, see Moghul and Safar-Aly, 2014). Hence, according to a recent policy paper published by the Islamic Research and Training Institute, green *sukuk* can be considered 'the *Shari'ah*-compliant version of a green bond' as they represent '*Shari'ah*-compliant investments in renewable energy and other environmental assets', such as 'clean energy, mass transit, water conservation, forestry, and low-carbon technologies' (Obaidullah, 2017, pp. 24–25).

If, generally speaking, investor appetite for green bonds has been largely driven by environmental and social responsible aims, a very strong potential for green *sukuk* can be foreseen in relation to the *Islamic Declaration on Global Climate Change* as released by the International Islamic Climate Change Symposium held in Istanbul in August 2015 (Obaidullah, 2017, p. 7). Indeed, commentators have already remarked on the strategic nature of green *sukuk* especially in relation to the infrastructure market, which 'plays a critical role in growth, competitiveness, job creation, and poverty alleviation, yet increasing access to basic infrastructure services remains a critical challenge in developing countries' (Dey *et al.*, 2016, p. 4).[21] Accordingly, the global appeal of green *sukuk* goes far beyond the boundaries of Islamic finance. In fact, if there is no doubt that Muslim clients can find in these innovative products the perfect match between their religious values and ecological concerns, the asset-backed structure of *sukuk* makes them a suitable form of investment for the financing of renewable energy infrastructures as well.

Hence, on the side of the Muslim demand, a Green *Sukuk* Working Group 'was established in 2012 by the Climate Bonds Initiative, the Clean Energy Business Council (CEBC) of the Middle East and North Africa, and the Gulf Bond and *Sukuk* Association' (Alam *et al.*, 2016, p. 175). Malaysia, as the most advanced *sukuk* market, has already embarked upon proactive initiatives in the field, in order to finance 'a greener world using ethical funding options' (Bank Negara Malaysia, 2014, p. 1). Reviewing the global trends, gaps and opportunities in the global green economy, the Central Bank of Malaysia has noted how

> [a]s the world economy gradually moves towards adopting a green and more sustainable development model, the Islamic finance industry has tremendous opportunities to develop *Shari'ah*-compliant green financing facilities to meet the expanding liquidity requirements in the sector.
> (Bank Negara Malaysia, 2014, p. 4)

Along with the conventional banks, since 2013 Islamic banks in Malaysia have been eligible to enter the Green Technology Financing Scheme Islamic (GTFS-i), and the Securities Commission Malaysia launched in August 2014 a SRI (social responsible investment) *sukuk* framework also to facilitate the green trend (Safar-Aly, 2015, p. 57).

On the side of the global appeal of green *sukuk*, it must be noticed that the first green *sukuk* was the French Orasis Sukuk, combining a *istisna'* and *ijarah* structure for an asset-backed investment in solar plants producing green energy (Alam *et al.*, 2016, pp. 178–182). Launched in 2012, as a France-based project, Orasis represents an important example to be replicated in the Middle East and North Africa, able to combine *Shari'ah* standards, infrastructure development purposes for developing countries and ecological concerns (Hassoune, 2012).[22] Looking at the other side of the globe, in late 2012 two Australian solar companies (Solar Guys International and Mitabu Australia) launched a photovoltaic project in Indonesia through a green *sukuk* based in Malaysia. 'The project ... is the first phase of the "One Solar Watt per Person" program in Indonesia. The solar project commenced in July 2015 ... and the first phase ... will be funded through an offer of a $150 million of green *sukuk*' (Alam *et al.*, 2016, pp. 175–176).

5.2. Green awqaf *and local environmental protection*

From a historical and socio-economic perspective the social purpose inherently embedded in *waqf* institutions can be interpreted within the frame of the informal economy that characterizes the institutes of Islamic microfinance in favour of the needy and the poor, and has been recently re-discovered in ethnographic research (see, for instance, the work by Effendi, 2013). At the same time, through the emergent rise of environmental consciousness within the Islamic economics circle, the 'green' evolution of traditional Islamic endowments (*awqaf*) is being presented as a significant advance to cope with the challenge of climate change, provide goods for humanitarian purposes in case of natural disasters, and promote environmental awareness among consumers and the general public.

> *Awqaf* may directly engage in provision of goods and services related to mitigation and adaptation. Such green *awqaf* may be established as dedicated entities for conservation of soil, water, plants, ... [they] may be dedicated to ... clean technology ... [as well as] consumer awareness and stronger support of action to mitigate climate change.
>
> (Obaidullah, 2017, pp. 20–21)

In actual fact, till recently the establishment of a *waqf* 'for the purpose of environmental protection ... has been less popular than any other form of *waqf*, such as for religious, education, health, and poverty alleviation purposes' (Budiman, 2011, p. 885). In line with what has been remarked in Section 4 of this chapter about the delay of a specific ecological approach in Islamic economics, both 'discourse and practices of *waqf* for this particular purpose seem very limited although the Islamic teachings and principles have extensively encouraged Muslim to maintain and protect the environment' (*ibidem*, p. 885). Despite this delay, Budiman registers pioneering 'tree *waqf*' programmes in Indonesia, in the form of 'tree planting and cultivating, making well and building clean water installation' in South Sumatera Province (2007), at Penagan village, West Mendo sub-district (2009), with the issuance of a religious decree regarding the permissibility of tree *awqaf* by Majelis Ulama Indonesia (Indonesian Ulama Council) in 2010 (*ibidem*, p. 886).

Without any doubt, although the constitution of green *awqaf* is still in its infancy, the combined purpose of environmental protection and sustainable development for local communities that they are able to foster suggests that the governments of Muslim countries, as well as non-governmental organizations, should look back at the tradition of *waqf* as a viable instrument for the promotion of modern Islamic green finance. This will at the same time depend on a more general intervention with regard to the incorporation of the current notion of environmental sustainability among the criteria of *Shari'ah*-compliance in use by Islamic financial institutions (see Section 5.3).

5.3. Shari'ah *compliance and green economy: future prospects for global impact*

The World Bank Report quoted at the beginning of this section, while arguing the potential of Islamic finance for contributing to the pursuit of SDGs, also certifies the persistent weaknesses in the *Shari'ah*-compliant market with regard to green economy standards.

> In a study of social reporting of 29 Islamic banks, Maali *et al.* (2006) find their charitable activities and employee-related issues to be moderately good. However, none of the Islamic banks report any activities related to environment. Similarly, interviews of 18 senior executives of Islamic financial institutions in the Gulf Cooperation Council (GCC) showed that corporate social responsibility is not the major concern for Islamic banks (Aribi and Arun, 2012). The focus of their operations is on *Shari'ah* compliance, and none reported anything of environmental issues.
>
> (Ahmed *et al.*, 2015, p. 25)

This chapter has underlined the extent to which, despite the Islamic tradition about environmental protection (see Part One), both the discipline of Islamic economics (Section 4) and the practice of Islamic finance (Section 5) have only recently embraced a 'green economy' approach. Without any doubt, green *sukuk* (5.1) and *awqaf* (5.2) do constitute important tools for the development of an Islamic eco-system able to reconcile objectives of economic development with environmental protection and sustainability.

But, as clearly remarked by Ahmed *et al.* (2015), the full integration of environmental goals into the general frame of the operations of Islamic financial institutions will require a 'cultural embedment' phase (p. 25) that this chapter has both emphasized at its inception (Section 2) and depicted in terms of a fruitful dialogical relation between Islamic and ecological economics (Section 4), by fully incorporating the contemporary notion of environment sustainability in the *maqasid* and *Shari'ah*-compliance screening criteria.

In fact, while the 'bulk of the Islamic investment screening used for the stock markets applies negative and exclusionary criteria' (i.e. prohibitions of *riba*, speculation, gambling...), the current practice 'does not apply positive screening criteria' such as those related to environmentally friendly production (Ahmed *et al.*, 2015, p. 25).

In the light of this, the launch by the Malaysian bourse, Bursa Malaysia, of a dedicated Environmental, Social and Governance (ESG) Index in December 2014 (as announced by Bank Negara Malaysia, 2014, p. 8) must be welcomed in relation to the convergent effort by the Malaysian capital market regulators to foster new green investments eligible both for the GTFS-i (see above) and for the ESG Index, hence nourishing Islamic green finance. Correspondingly, a positive evaluation has to be advanced, in terms of *Shari'ah*-compliance, with regard to the Policy Guidelines for Green Banking (PGGB) introduced by the Bangladesh Central Bank in 2011 (Julia *et al.*, 2016).

Despite these efforts by local national authorities, the need for further *Shari'ah*-compliance improvements in the light of the green economy still remains an open issue for the future of Islamic finance and, more broadly, for the sustainable development of Muslim countries (Vaghefi *et al.*, 2015) and the global economy as a whole.

6. Conclusions: the social value of Islamic green finance

Moving from the core principles of the Islamic tradition with regard to environmental protection and sustainable development (Part One) to their contemporary implementation in the paradigm of Islamic economics and application in the emergent field of Islamic green finance (Part Two), this chapter has outlined the potential of all these instruments to contribute to a more responsible economic growth at a local and global stage, both at an intra- and inter-generational perspective.

A guiding principle in the study has been the recognition of the deep interrelation between religion, culture, ecology and economics for a sustainable development in human societies.

With regard to Muslim nations, there is no doubt that the holistic approach of the *tawhidi* framework in Islam, with its inherent attention to economic and ecological balance (*mizan*) and the assertion of human responsibility (*khalifah*) towards the nature as God's creation, can represent the background for a viable paradigm of sustainable development and an alternative to the classic profit-oriented model of capitalism.

The chapter has shown that, if persistent shortcomings still affect the theory of Islamic economics, the practice of Islamic green finance offers examples of operative tools (*sukuk* and *awqaf*) that are able to embrace an 'ecological revolution' necessary to guarantee the prosperity of present and future generations. Hence, although further efforts are required in terms of a stronger overlap between criteria of *Shari'ah* compliance and the green economy, the 'seeds' of a fruitful segment for social finance (able to reconcile Muslim ethics, economic development and the preservation of natural resources) have already been planted.

The growth of this 'tree' will depend both on the adherence to Islamic principles and the capability by private and public actors, at a national and international level, to effectively act for their implementation in the governance of natural resources and of environment protection. To this objective, the community-oriented approach that intrinsically belongs to Islamic economics (in terms of cooperation among the market participants, and the sharing of resources) can offer the appropriate background to transform Islamic green finance in a core operative branch of the social finance sector, both for Muslims and non-Muslims alike.

Notes

1 Held in conjunction with the 25th anniversary of its establishment, the Conference was organized by the Institute of Islamic Understanding Malaysia (IKIM, from the Malay official denomination 'Institut Kefehaman Islam Malaysia':

www.ikim.gov.my), founded on 18 February 1992 to promote the study and implementation of the teachings of Islam, both at a national and global scale.

2　Dato' Sri Haji Mohammad Najib bin Tun Haji Abdul Razak (born 1953) is the sixth Prime Minister of Malaysia. President of the United Malays National Organisation, he succeeded Prime Minister Tun Dato' Sri Haji Abdullah bin Haji Ahmad Badawi on 3 April 2009.

3　See *inter alia* Kyoto Protocol to the United Nations Framework Convention on Climate Change, entered into force on 16 February 2005, UN Treaty Series, Vol. 2303, 2005, N. 30822.

4　The Declaration is a non-binding instrument adopted by the International Islamic Climate Change Symposium held in Istanbul, which is available at: www.ifees.org. uk/wp-content/uploads/2016/10/climate_declarationmMWB.pdf. It deserves to be noted that the *Declaration* follows by a few days the adoption by the General Assembly of the United Nations of the Draft Resolution submitted by the President of the General Assembly for the adoption of the post-2015 development agenda (A/69/L.85, 12 August 2015), that was the basis for the Resolution *Transforming Our World: The 2030 Agenda for Sustainable Development* (A/RES/ 70/1, 21 October 2015, adopted on 25 September 2015). See also in this chapter, Section 4.3.

5　In particular Art. 3 requires that 'The right to development must be fulfilled so as to equitably meet developmental and environmental needs of present and future generations' (United Nations, 1992). The International Court of Justice has also reaffirmed how 'This need to reconcile economic development with protection of the environment is aptly expressed in the concept of sustainable development' (ICJ, 1997, § 140). On the matter see McCormick, 1986, and, recently, Sachs, 2015.

6

> Thus, we can see that there is no conflict between the principles of Islam and the fundamental objectives of capitalism (profits from commercial activity, financial returns from investment at risk, private property, etc.). Islam, however, accepts capitalist practices only to the extent that they do not harm social welfare. The preferences of Islam therefore go to a relatively egalitarian capitalism, the State being fit to take measures to that end. Finally, for Islam, there are limits to the appropriation of natural resources by man and to the general exercise of the right to property.
>
> (English translation by this chapter's author)

7

> The ultimate objective of Islamic law is the universal common good of all created beings, encompassing both our immediate welfare in the present and our ultimate welfare in the hereafter. This objective of the universal common good is a distinctive characteristic of Islamic law. It means that no species or generation may be excluded from consideration in the course of planning and administration ... The ultimate responsibility for right action lies with the individual who will be judged on the Day of Judgment for what he did with his life, regardless of what the governing authorities with their various administrative and municipal agencies and courts of law required him. Therefore the protection, conservation, and development of the environment and natural resources is a mandatory religious duty to which every Muslim should be committed. This commitment emanated from the individual's responsibility before God to protect himself and his community.
>
> (Bagader *et al.*, 1994, p. 17; on the topic see also Mekouar, 1988, p. 49)

8 With regard to this divergence between Islam and the West, it deserves to be mentioned here the separate opinion by Judge Weeramantry, in the above quoted case of the ICJ (see note 5): 'Europe, likewise, had a deep-seated tradition of love for the environment, a prominent feature of European culture, until the industrial revolution pushed these concerns into the background'; while

> the principles of Islamic law that inasmuch as all land belongs to God, land is never the subject of human ownership, but is only held in trust, with all the connotations that follow of due care, wise management, and custody for future generations. The first principle of modern environmental law – the principle of trusteeship of earth resources – is thus categorically formulated in this system.
> (ICJ, 1997, separate opinion of Vice-President Weeramantry, p. 108)

9 On the point it can be mentioned here the *Encyclical Letter 'Laudato Si'* by Pope Francis (2015).

10 Unfortunately, as Hamed argues,

> [u]ntil now, efforts to achieve sustainable development in the Muslim countries have rarely capitalized on the cultural heritage of the *Shari'ah*. The programs implemented throughout these countries suggest an elitist bias. Their conceptual underpinning is rooted in Western values and/or serving foreign users. The proposals that have been presented by different scholars to revitalize traditional Islamic institutions (such as *hisba, haram, hima, waqf, ihya*, and others) are few in number, sketchy in content, and overly optimistic in spirit. All of these proposals have avoided any serious assessment of implementing their schemes under the political conditions that prevail in Muslim countries today.
> (Hamed, 2003, pp. 416–417)

11 For the different ways in which the modern concept of 'environment' finds an expression in the *Qur'an* see: Chittick, 1986, pp. 672–673.

12 The principle of *tawhid* has some economical implications as well: the payment of *zakat* (Q. 9:60) has to be considered as an obligation that God imposed for the welfare of the community and not in the sense of a tax to be paid to the State, the premise being that those who have benefited from God's munificence are required to share it with those who were excluded, see Sid Ahmed, 1990, p. 410.

13 Since natural resources (and related issues, such as air pollution, water distribution, global warming, governance of public and common goods) represent a core subject of environmental economics analysis, this field is also known under the label of 'environmental and resource economics'.

14 While the Association of Environmental and Resource Economics (AERE) was established in 1979, the International Society for Ecological Economics (ISEE) 'was founded by participants at a workshop in Barcelona in 1987', though 'its roots go back at least to a meeting on the integration of economics and ecology in Sweden in 1982' (Van den Bergh, 2001, p. 13 note 1).

15 Formally known as the 'World Commission on Environment and Development' (WCED), the 'Brundtland Commission' (after the name of the chairperson, Gro Harlem Brundtland), was established by the United Nations to define a common framework for sustainable development for all the UN member states. The Commission released in 1987 the Report *Our Common Future* (also known as the *Brundtland Report*), which coined the definition of 'sustainable development' as quoted in the main text.

16 Traditional environmental economics is based on neoclassical welfare theory and microeconomics. Its core insights are critically dependent on the assumption of rational behavior (utility or profit maximization), which together with an additional assumption of market clearing generates a unique economics equilibrium, that is, a unique combination of prices and tradable quantities of each product on each market (including the ones of labour and capital).

(Van den Bergh, 2001, p. 13, note 2)

17 In a recent paper (which builds on the contents of his previous work of 2006) Hasan recognizes the delay that Muslim countries and Islamic education institutions are still experiencing in embodying environmental issues in their research agenda:

Many colleges and universities in the developed world have a designated environmental finance center. Some colleges and universities offer environmental finance degrees that focus on economic and policy analysis, financial analytics, science and technology, markets and regulation. Developing countries, Muslim especially, are lagging far behind in environmental teaching and research.

(Hasan, 2017, p. 10)

'INCEIF the Global University of Islamic finance remain one glaring example of such omission but they are planning to fill the gap in due course' (*ibidem*, note 9). In summary, it seems that this educational challenge, though well-known, still has a way to go.

18 Officially known as *Transforming Our World: The 2030 Agenda for Sustainable Development* (United Nations, 2015), the Resolution indicates as fundamental goals for the period 2015–2030: (1) no poverty; (2) zero hunger; (3) good health and well-being; (4) quality education; (5) gender equality; (6) clean water and sanitation; (7) affordable and clean energy; (8) decent work and economic growth; (9) industry, innovation and infrastructure; (10) reduced inequalities; (11) sustainable cities and communities; (12) responsible consumption and production; (13) climate action; (14) life below water; (15) life on land; (16) peace, justice and strong institutions; (17) partnerships for the goals. This list succeeded the *Millennium Development Goals* fixed for the period 2000–2015.

19 The fundamentally different conception of the interaction between economy, society and environment from (a) to (b) (see Figure 9.1) is perfectly depicted by Molly Scott Cato in describing the move from conventional to green economics:

The three circles model ... helps to explain the different view of the economy that results from taking sustainability seriously. In the conventional view ... [diagram (a) in Figure 9.1] the economy, environment and society interact but are not interdependent. They are drawn as of equal size and therefore importance, although in reality the economy carries much more sway in decision making, with society bearing the cost and the environment paying the highest price of all. This figure makes clear why economists refer to the negative consequences of production processes – say, pollution from a nuclear power station – as an 'externality', because in their view of the world what happens to the environment and the people who live in it happens somewhere else. It can be pushed outside the 'economy' circle and dealt with elsewhere. Once you realize that there is no 'elsewhere' you have to consider the wastes you produce in all your economic activities differently. This is illustrated on the right-hand side of the graphic [diagram (b) in Figure 9.1], where society nestles inside the environment and the economy is a part of society. In this view, both society and economy are dependent on the environment. It also implies that economic activity takes place within a network of social relationships … This is the world as viewed by green economics[.]

(Scott Cato, 2009, pp. 36–37)

20 On Sustainable Development Goals (SDGs) see note 18.
21

Although banks are the traditional providers of debt finance for infrastructure, there has been significant interest in introducing infrastructure *sukuk* … A *sukuk* product to fund a specific environmentally sustainable infrastructure project, such as the construction of renewable energy generation facility, could appeal to both conventional environment-focused 'green' investors and *sukuk* investors.

(Dey *et al.*, 2016, p. 4)

22 Alam *et al.* (2016) note that despite its appeal, 'the investment was not deemed successful 2 years into its issuance' for a series of factors, also linked to the financial crisis in Europe. 'Notwithstanding these setbacks, the features of this green *sukuk* were a first of their kind. The positive and negative lessons of this initial French experience may well provide the basis for developing broader *Sharia*-compliant solutions to green investments' (p. 182).

References

Adams, W.M. (2006) *The Future of Sustainability: Re-Thinking Environment and Development in the Twenty-First Century*. [online]. IUCN Report, The World Conservation Union. Available from: www.iucn.org [Accessed 18 April 2017].

Afsaruddin, A. (2013) The *siyar* law of aggression: juridical re-interpretations of Qur'anic *jihad* and their contemporary implications for international law. In: Frick, M.L., and Müller, A.T. (eds) *Islam and International Law: Engaging Self Centrism from Plurality of Perspectives*. Leiden: Martinus Nijhoff Publ., pp. 45–63.

Ahmed, H., Mohieldin, M., *et al.* (2015) *On the Sustainable Development Goals and the Role of Islamic Finance*. [online]. Policy Research Working Paper 7166, World Bank Group. Available from www.worldbank.org [Accessed 22 April 2017].

Akbar, K.F. (1992) Environmental crisis and religion: the Islamic viewpoint. *Islamic Thought and Scientific Creativity*. 3(1).

Akhtar, M.R. (1996) Towards an Islamic approach for environmental balance. *Islamic Economic Studies*. 3(2), pp. 57–76.

Alam, N., Duygun, M. and Ariss, R.T. (2016) Green *sukuk*: an innovation in Islamic capital markets. In: Dorsman, A., Arslan-Ayaydin, Ö. and Karan, M.B. (eds) *Energy and Finance: Sustainability in the Energy Industry*. Switzerland: Springer, pp. 167–185.

Aldeeb Abu-Sahlieh, S.A. (2008) *Il Diritto Islamico*. Roma: Carocci (translation from the French ed., 2006: *Introduction à la Société Musulmane*. Paris: Éditions d'Organisation).

Aribi, Z.A., and Arun, T.G. (2012) *Corporate Social Responsibility in Islamic Financial Institutions (IFIs): A Management Insight*. [online]. Available from: www.ssrn.com [Accessed 16 April 2017].

Ba Kader, A.B.A., *et al.* (1983) *Islamic Principles for the Conservation of the Natural Environment.* International Union for Conservation of Nature and Natural Resources (IUCN), Gland, Switzerland, and Meteorological and Environmental Protection Administration (MEPA). Siegburg: Daemisch Mohr.

Bagader, A.A., *et al.* (1994) *Environmental Protection in Islam.* International Union for Conservation of Nature and Natural Resources (IUCN), Gland, Switzerland, and Meteorological and Environmental Protection Administration (MEPA). Gland, Switzerland, and Cambridge, UK: IUCN.

Bakhashab, O.A. (1988) Islamic law and the environment: some basic principles. *Arab Law Quarterly.* **3**(3), pp. 287–298.

Bank Negara Malaysia (2014) *Islamic Finance. Ready to Finance a Greener World.* [online] MIFC Insight Report – Green Financing. Available from: www.mifc.com [Accessed 23 April 2017].

Ben Achour, Y. (2011) *La Deuxième Fatiha. L'Islam et la Pensée des Droits de l'Homme.* Paris: Presses Universitaires de France.

Budiman, M.A. (2011) *The Role of Waqf for Environmental Protection in Indonesia.* [online]. Paper presented at the Aceh Development International Conference 2011, 26–28 March, Bangi, Malaysia, pp. 880–889. Available from: www.ssrn.com [Accessed 23 April 2017].

Cattelan, V. (2013) *Shariʿah* economics as autonomous paradigm: theoretical approach and operative outcomes. *Journal of Islamic Perspective on Science, Technology and Society.* **1**(1), pp. 3–11.

Chapra, M.U. (1993) *Islam and Economic Development: A Strategy for Development with Justice and Stability.* Islamabad: International Institute of Islamic Thought and Islamic Research Institute.

Chishti, S.K.K. (2003) *Fitra*: an Islamic model for humans and environment. In: Foltz, R.C., Denny, F.M. and Baharuddin, A. (eds) *Islam and Ecology: A Bestowed Trust.* Center for the Study of World Religion, Harvard Divinity School. Cambridge, MA: Harvard University Press, pp. 67–82.

Chittick, W.C. (1986) 'God surrounds all things': an Islamic perspective on the environment. *The World & I.* **1**(6), pp. 671–678.

Dey, D., Hussain, T. and Hauman, M. (2016) *Green Bonds & Islamic Finance.* [online]. New York: White & Case. Available from: www.whitecase.com [Accessed 23 April 2017].

Dutton, Y. (2003) The environmental crisis of our time: a Muslim response. In: Foltz, R.C., Denny, F.M. and Baharuddin, A. (eds) *Islam and Ecology: A Bestowed Trust.* Center for the Study of World Religion, Harvard Divinity School. Cambridge, MA: Harvard University Press, pp. 323–340.

Effendi, J. (2013) *The Role of Islamic Microfinance in Poverty Alleviation and Environmental Awareness in Pasuruan, East Java, Indonesia: A Comparative Research.* PhD dissertation. Göttingen: unpublished.

Erdur, O. (1997) Reappropriating the 'green': Islamist environmentalism. *New Perspectives on Turkey.* **17**, pp. 151–156.

Greenstone, M., and Jack, B.K. (2015) Envirodevonomics: a research agenda for an emerging field. *Journal of Economic Literature.* **53**(1), pp. 5–42.

Hamed, S-E. A. (2003) Capacity building for sustainable development: the dilemma of Islamization of environmental institutions. In: Foltz, R.C., Denny, F.M. and Baharuddin, A. (eds) *Islam and Ecology: A Bestowed Trust.* Center for the Study of World Religion, Harvard Divinity School. Cambridge, MA: Harvard University Press, pp. 403–421.

Hasan, Z. (2006) Sustainable development from an Islamic perspective: meaning, implications, and policy concerns. *JKAU Islamic Economics*. **19**(1), pp. 3–18.

Hasan, Z. (2017) Growth, environment and Islam. [online]. MPRA Paper no. 76347. Available from: https://mpra.ub.uni-muenchen.de/76347 [Accessed 18 April 2017].

Hassan, A. (2005) Islamic economics and the environment: material flow analysis in society-nature interrelationships. *JKAU Islamic Economics*. **18**(1), pp. 15–31.

Hassoune, A. (2012) *Orasis: First French Sukuk. Islamic Financial Solution for Green Energy in France*. [online]. Paris: Hassoune Conseil. Available from: https://cenf.univ-paris1.fr/fileadmin/Chaire_CENF/HC_-_Orasis_Sukuk_presentation_10-2012.pdf [Accessed 23 April 2017].

Heinrichs, P.W. (2002) *Qawaʻid* as a genre of legal literature. In: Weiss, B.G. (ed.) *Studies in Islamic Legal Theory*. Leiden: Brill, pp. 365–384.

Husaini, S.W.A. (1980) *Islamic Environmental Systems Engineering: A Systems Study of Environmental Engineering, and the Law, Politics, Education, Economics and Sociology of Science and Culture of Islam*. London: Macmillan.

International Court of Justice (ICJ) (1997) *Gabčíkovo-Nagymaros Project (Hungary/ Slovakia), Judgment, ICJ Reports*.

Izzi Dien, M.Y. (1992) Islamic ethics and the environment. In: Khalid, F.M., and O'Brien, J. (eds) *Islam and Ecology*. London: Cassell, pp. 25–35.

James, P. (2015) *Urban Sustainability in Theory and Practice: Circles of Sustainability*. London and New York: Earthscan, Routledge.

Julia, T., Rahman, M.P. and Kassim, S. (2016) *Shariah* compliance of green banking policy in Bangladesh. *Humanomics*. **32**(4), pp. 390–404.

Kamali, M.H. (1989) Source, nature and objectives of *Shariʻah*. *The Islamic Quarterly*. **33**, pp. 215–236.

Kamali, M.H. (1997) *Principles of Islamic Jurisprudence*. Revised Edition. Cambridge, UK: The Islamic Texts Society.

Kamali, M.H. (1999) '*Maqasid al-Shariʻah*': the objectives of Islamic law. *Islamic Studies*. **38**(2), pp. 193–208.

Khalid, F.M. (2002) Islam and the environment: social and economic dimensions of global environmental change. In: Timmerman, P. (ed.) *Encyclopedia of Global Environmental Change*. Chichester: John Wiley, pp. 332–339.

Khalid, F.M. (2003) Islam, ecology, and modernity: an Islamic critique of the root causes of environmental degradation. In: Foltz, R.C., Denny, F.M. and Baharuddin, A. (eds) *Islam and Ecology: A Bestowed Trust*. Center for the Study of World Religion, Harvard Divinity School. Cambridge, MA: Harvard University Press, pp. 299–322.

Llewellyn, O. (1992) Desert reclamation and conservation in Islamic law. In: Khalid, F.M., and O'Brien, J. (eds) *Islam and Ecology*. London: Cassell, pp. 87–97.

Llewellyn, O.A. (1984) Islamic jurisprudence and environmental planning. *Journal of Research in Islamic Economics*. **1**(2), pp. 27–46.

Llewellyn, O.A. (2003) The basis for a discipline of Islamic environmental law. In: Foltz, R.C., Denny, F.M. and Baharuddin, A. (eds) *Islam and Ecology: A Bestowed Trust*. Center for the Study of World Religion, Harvard Divinity School. Cambridge, MA: Harvard University Press, pp. 185–248.

Maali, B., Casson, P. and Napier, C. (2006) Social reporting by Islamic banks. *ABACUS*. **42**(2), pp. 266–289.

Mahmassani, S. (1966) The principles of international law in the light of Islamic doctrine. *Collected Courses of The Hague Academy of International Law*. Vol. 117, pp. 201–328.

McCormick, J. (1986) The origins of the world conservation strategy. *Environmental Review*. **10**(3), pp. 177–187.

Mekouar, M.A. (1988) *Études en Droit de l'Environnement*. Rabat: Editions Okad.

Moghul, U.F., and Safar-Aly, S.H.K. (2014) Green *sukuk*: the introduction of Islam's environmental ethics to contemporary Islamic finance. *The Georgetown International Environmental Law Review*. **27**(1), pp. 1–60.

Mohamed, Y. (1996) *Fitrah: The Islamic Concept of Human Nature*. London: Ta Ha Publ.

Naiya, I.I. (2007) Environmental issues and Islamic economics: nature and solutions. [online]. Proceedings of the 2nd Islamic Conference (iECONS2007), Faculty of Economics and Muamalat, Islamic Science University of Malaysia. Available from: www.islamiceconomichome.com/uploads/iecons052.pdf [Accessed 14 April 2017].

Nasr, S.H. (1964) *An Introduction to Islamic Cosmological Doctrines*. Cambridge, MA: Belknap Press.

Nasr, S.H. (1990) Islam and the environmental crisis. *The Islamic Quarterly*. **34**(4), pp. 217–234.

Nomanul Haq, S. (2003) Islam and ecology: toward retrieval and reconstruction. In: Foltz, R.C., Denny, F.M. and Baharuddin, A. (eds) *Islam and Ecology: A Bestowed Trust*. Center for the Study of World Religion, Harvard Divinity School, Cambridge, MA: Harvard University Press, pp. 121–154.

Obaidullah, M. (2017) *Managing Climate Change: The Role of Islamic Finance*, IRTI Policy Paper Series PP/2017/01. Jeddah: Islamic Research and Training Institute.

Orhan Aström, Z.H. (2011) Paradigm shift for sustainable development: the contribution of Islamic economics. *Journal of Economic and Social Studies*. **1**(1), pp. 73–82.

Özdemir, İ. (2003) Toward an understanding of environmental ethics from a Qur'anic perspective. In: Foltz, R.C., Denny, F.M. and Baharuddin, A. (eds) *Islam and Ecology: A Bestowed Trust*. Center for the Study of World Religion, Harvard Divinity School. Cambridge, MA: Harvard University Press, pp. 3–37.

Pope Francis (2015) *Encyclical Letter 'Laudato Si' of the Holy Father Francis on Care for Our Common Home*. Rome: Vatican Press.

Razak, N. (2017) *Official Speech*. [online]. IKIM International Conference on Religion and Civilizational Sustainability, Kuala Lumpur, 20 February 2017. Available from: Razak's blog www.najibrazak.com/bm/blog/ikim-international-conference-on-religion-and-civilization-sustainability/ [Accessed 3 April 2017].

Sachs, J.D. (2015) *The Age of Sustainable Development*. New York: Columbia University Press.

Saeed, A. (1996) *Islamic Banking and Interest: A Study of the Prohibition of Riba and Its Contemporary Interpretation*. Leiden: Brill.

Safar-Aly, S. (2015) Environmentally-conscious and socially responsible investment: a growth opportunity for Islamic finance. *Islamic Finance News*, March, pp. 56–57.

Said, A.A., and Funk, N.C. (2003) Peace in Islam: an ecology of the spirit. In: Foltz, R.C., Denny, F.M. and Baharuddin, A. (eds), *Islam and Ecology: A Bestowed Trust*. Center for the Study of World Religion, Harvard Divinity School. Cambridge, MA: Harvard University Press, pp. 155–184.

Saleh, N.A. (1992, 2nd ed.) *Unlawful Gain and Legitimate Profit in Islamic Law: Riba, Gharar and Islamic Banking*. London: Graham & Trotman Ltd.

Sarkawi, A.A., and Abdullah, A. (2015) Contextualising the Islamic fundamentals in the contemporary concepts of sustainability, livability and quality of life in the built environment. *Middle-East Journal of Scientific Research*. **23**(6), pp. 1249–1256.

Sarwaki, A.A., Abdullah, A. and Dali, N.M. (2016) The concept of sustainability from the Islamic perspective. *International Journal of Business, Economics and Law*. **9**(5), pp. 112–116.

Scott Cato, M. (2009) *Green Economics: An Introduction to Theory, Policy and Practice*. London and Sterling, VA: Earthscan.

Shah Haneef, S.S. (2002) Principles of environmental law in Islam. *Arab Law Quarterly*. **17**(3), pp. 241–254.

Shaikh, S.A. (2013) *Islam and Environmental Economics*. [online]. MPRA Paper no. 53799. Available from https://mpra.ub.uni-muenchen.de/53799/ [Accessed 12 April 2017].

Sid Ahmed, A. (1982) Finance islamique et développement. *Tiers-Monde*. **23**(92), *L'Islam et son Actualité pour le Tiers Monde*, pp. 877–890.

Sid Ahmed, A. (1990) Économie islamique, principes et réalités: l'expérience récente des pays arabes. Une première évaluation. *Tiers-Monde*. **31**(122), *Technologie et développement*, pp. 405–435.

Sonbol, A. (2009) Norms of war in Sunni Islam. In: Popovski, V., *et al.* (eds) *World Religions and Norms of War*. Tokyo; New York; Paris: United Nations University Press, pp. 282–302.

United Nations (1987) *Report of the World Commission on Environment and Development: Our Common Future*. Transmitted to the United Nations General Assembly as an Annex to document A/42/427.

United Nations (1992) *Rio Declaration on Environment and Development*, Report of the UN Conference on Environment and Development (Rio de Janeiro, 3–14 June 1992), A/CONF. 151/26 (Vol. I) 12 August 1992, Annex I.

United Nations (2015) *Transforming Our World: The 2030 Agenda for Sustainable Development*, Resolution adopted by the General Assembly on 25 September 2015, A/RES/70/1.

Vadillo, U.I., and Khalid, F.M. (1992) Trade and commerce in Islam. In: Khalid, F.M., and O'Brien, J. (eds), *Islam and Ecology*. London: Cassell, pp. 69–85.

Vaghefi, N., Siwar, C. and Aziz, S.A.A.G. (2015) Green economy: issues, approach and challenges in Muslim countries. *Theoretical Economics Letters*. **5**, pp. 28–35.

Van den Bergh, J.C.J.M. (2001) Ecological economics: themes, approaches, and differences with environmental economics. *Regional Environmental Change*. **2**(1), pp. 13–23.

Warde, I. (2012) Status of the global Islamic finance industry. In: Nethercott, C.R., and Eisenberg, D.M. (eds) *Islamic Finance: Law and Practice*. Oxford: Oxford University Press, pp. 1–14.

White, L. Jr (1967) The historical roots of our ecologic crises. *Science, New Series*. **155**(3767), pp. 1203–1207.

10 *Salam* finance

Securing the purpose of microfinancing

Atiq-ur-Rehman

1. The role of microfinance in poverty reduction and development: successful experiences and persistent scepticism

Microfinancing has been used as a tool for poverty eradication and rural development in many parts of the world and its success to achieve these objectives is well recognized.

There are in fact many success stories of microfinance initiatives, the most famous one being the experience developed by Prof. Muhammad Yunus, the founder of Grameen Bank. As is well known, the success of his microfinance programmes enabled Prof. Yunus to win the prestigious Nobel Peace Prize in 2006. The scientific studies finding significant impacts of microcredit on recipients' social and economic status are very large in number, and confirm the effectiveness of microfinancing as a means of development. These include, for instance, Pitt and Khandker (1998) and Khandker (2005), who investigated this relationship for Bangladesh; Crépon *et al.* (2015) for Morocco; Shirazi and Khan (2009) for Pakistan; Angelucci *et al.* (2015) for Mexico; Dunn and Arbuckle (2001) for Peru; etc.

However, there is also a large number of researchers who are sceptical about the success of microfinancing. For instance, Hulme and Mosley (1996) argue that 'poor households do not benefit from microfinance; it is only non-poor borrowers (with incomes above poverty lines) who can do well with microfinance and enjoy sizable positive impacts' (as quoted by Chowdhury, 2011, p. 166). The study also argues that a large proportion of those under the poverty line, after getting microfinance loans, ended up with less incremental income compared to those who didn't get any borrowing. Some people suggest that the poorest people ending up in an even worse state is related to the entrepreneurial mindset of the recipient. For example, Banerjee *et al.* (2013) failed to find any impact of microcredit on health, education, and women's empowerment in suburbs of Hyderabad, India. They conclude that households with an existing business at the time of the programme invest in durable goods, and their profits increase, but they also remarked that they find no impact of microfinance on measures of health, education or women's decision-making. Van Rooyen *et al.* (2012) report that in South Africa, in some cases microfinancing has even increased poverty and reduced children's education and women's empowerment.

Furthermore, there are many questions regarding the outreach of microfinance programmes and many researchers have accused microfinance programmes of not targeting the poorest people. For example, Morduch and Haley (2002) argue that even a well-designed microfinance programme is unlikely to have a positive impact on the poorest unless it specifically seeks to reach them through appropriate product design and targeting. Navajas *et al.* (2000) also support this idea and argue that in the absence of a well-specified targeting tool, the poorest will either be missed or they will tend to exclude themselves because they do not recognize the programmes as being conceived for them and their needs. Weiss and Montgomery (2005) summarize their analysis about microfinancing by saying that '[r]eaching the core poor is difficult and some of the reasons that made them difficult to reach with conventional financial instruments mean that they may also be high risk and therefore unattractive microfinance clients' (p. 412).

2. Why does microfinance fail?

As mentioned above, there are several pieces of evidence showing that microcredit programmes have been successful in alleviating poverty and uplifting the standard of life. However, at the same time, there are also studies that argue about the lack of relevant impact of microfinancing on the living standards of borrowers, particularly of those who are at the poorest level of income and/or wealth. Some authors even blame microfinance programmes for creating a debt trap, worsening the lives of borrowers.

Microcredit, if forwarded for the purpose of household enterprise, can enable the household to produce, therefore the result should be a positive change in the quality of life of the borrowers. So, what may be wrong with microfinance if it is unable to create positive impacts on society?

Academic literature presents different reasons for the negative or insignificant impacts of microfinance programmes on the recipient's living standards.

i.   First, a number of authors point out that the entrepreneurial aptitude of the borrowers determines the gains of microcredit. For example, Banerjee *et al.* (2013) argue that generally people with entrepreneurial skills enter into borrowing and produce better results. Those entering into borrowing without much entrepreneurial skill end up in an even worse situation.

ii. Second, the literature points out that there are large numbers of borrowers who are theoretically supposed to initiate a business out of the microcredit. However, they use the loan for some activity other than business, and therefore no impact of credit on level of poverty could be observed.

iii. Third, some studies argue that microcredit creates a debt trap which engulfs the earning of the borrowers and no impact of microcredit on poverty can be observed. This may happen if the productivity of capital is less than the interest payable on the microcredit.

iv. Many studies have pointed out that the outreach of microfinance programmes doesn't include the poorest because of their obvious inability to pay back: therefore, no benefit of microfinance is transmitted to these individuals.

The entrepreneurial skills mentioned above as a reason for the failure of microcredit (i) could be more precisely specified as the skill to market the product produced by the household enterprise. The rural household can often learn the skills to produce the goods, e.g. handicrafts or agricultural products, but these households may not be very capable of searching for suitable venues for the marketing of these goods. The middlemen responsible for selling the goods often exploit their position and extend very little share of the revenue generated by the product to the producer. The financer might be interested in the noble goals of eradicating poverty and improving the living standards of the recipient, but the middleman supposed to sell the products of the borrower in the market may not have any interest in any such thing. Having the typical profit-maximizing mindset, the middleman exploits the producer and may give him a part of the price which is insufficient for the improvement of living standards. Accordingly, the final result can be either a failure or a lower efficiency of the financing arrangement.

A large number of studies (e.g. Khan, 2014) have found that microcredit money has not been used by the recipients for income-generating activities (ii); rather, recipients use it for consumption on durables or some other non-productive activities. Therefore, because of absence of any new income-generating activity, no improvement in the living standard of recipients can be expected.

The third problem mentioned in the literature (iii) is the debt trap created by the microcredit. If the interest on microcredit is more than the productivity of capital, the recipient would have to pay more compared to what can be earned with this capital and, as a result, the burden of debt on the recipient shall keep increasing day by day, and the credit would worsen the living standards instead of improving them. Taylor (2012) analyses the microfinance crisis of Andhra Pradesh and found the debt trap to be an important reason. Bateman *et al.* (2012) analyse the microfinance loans in Bosnia and report that many individuals in Bosnia got hooked into taking out multiple microloans, using each new microloan to repay existing ones, hence in the process building up a mountain of personal debt that at some point needed to be repaid. A detailed history of over-indebtedness and the role of microfinance is also provided by Bateman and Chang (2012), reporting many cases where microfinance ended up with a debt trap.

As far as the fourth problem (iv) is concerned, specific discussion will be made later on, with regard to the *salam* contract in the Islamic legal tradition, and its advantages in coping with this issue.

3. How to manage microfinance problems? Advancing some practical solutions

The problems that put a limit on the functionality of microfinance institutions have to be taken into careful consideration in order to overcome any negative effect related to them.

The first problem (i) assumed to be responsible for undesirable impacts of microcredit is the lack of entrepreneurial skills. The lack of entrepreneurial skills specifically means inability of the recipient to market his products. This can happen due to three main reasons.

a. Rural communities may be easily trained for the production of some particular industrial or agricultural product, but it is not easy to teach them the marketing skills in the current highly competitive marketing environment.
b. Many microcredit programmes have been focused on women and their empowerment. Despite their remarkable social value and inner potential, even today in many traditional societies, women don't have sufficient access to the market. They are not so free yet to open up shops and sell their products, and still have limited freedom outside their homes. This also causes failure of household enterprises.
c. Even if the producer has access to the market and has sufficient skills to sell his/her products, managing both production and marketing issues can affect the efficiency of enterprise governance. Especially when markets are some distance away, it may not be very easy for the producer to manage both aspects, hence his production unit and his showroom/selling point. As a consequence, he may not be able to get appropriate payoff on his business.

To overcome these problems, one can suggest that the financer/microfinance institution (MFI) should agree to purchase the products and should take the responsibility of marketing them.

The financer, while forwarding the loan to the recipient, should enter into a contract to purchase the recipient's products. Therefore no recovery should be made to the MFI in form of cash. The marketing of the products would become the responsibility of the MFI, which has a sufficiently large set of resources to market the product in an appropriate way. This would shift the responsibility of marketing from the recipient to the financer. The financer, typically having a large pool of resources, in fact, can get a higher return by fostering a better market strategy. The producer won't have to pay back in the form of cash, therefore there would be very small chances of default. Another advantage would be that the producer can engage all his energies in the production process, which will increase the whole efficiency of the finance arrangement.

The second problem (ii) that earlier studies have found in the microcredit schemes is that the recipient may not utilize the loans in income-generating activities. This problem could be managed in two ways.

a. Financing should be done partly in the form of goods production and partly in the form of cash to meet the consumption needs of the recipient. For example, if a borrower needs a loan for the production of maize, the agreed loan could be given in the form of seeds, fertilizers and the use of a tractor vehicle instead of cash financing only. If someone wants to borrow for the production of garments, the financing could be provided in the form of stitching machines, unstitched cloths, etc. This would ensure that the loan is utilized for the purpose declared in the loan agreement.

b. The return is to be made (at least partially) in terms of product delivery; therefore the recipient must have to be engaged in production so that he/she can reimburse the obligation. Accordingly, a microfinance arrangement that bounds the financer to purchase the product would prevent the use of the loan for non-productive purposes, and can more easily result in an improvement in the living standard of the recipient.

The third problem mentioned in the literature (iii) that can limit the success of microcredit initiatives is the creation of the debt trap. If the productivity of capital is less than the interest to be paid, this will create a debt trap and the debt will keep increasing. This happens typically when the products don't get the prices they deserve. In the arrangement mentioned above, the chances of creating the debt trap are very low because of two reasons: (a) the borrowers don't need to pay interest. It is the product of the borrower that repays the financer as a return of the loan; (b) the product is expected to get a higher price because it is to be marketed by a financier who has access to the appropriate market. Therefore a microcredit arrangement in which the borrower reimburses its debt in the form of produced goods is expected to better overcome the problems associated with microfinancing and can enhance the usefulness of microcredit.

4. *Salam* financing

It is remarkable to note that the Islamic legal tradition seems to offer an appropriate tool to deal successfully with the problems related to the efficiency of microcredit initiatives, as discussed in the previous sections: namely, the contract of *salam* (i.e. future sale with advance payment).

Salam is an ancient mode of agricultural financing, popular in Arab societies. It consists of a contract of future sale, in which the buyer pays the price of the commodity in advance to the producer, who makes a commitment to deliver the commodity in a predefined date in the future. *Salam* was originally sanctioned during the time of the Prophet Muhammad (PBUH) to facilitate the trading activities of farmers who were awaiting the harvest of crops. In modern times it has also been applied to the production of raw materials and fungible goods in general (Mansuri, 2006; Ehsan and Shahzad, 2015; Rehman and Shahzad, 2017). *Istisna'* (i.e. contract of manufacture) is the counterpart of *salam* used for financing industrial goods, whereas the term *salam* is used for financing agricultural goods. Typically a *salam* contract works as follows.

- The financer agrees to purchase the goods produced by the recipient in a fixed amount at a fixed time.
- The quality and quantity of the goods to be traded have to be specified.
- The price of the good to be produced and payable by the financer is also specified in advance, and full payment has to be made at the conclusion of the contract.
- If the producer produces goods above the quantity agreed with the financer, he is free to sell/consume this surplus as he wants.
- Payment to the recipient can be made in terms of cash or commodity.
- If for some inevitable reason the producer fails to fulfil his obligation at the pre-specified time, he can be given further time by the financer to fulfil the obligation.

5. *Salam* as an instrument to finance the poorest

The *salam* mode of financing, with all its peculiarities as described in the previous section, can offer relevant means to include the poorest among the poor within microfinance initiatives, thus facing the issue of their economic inclusion as a persistent problem (Section 2, iv) in microcredit programmes (Aburaida, 2011; Rehman and Shahzad, 2017).

There is a quote by the famous British-born American comedian and actor Bob Hope (1903–2003) that says that 'A bank is a place that will lend you money if you can prove that you don't need it.' This is true in the sense that to get a loan from a bank one has to provide a guarantee with a value greater than the financing that has been requested. Therefore, the extremely marginalized classes, i.e. the people who are most in need, remain out of the finance circle. Under this condition, when applied to microfinance, also microcredit remains unable to reduce extreme poverty, and it is in this light that there are many criticisms of the current practices of micro financing for ignoring the poorest of poor.

Every bank tries to reduce chances of default; therefore, the institution focuses its activities on those who are capable of providing a reasonable mortgage or collateral. For microfinance institutions, it becomes more challenging to manage the defaults. Suppose someone is providing microfinance using interest-free loans. Every single default will reduce the capital invested in microfinance. There is no source of covering this loss and ultimately the sustainability of microfinance institutions (MFIs) will be at stake. This urges the search for a financial mode that can have greater sustainability, and *salam* arrangements can be considered as a viable tool in this direction.

In *salam* finance, in fact, where the financer agrees to purchase the goods produced by the recipient, it is possible to modify the finance arrangement to minimize the need of collateral. The MFI only needs to ensure that the finance is used for the purpose mentioned in the contract.

This could be done in two ways.

a. The financer pays most of the payment to the recipient in the form of goods needed for the production, e.g. seeds and fertilizers, machinery, raw materials. The financer can also make some cash payment for the urgent consumption needs of the recipient, but most of the financing could be done in terms of production goods. This will ensure that the financing will be used for production. As a consequence, there will be no or small need of external collateral if the financer can ensure that the financing is utilized for the purpose declared.

b. The financer will be reimbursed in terms of produced goods. This will reduce the chances of default because under this condition the recipient doesn't need to search a market for the products that the financer agrees to purchase.

In a nutshell, if the financer can somehow ensure himself that the finance is used for production, the need for external collateral can be reduced. The financer can achieve this by making most of the payment in the form of production goods instead of cash: in this way, also those having no collateral can become eligible to access microfinance.

6. Advantages of the proposed *salam* model, and foreseeable limits

There are numerous advantages related to *salam* financing, as outlined in the previous section, some of which can be summarized as follows, also in comparison with other financial models of Islamic finance (e.g. *murabahah* and *mudarabah*).

1. The *salam* model works according to cooperative principles in which the efficiency can increase through the sharing of the tasks. In reverse, in conventional investment models, the enterprise has to do many tasks simultaneously. The entrepreneur has to search for the productive skills, the capital as well as marketing. Therefore, for the households, it becomes very difficult to manage an enterprise. Many individuals who can produce, fail to find a marketing opportunity for their product and remain unable to get the rewards for their efforts. Many times this leads to the failure of the business venture. In the proposed model, the producer works only according to his specialty, without getting involved in marketing work.

2. The proposed mechanism avoids the criticism faced by *murabahah* financing (i.e. double sale with mark-up), where the financer's earning is not subject to any risk. In the *salam* model, the financer earns only when the recipient earns. The similarity between *murabahah* arrangements and

interest-based loans, which prevents many practising Muslims from fully embracing the core principles of risk sharing in Islamic finance, would gradually disappear by adapting the *salam* financing model.

3. The MFI does not need a guarantee or mortgage. The recipient purchases equipment/material for the production as per the terms decided in the agreement. The equipment serves as the mortgage for the financing.

4. The producer doesn't have to look for a market for his products if he is already ensured that his product is already sold. Therefore, he can utilize his full energy for production.

5. The poorest cohort of a society remains unable to get a benefit from microfinancing because of their inability to provide a reasonable guarantee. The conventional financing as well as the existing Islamic microfinance models need a collateral for the provision of loans which these individuals are unable to provide. In the *salam* model, as proposed above, the recipient makes an agreement with the financer to use the finance for purchasing the equipment required for production. This equipment can serve as a guarantee eliminating the need for an external mortgage. In this way the extremely marginalized class can gain the benefit of microfinancing.

6. The *salam* structure presents some advantages also in comparison with the model of *mudarabah* (i.e. silent partnership). In fact, the *mudarabah* model presupposes a lot of trust between the partners to be operational. As inter-personal trust may be lacking on many occasions, as the financer and the manager are strangers to one another, this impairs a widespread use of the *mudarabah* model in the practice. For instance, in the *mudarabah*, if the recipient declares a financial loss, this loss would have to be borne by the financer, who has then the need to verify the loss: this may prevent the financer from the provision of financing, when this review is difficult. But in the *salam* model, if the recipient is unable to fulfil his obligation at the pre-decided time, his obligation would not terminate, as the recipient would have to pay the financer at some later time. Therefore, there is no incentive for the recipient to declare a loss; furthermore, when there is a repayment based on the distribution of the products, the financer can be entitled to verify the progress of the production.

The major disadvantage of the proposed model is that the financer has to serve both as financial intermediary and as an enterprise responsible for selling goods produced by its clients. However, this disadvantage also creates an opportunity in that the financer can get an appropriate price for the product by better marketing the produced goods. Moreover, since the financer purchases goods in advance, the market fluctuation of prices cannot affect his business. The time between the sale agreement and the delivery also provides an opportunity of marketing before the commodity comes into the hands of the financer: therefore the financer can ensure a timely sale of his commodity with an appropriate profit.

7. Conclusions

Microfinance is a popular tool for financing poor and marginalized classes and there are many stories that witness its success. However, there are at the same time failed experiments of microfinance schemes, with many documented cases where microfinance remains unable to bring significant change to the lives of target communities.

As this chapter has shown, there are many reasons for the failure of these schemes.

First, there is the inability of the recipient of microfinance to market his/her product, hence a lack of entrepreneurial aptitude and skills (Banerjee *et al.*, 2013). Second, the borrowers are theoretically supposed to initiate a business out of the microcredit; but many times they use the loan for some other activities, therefore no impact of credit on poverty reduction can be observed. Third, some researchers argue that microcredit programmes create a debt trap which engulfs the earning of the borrowers. Last but not least, some researchers have pointed out that the outreach of microfinance programmes doesn't include the poorest because of their obvious inability to pay back: therefore, no benefit of microfinance is transmitted to these individuals.

Fortunately, *salam* finance has the ability to overcome all the problems mentioned above and can lead to a microfinance model free of the weaknesses that affect existing schemes.

In *salam* finance, the marketing strategy becomes a responsibility for the financer, so clients with lack of entrepreneurial skills can be engaged in production, while they don't need to worry about the marketing of their products. Moreover, in a *salam* agreement, the recipient of the loan would have to return the produced good, therefore it becomes highly unlikely that he/she uses the loan for some purpose other than production. Similarly, *salam* finance reduces the lack of external collateral and can easily be provided to the poorest cohort of society. It also enhances productivity by sharing the responsibilities of production and marketing.

In summary, *salam* represents a major opportunity for enhancing the productivity and efficiency of microfinance schemes, although this is not yet fully recognized even by the practitioners of Islamic microfinance. This chapter, on the contrary, suggests that it is now time to re-appreciate all the advantages related to the *salam* model as an effective tool of poverty reduction, and to promote its employ for social impact investments and financial inclusion.

References

Aburaida, K.M.M. (2011) Rural finance as a mechanism for poverty alleviation in Sudan, with an emphasis on '*salam*' mode. *European Scientific Journal*. **7**(26), pp. 157–166.

Angelucci, M., Karlan, D. and Zinman, J. (2015) Microcredit impacts: evidence from a randomized microcredit program placement experiment by Compartamos Banco. *American Economic Journal: Applied Economics*. **7**(1), pp. 151–182.

Banerjee, A., Chandrasekhar, A.G., Duflo, E. and Jackson, M.O. (2013) The diffusion of microfinance. *Science.* **341**, 1236498.

Bateman, M. and Chang, H.-J. (2012) Microfinance and the illusion of development: from hubris to nemesis in thirty years. *World Economic Review.* **1**, pp. 13–36.

Bateman, M., Sinković, D. and Škare, M. (2012) The contribution of the microfinance model to Bosnia's post-war reconstruction and development: how to destroy an economy and society without really trying. *ÖFSE Working Paper Series*, **36**. Vienna: Austrian Research Foundation for International Development.

Chowdhury, A. (2011) How effective is microfinance as a poverty reduction tool?. In: Sundaram, J.K., and Chowdhury, A. (eds) *Poor Poverty: The Impoverishment of Analysis, Measurement and Policies.* London and New York: Bloomsbury Academic and United Nations, pp. 165–183.

Crépon, B., Devoto, F., Duflo, E. and Parienté, W. (2015) Estimating the impact of microcredit on those who take it up: evidence from a randomized experiment in Morocco. *American Economic Journal: Applied Economics.* **7**(1), pp. 123–150.

Dunn, E. and Arbuckle, J.G. (2001) Microcredit and microenterprise performance: impact evidence from Peru. *Small Enterprise Development.* **12**(4), pp. 22–33.

Ehsan, A. and Shahzad, M.A. (2015) *Bayʿ salam*: a proposed model for *Shariʿah* compliant agriculture financing. *Business & Economic Review*, University of Peshawar. **7**(1), pp. 67–80.

Hulme, D. and Mosley, P. (1996) *Finance against Poverty* (2 Vols.). London: Routledge.

Khan, M.B. (2014) *Microfinance – A Poverty Reducing Agent in Pakistan.* [online]. Available from: https://ssrn.com/abstract=2426755 [Accessed 25 May 2017].

Khandker, S.R. (2005) Microfinance and poverty: evidence using panel data from Bangladesh. *The World Bank Economic Review.* **19**(2), pp. 263–286.

Mansuri, M.T. (2006) *Islamic Law of Contracts and Business Transactions.* New Delhi: Adam Publishers and Distributors.

Morduch, J. and Haley, B. (2002) Analysis of the effects of microfinance on poverty reduction. *NYU Wagner Working Papers Series*, **1014**.

Navajas, S., Schreiner, M., Meyer, R.L., Gonzalez-Vega, C. and Rodriguez-Meza, J. (2000) Microcredit and the poorest of the poor: theory and evidence from Bolivia. *World Development.* **28**(2), pp. 333–346.

Pitt, M.M. and Khandker, S.R. (1998) The impact of group based credit programs on poor households in Bangladesh: does the gender of participants matter?. *Journal of Political Economy.* **106**(5), pp. 958–996.

Rehman, A. and Shahzad M.A. (2017) Eradicating poverty through *salam* and *istisnaʿ*. Strategy for poverty reduction in rural Pakistan. *Maʿarif Research Journal.* January–June 2017.

Shirazi, N.S. and Khan, A.U. (2009) Role of Pakistan Poverty Alleviation Fund's micro credit in poverty alleviation: a case of Pakistan. *Pakistan Economic and Social Review.* **47**(2), pp. 215–228.

Taylor, M. (2012) The microfinance crisis in Andhra Pradesh, India: a window on rural distress?. *Food First Backgrounder.* **18**(3), pp. 1–4.

Van Rooyen, C., Stewart, R. and De Wet, T. (2012) The impact of microfinance in sub-Saharan Africa: a systematic review of the evidence. *World Development.* **40**(11), pp. 2249–2262.

Weiss, J. and Montgomery, H. (2005) Great expectations: microfinance and poverty reduction in Asia and Latin America. *Oxford Development Studies.* **33**(3–4), pp. 391–416.

11 *Waqf* based *takaful* model

A challenge for entrepreneurship

*Germán Rodríguez-Moreno**

1. Introduction

No one familiar with *waqf* ('charitable trust', pl. *awqaf*) would fail to acknowledge its importance as a concept and resilience as an institution.

Waqf as an institution 'stands out as one of the major achievements of Islamic civilisation' which has provided throughout history 'a myriad of the essential services such as health, education, municipal, etc. … at no cost whatsoever to the government' (Çizakça, 1998, pp. 43–44). It is a 'time-tested institution' (Shirazi *et al.*, 2015) which in its long history has made a deep and significant impact well beyond Islam and the Islamic world (Gaudiosi, 1988); and one which, as argued by Daud Vicary Abdullah, INCEIF (International Centre for Education in Islamic Finance) President and CEO from August 2011 to July 2017, '…with effective administration and implementation,[1] has a great spiritual and economic potential' (cited by Zainol *et al.*, 2014, p. 50), among other things, to 'eradicate urban poverty' (*ibidem*, p. 52).

Nevertheless, it is essential not to get carried away with grandiloquent statements and wishful thinking. The institution of *waqf* may be a (very) useful tool, but it is not, neither is it meant to be, a panacea. *Waqf* is not here to replace the role of the modern state appealing to a glorious past. As Timur Kuran has pointed out, 'the *waqf* system lack[ed the] flexibility necessary for efficient resource utilization', proving 'unsuitable to the relatively dynamic economy of the industrial age' (2001, pp. 841 and 843). In the same manner, it is important to acknowledge recent developments in the *waqf* institution that provides it with the flexibility it traditionally lacked. It 'now enjoys juristic personality, which means that it can sue and be sued as a legal entity[2] … Another major reform is that a modern *waqf* is overseen by a board of *mutawallis* endowed with powers similar to those of a corporate board of trustees' (*ibidem*).

In this light, the aim of this chapter is a modest (in terms of width of contents) but relevant (with regard to possible applications for social finance) one. It aims to test whether there is a role for *waqf* in a modern economy; or, looking at the other side of the coin, whether the private sector can be up to the challenge of employing *waqf* for social entrepreneurship.

More specifically, the study will focus on the potential relationship between *waqf* and *takaful*, i.e. 'Islamic insurance', for social entrepreneurial purposes; and the extent to which this alliance can satisfy at the same time both *Shariʿah* compliance criteria, belonging to the Islamic financial industry, and regulatory requirements that characterize contemporary financial services. *Takaful* is a capital intensive industry; *waqf* has to have a charitable purpose at all times – it would otherwise cease to be *waqf*, according to the principles of Islamic law. So, can this 'marriage' work?

To answer this question, the chapter will provide a description of *waqf* in the Islamic legal tradition (Section 2) and of a *takaful* undertaking according to current regulatory parameters (Section 3). Section 4 will advance the model of a *waqf* general *takaful* undertaking, while Section 5 will discuss the proposed model and certain fundamental related issues surrounding it. Some final considerations will conclude the discussion (Section 6).

2. The *waqf* as charitable trust and its conditions of validity[3]

The Hanafi school of law defines *waqf* as 'the detention of the corpus from the ownership of any person and the gift of its income or usufruct either presently or in the future, to some *charitable purpose*' (my emphasis) (cited in Gaudiosi, 1988, p. 1234).

The corpus (i.e. the *waqf* properties) is relinquished by the founder, but it is not acquired by any other person; it is said to be 'arrested' or 'detained'. The beneficiaries, while not the owners of the *waqf* property, have a legal interest in the usufruct of the *waqf* itself.

Four basic conditions of validity govern the *waqf*: it is required to be (i) irrevocable; (ii) perpetual; (iii) inalienable; and to have (iv) a charitable purpose.

(i) Once the property is declared *waqf* by its owner (known as the *waqif*), the *waqf* thereby created becomes irrevocable without any need to deliver possession to the beneficiary. The *waqif* may retain certain rights as to the management of the *waqf*, but the endowment itself is invalid unless it is irrevocable.

(ii) The *waqf* is perpetual.[4] The specific object of the *waqf* does not need to be permanent, however. If said object ceases to exist, the *waqf* income is applied to a similar charitable purpose. What is intended is the perpetuity of dedication and not necessarily the perpetuity of the object (Mohammad and Iman, 2010, p. 29).

(iii) The *waqf* is inalienable (as a *hadith* by 'Umar reports). The corpus cannot be the subject of 'any sale, disposition, mortgage, gift, inheritance, attachment, or any alienation whatsoever by the *waqif* or *mutawalli'* or their heirs (Gaudiosi, 1988, p.1235; Mohammad and Iman, 2010, p. 30).

(iv) The *waqf* must have a charitable purpose. The intention behind the creation of a *waqf* is the performance of 'good works pleasing to God' (Gaudiosi, 1988, p. 1237). This is a *sine qua non* condition without which the *waqf* would be void. The *waqf* throughout its history has commonly been used to endow mosques, schools and universities, hospitals and other charitable institutions where the beneficiaries have a right 'to be as informed as the *mutawalli'* regarding the provisions of the *waqf* instrument (*ibidem*, p. 1239). Once a *waqf* is established, its preservation and sustainability become paramount.

3. The t*akaful* undertaking as a tool for mutual assistance

Article 2 of the *Takaful* Act of Malaysia (1984) defines *takaful* as

> a scheme based on brotherhood, solidarity and mutual assistance which provides for *mutual financial aid and assistance* to the participants in case of need whereby the participants *mutually agree to contribute* for that purpose [my emphasis].

In turn, the Islamic Financial Services Board (IFSB) defines a *takaful* undertaking as

> a group of participants [who] agree among themselves to support one another jointly from the losses arising from specified risks. In a *takaful* arrangement the participants *contribute a sum of money as a* tabarruʿ [i.e. contribution in form of donation] *commitment* into a common fund that will be used mutually to assist the members against a specified type of loss or damage.
>
> (IFSB, 2009, p. 2; my emphasis)

In the light of the above definitions, the participants in a *takaful* undertaking become so only on the basis of contributing a sum of money, however small. If there is no contribution by them or on their behalf, a person cannot become a participant. This monetary contribution is in the form of a *tabarruʿ* commitment, i.e. a donation. This is important given that the participants in a *takaful* scheme structured around a *waqf* fund will probably not be able to make a full contribution.[5] However, they must make a contribution, however nominal in value, to be classed as a participant.

In a normal *takaful* undertaking, the level of contributions that a participant has to make is the result of a rather complex actuarial formula, the aim of which is to meet and preserve solvency ratio requirements. The Participants Risk Fund (PRF) has to be funded at all times to allow the *takaful* undertaking to meet all claims as they arise. As a rule of thumb, a newly set up general insurance undertaking takes around four years to break even. Given the capital requirements, the cash flow in the initial period is one way, i.e. investment and expense, some income but certainly not profits. In a *waqf* model, the level of participants' contributions not met by the participants will have to be met by the Takaful Operator (TO) and other donors. Such potential demands over a long period of time will have to be taken into consideration by a TO prior to establishing a *waqf* fund. Given the relatively small contributions made by the participants, any breakeven point may have to wait longer than what it would be otherwise. This is an issue that would undermine the viability of any venture, not to mention a venture of this type in a heavily regulated industry.

Nevertheless, the long term aim of a *waqf* based model *takaful* undertaking ought to be a viable going concern in its own right, independent of the TO's philanthropy. Any deficit thereafter, in the event there is one, would be obtained as a *qard hasan* (i.e. 'benevolent loan' according to Islamic law) from the TO and/or other sources.

4. The *Waqf* General *Takaful* Undertaking: advancing a *waqf/takaful* combined structure

A *Waqf* General *Takaful* Undertaking,[6] matching *waqf* and *takaful* in a marriage between entrepreneurial and philanthropic purposes, should meet the following features (see Figure 11.1 for a graphical representation).

1) A *Waqf* Fund (WF) is established from the initial donation of seed money by the TO, a limited liability company.[7]
2) Donation of seed money (if the capital donated by TO is not sufficient to reach the minimum regulatory capital) and/or operating capital by one or more donors different to the TO.[8]
3) Participants pay contributions into the Participants' Fund (PF).
4) The PF is channelled into the Participants' Risk Fund (PRF),[9] i.e. the *tabarru'* account.
5) The funds in the PRF are donated by the Participants (the *tabarru'* commitment) to the WF.
6) The WF is divided into, at least, two sub-funds: (i) the underwriting fund (WUF); and (ii) the investment fund (WIF). The WIF is invested in *Shari'ah* compliant asset investments.
7) The investment profit, if any, is returned to the WUF.
8) The *wakalah* fee is paid to the TO out of the WUF. The fee, which consists of agency commission and administration expenses, is channelled into the TO Shareholders' Fund (8a).
9) At year end, the surplus (after deducting claims, re-*takaful* and reserves) in WF will be retained in the WUF.[10]

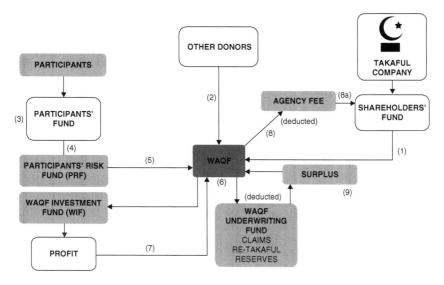

Figure 11.1. Waqf based general *takaful* model (*wakalah waqf* general insurance)
(Author's personal elaboration)

5. Discussing the proposed model

5.1. Takaful *operator as* waqif: *essential or necessary?*

Regardless of what model is adopted for a *takaful* company, what seems to be an immovable fixture in all analyses on the subject is the figure of the TO.

However, the IFSB clarifies at the end of its definition of Takaful Undertaking that 'in principle it could be a pure mutual structure' (IFSB, 2009, p. 2). In other words, a Takaful Undertaking need not outsource its management. In a seldom referred to footnote, the IFSB adds the two reasons that, in its view, explain why pure mutual structures are not normally used. First they 'are not recognised in a number of countries' legal systems. Second, and more fundamentally, '*a newly formed* mutual insurance company would hardly be able to meet the capital adequacy requirements that are now standard' (emphasis added) (IFSB, 2009, p. 2, footnote 4). It is thus clear that the TO is not an indispensable feature of a Takaful Undertaking. The existence of the TO is not a *Shari'ah* requirement. It is rather the product of a business model which owes more to necessity than to best practice.

The above consideration takes on greater importance when discussing specifically the *waqf* model in a Takaful Undertaking. The pure mutual structure (see Figure 11.2) is the closest to a *waqf*, and *vice versa:* (i) the participants

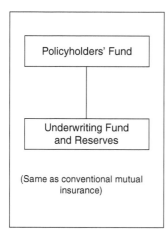

- In principle a Takaful under-taking could be a pure mutual structure

- Management and underwriting are done in-house by the same legal entity

- There is no Qur'anic doctrine requiring otherwise
- A newly formed mutual insurance company, however, would probably be unable to meet the capital adequacy requirements that are now standard

- Therefore, one important role of the TO is to provide the capital backing that allows such requirements to be met

Figure 11.2. Mutual basic structure
(Author's personal elaboration)

(beneficiaries) and the owners of the (*waqf*/mutual) fund are one and the same; (ii) the objective of both is not to profit from but to benefit the participants; and (iii) to the extent profits are generated, these are not distributed but reinvested.

The two obvious differences are that: (i) in a pure mutual insurance structure, management and underwriting are done in-house by the same legal entity; and (ii) a mutual insurance undertaking is not obliged to invest its assets in *Shari'ah* compliant instruments. But investment in *Shari'ah* compliant instruments does not require the existence of a TO. In other words, the existence of a TO does not make a Takaful Undertaking more or less *Shari'ah* compliant; nor is it the result of best practice, i.e. it does not make said undertaking more efficient or more prudent.[11] The existence and role of the TO have more to do with the difficulty of raising the required (seed) regulatory capital and/or maintaining the required solvency ratio.[12]

Therefore, accepting that there will be a TO as part of a Takaful Undertaking, the question is how this should work if there were a *waqf* fund. It is interesting to notice that in its 'stock-taking exercise', the IFSB confirmed that 'the most frequently used models ... are the *mudarabah, wakalah* and *wakalah-mudarabah* models' (IFSB, 2009, p. 3). In other words, the IFSB does not include in its Governance Guidelines the *waqf* model. It does not mean that the *waqf* model is not financially viable. It suggests, however, that the other models are more financially interesting and/or rewarding to the TO. And herein lies the challenge referred to above: Who chooses the model to use? And who should be the primary beneficiary of any model adopted?

5.2. *Sources of funds*

One thing that seems to be taken for granted in a lot of the literature on the topic is that a *waqf* fund in a Takaful Undertaking has only two sources of funds: the Participants and the TO. There is, however, nothing anywhere that proscribes that a *waqf* fund should or could not receive donations from other sources, i.e. donors different from the TO.[13] The development of *waqf* from being the product of a donation of exclusively immovable property to cash *waqf* to corporate *waqf* opens up a plethora of opportunities and alternatives. A *waqf* fund may now be the recipient of donations from a multiplicity of donors different from and in addition to the participants, not to mention the TO.

Given that there is a TO which is not only a donor but also the manager of the *waqf* fund, we need to think of an appropriate commercial structure for that relationship to occur. The single criterion to adopt is that model which allows the long term preservation of the *waqf* fund. In a Takaful Undertaking (as in any conventional general insurance company), the most important thing is the welfare of the technical reserves, i.e. the capacity of the Takaful Undertaking to meet claims as and when they arise. Therefore, the management model to adopt is the one that siphons out the least amount of capital from the *waqf* fund. In this context, and for the reasons explained later, the *wakalah* model may be the most appropriate.

In this light, we need to dissect each one of the elements in turn making up a combined *wakalah waqf* model General Takaful Undertaking with a view to establish the nature and size of the challenge.

Wakalah *model and fee*

The aim in a *waqf* model is to ensure the sustainability and viability of the *waqf*. In the context of a Takaful Undertaking, the TO provides two functions: management and underwriting. Underwriting (insurance services) includes: (i) product development; (ii) the preparation of the insurance policy; (iii) the collection of contributions; (iv) the assessment of claims; and (v) the distribution of compensations. Management services include the management of investment funds on either a *mudarabah*, *wakalah* or *waqf* basis.

The *waqf* model in the context of a Takaful Undertaking resembles in almost all features a mutual insurance company. However, for the reasons explained above regarding the difficulty of meeting the capital adequacy requirements, a mutual insurance company structure is not a viable option at inception.[14]

To ensure the long term sustainability and viability of a General Takaful Undertaking, the most important task is to ensure the health of the technical provisions.[15] Therefore, the optimum structure is that which allows the WF to retain the largest amount of capital. The *wakalah* model, *prima facie*, meets this requirement to the extent that the TO as *wakil* receives a fee for its services and nothing more. Schematically, it works as follows:

1) There is a principal-agent relationship. The *waqf* fund is the principal; and the TO the agent.[16]
2) The *wakalah* fee is paid out of the contributions, made by way of donations, into the *waqf* fund.
3) The level of the *wakalah* fee is agreed upfront and must be expressly stated in the contract between the parties. The criterion upon which the fee is calculated may be, for example, a percentage of contributions.
4) The *wakalah* fee consists of (i) management expenses; (ii) distribution costs, including intermediaries' remuneration; and (iii) a margin of operational profit.

There is no objection to the TO being paid for services rendered. Further, the TO is entitled to recover its expenses and costs incurred in providing those services.[17] And arguably, the TO may also be entitled to a reasonable (under the circumstances) margin of operational profit, which should be included in the fee. But the fee should be all the TO receives as *wakil*.

The TO is not entitled to share in the distribution of profit generated by the *waqf* fund, even though said profit may owe, no doubt, something to the investment skills of the TO. Perversely, some have argued that the *wakil* may need to be given a performance incentive (as if the fee were not sufficient). Were this not bad enough, some argue that said incentive should come out of the underwriting surplus.[18] To put it bluntly, if the TO wants to make money for its shareholders (and the TO is perfectly entitled to do so), then the TO should be well advised to put its money into a different venture. The TO, however, cannot make a donation to establish and/or to develop a *waqf* fund expecting to profit from it.[19] All profit created by a *waqf* fund belongs exclusively to the *waqf* and its use is for the benefit of the beneficiaries as per the *waqf* instrument. Furthermore, the reason to opt for a *waqf* model in the first instance is that the beneficiaries are, by definition, unable to make a contribution expected of a participant if they were to adopt a different Takaful Undertaking model. Were the Participants able to meet the expected contributions in accordance with underwriting standards, there would not be a need to structure a Takaful Undertaking around a *waqf* fund.

5.3. The relationship between the takaful operator and the participants

The literature on *waqf* tends to praise (very) highly the role of the *waqif*: 'the natural tendency among the Muslim rich to do good deeds' (Çizakça, 1998, p. 50) whilst either completely ignoring the beneficiaries or looking at them rather patronisingly as mere passive recipients: 'We can grant charity to poor people …' (Abdullah, 2014, p. 20) or 'assist[ing] these "unfortunate people" ' (Salman and Htay, 2012, p. 234) as if poverty were the result of bad luck or charity were something that could possibly substitute the question of social rights. The IFSB, in its Guiding Principles on Governance for Takaful Undertakings, has alerted to the existence of an uneven relationship between the Takaful Operator and the participants which is characterized by information asymmetry and misalignment of incentives (IFSB, 2009, p. 8).

Conflicts of interest

In its paper on Governance (2009), the IFSB aims to champion the Governance of Takaful Undertakings in accordance with internationally recognized best practice standards. The IFSB recognizes that a 'hybrid' structure between a mutual (WF, in this case) and a proprietary entity (the TO) may lead to conflicts of interest between the shareholders and the participants. The IFSB recommends that the TO has in place a comprehensive governance framework appropriate for *takaful* business models adopted to define and preserve the independence and integrity of each organ of governance. The rationale behind this recommendation is that the TO (as *wakil* or *mudarib*) has considerable discretion. The TO, for example, initiates and/or manages the *takaful* scheme, including determining the range of products, pricing, terms and conditions of each contract, etc.; and there is no clear mechanism by which the Participants can control, influence and/or sanction the behaviour of the TO. The Participants lack the power or information to monitor and control the TO (information asymmetry). The IFSB proposes a balanced approach that considers the interests of all stakeholders and calls for their fair treatment. The governance structure to be put in place shall represent the rights and interests of all stakeholders, including the Participants. This obviously includes the Participants in a *waqf* scheme based Takaful Undertaking.

Further, the IFSB recommends that a Governance Committee (GC) is established, and that it includes (i) an independent non-executive director (experienced and able to contribute), (ii) a *Shari'ah* scholar, and (iii) an actuary. And it adds, that any increase in membership is to be made up of independents. Said independents, I would argue, need to include at least one representative of the Participants. The more effective checks and balances are inserted into the system, the more likely it is that the otherwise unbalanced relationship between the TO and the Participants and the risks attached to it are minimized.

Multiple financing as a democratizing factor

Traditionally, the parties to a *waqf* are the founder (*waqif*), the trustee (*mutawalli*), the judge (*qadi*) and the beneficiaries. The founder may appoint himself a trustee. As a *waqif*, the founder has considerable latitude in setting out the terms and conditions of the operation of the *waqf*, including (i) the appointment/dismissal of the *mutawalli*, (ii) the selection of the beneficiaries, and (iii) the distribution of the *waqf* income. To the *waqif* and *mutawalli* roles, we need to add the role as agent (*wakil*) of the *waqf* fund. The founder thus becomes an all powerful figure with all the risks attached to it referred to by the IFBS, as detailed above.

However, three relatively recent developments may act as effective checks and balances: (i) the *waqf* as a juristic person which may sue and be sued; (ii) the power and composition of the *mutawallis*, now structured as a board of directors with executive powers, including the ability to alter investments and spending; and (iii) the sources of finance which now include movables such as cash and company shares. The *waqf* structure may become more flexible and responsive to the needs of its stakeholders and the *waqf* instrument should reflect this.[20] The era of the single, all powerful *waqif* is reaching its twilight and perhaps not before time.

The fact that the sources of financing of a *waqf* may be both movable and immovable property open up an opportunity not only of multiplying the sources of funds but also the number of parties funding a *waqf* project. If the board of *mutawallis* procures representation for all the stakeholders (included, but not limited to, funders and beneficiaries),[21] this may democratize the decision-making process by procuring efficiency and fairness. In the context of a Takaful Undertaking, this multiplicity of funding parties may contribute to minimizing the conflicts of interests that traditionally have marred the relationship between the TO and the beneficiaries. This accords with the principles of and best practice recommendations promoted by the IFSB in its Governance Paper (2009).

6. Conclusions

We cannot underestimate the challenges facing a newly formed *waqf* based model general Takaful Undertaking to become a viable going concern in its own right. It is not a model popular with TOs, which legitimately seek a profitable venture for their own shareholders. As observed by Timur Kuran, 'the *waqf* system is no longer seen as the most reliable vehicle for sheltering wealth' (2001, p. 890). In addition, modern governance standards demand professional, responsive, transparent and fair management of both resources and stakeholders. Donating is no longer a matter of acquiring the right to manage, appoint and set up investment strategies. It now requires being accountable to stakeholders, regulators and government agencies. Many may not have an appetite to get involved in a venture of this type. But the need is there.

On the other hand, a *waqf* fund may now be the recipient of funds from several sources and a multiplicity of parties (from government agencies to small crowdfunding contributors). The financing responsibility need not rest on a sole philanthropist. This undoubtedly opens up opportunities for financing a plethora of charitable ventures which would find it difficult to raise sufficient capital. Ventures which would otherwise be unviable for lack of sufficient capital and a long lead prior to breaking even, may now become viable as venture-financing is a shared responsibility.

This chapter has deliberately dealt with a case in the highly regulated industry of insurance services to make a simple statement: if a *waqf* model can work here, it can work anywhere.

Notes

* **Acknowledgment**: I am grateful to Gen Rodríguez for her review of and comments on an earlier draft.
1 Whilst it is not the aim of this chapter to look at the history of *waqf* as an institution, Daud Vicary's reference to 'effective administration and implementation' tacitly acknowledges a major problem that has confronted this institution throughout its long history: ineffective administration and poor management.
2 Paradoxically, as Gaudiosi (1988) acknowledges, Merton College ceases to be a *waqf* ten years after its creation when in becomes incorporated in 1274. It has taken the *waqf* institution over 800 years to reach this point, i.e. to be recognized as having its own juristic personality, in the Muslim world.
3 The review of the origins of *waqf* heavily borrows in Section 2 from Gaudiosi (1988).
4 There have always been exceptions to this rule. Temporal *waqf* was allowed by Imam Abu Yusuf and the Maliki school of law; and it is currently recognized in Sudan and Egypt.
5 For the sake of simplicity, let us assume that our case study is the provision of dental (including orthodontic) care for the poor and college students on a grant living in a given city. Imagine that a normal insurance premium for dental care is 300 euro equivalent per person per year, and that this premium gives you an annual free check up and up to 40 per cent discount (50 per cent in the case of children under 12) on normal dental treatment. In other words, this is the kind of service that low income families and young students on a grant would not be able to afford. Using dental health care as an example is appropriate as it is the kind of service that is not covered fully or at all as part of the otherwise universal health care provided in many countries.
6 Given that we are talking about a *waqf* structure, I am working on the assumption that the venture contemplated here is General Takaful as it is less capital intensive than Family Takaful. The viability and sustainability challenges facing a *waqf* Family Takaful venture would be considerable to say the least.
7 For example, minimum regulatory capital in the case of Malaysia is RM 100 million (approx. USD 23 million); and in Indonesia, it is IDR 100 billion (approx. USD 7 million).
8 It is assumed that the TO would hold the *takaful* licence and not any other direct donor.
9 I have adopted the IFSB terminology to refer to the Participants' Investment Fund and Participants' Risk Fund, which are otherwise referred to by different authors as the Participants' Account and the Participants' Special Account respectively.
10 A general *takaful* undertaking does not need to generate an underwriting surplus. To the extent it does, it must be distributed exclusively to the beneficiaries in the form of lower contributions in future years. To the extent that some part of the surplus is not so distributed to the beneficiaries, it should be retained in the WUF. What should never happen is that the TO benefits from said distribution. The *Shari'ah* Committee of the Islamic Development Bank (IDB) does not agree with the TO benefiting from any underwriting surplus as it is not a profit; and

generating a surplus may be not more than an artificial mechanism used by the TO to increase contributions to the detriment of the beneficiaries for the exclusive benefit of the TO's shareholders (see IFSB, 2009, p. 4, footnote 7; and p. 15, footnote 24).

11 It may be argued that, unless a Takaful Operator acts with responsibility and solidarity, the *waqf* model for a Takaful Undertaking is doomed to failure.

12 Challenging the IFSB's premise is not part of this chapter, but I must admit that we need not accept it as a truism.

13 We will discuss below the issue of management and management rights of a *waqf* fund. But in principle, good management should be exclusively based on the sustainability of the model and the welfare of the beneficiaries.

14 It is beyond the remit of this chapter to explore the possibility of starting with one structure (WF and TO as separate entities) with a view to ending up with a single entity in the form of a mutual structure. But it would be worth testing the IFSB's premise that a mutual structure becomes prohibitive given the capital adequacy requirements.

15 Technical provisions are the estimates of future claims payable in respect of insured events that *have already happened* (or the consequence of such events) that are covered by the policy. Technical provisions are *liabilities* and not part of capital. Technical provisions or reserves are normally the largest item on a general insurer's balance sheet. The balance sheet is a management tool to assess the Takaful Undertaking's solvency (Dreksler *et al.*, 2013, p. 3).

16 Under any other Takaful model, the principal will be the Participants, but not in the case of a *waqf* which, by definition, is itself the owner of the fund.

17 I am assuming that these costs are not part of the donation, although they could be.

18 See Salman *et al.* (2015, p. 13), where we are told that the *waqf* model

> has additional features [*sic*] to the hybrid *wakalah-mudarabah* model. That additional feature is that the shareholders need to put up the same amount of money in the PRF to start the *waqf*. *Other than the initial donation as* waqf, *the rest will be similar to the hybrid* wakalah-mudarabah *model*. This is demonstrated by Diagram 4.7.
>
> (emphasis added)

And what we see when we look at said diagram in detail is that both the underwriting surplus from the PRF and the profit from the PIF are shared with the TO Shareholders' Fund [*sic*].

19 Given that the Takaful Operator has made a donation, i.e. a gift, the narration of Ibn Abbas becomes relevant: 'He who goes back on his gift is like a dog that eats its vomit.'

20 *Waqfs*, in the words of Timur Kuran, 'may be formed by pooling the resources of thousands of small contributors. Their founders may include governments and firms' (2001, p. 890). Writing almost 20 years ago, Timur Kuran probably did not have crowdfunding in mind, but there is no reason to exclude it as a source of finance of the modern *waqf*.

21 In accordance with the IFSB Governance Principle 2.1: 'TOs shall have in place an appropriate governance structure that represents the rights and interests of *takaful* participants' (2009, p. 12).

Bibliography

Abdullah, M. (2014) *Waqf*: a proposed model for Islamic finance. *Market Forces: College of Management Sciences.* 9(1), pp. 15–28.

Ahmad, M. (2015) Cash *waqf*: historical evolution, nature and role as an alternative to *riba*-based financing for the grass root. *Journal of Islamic Finance.* 4(1), pp. 63–74.

Asharaf Mohd, R., and Adbullaah, J. (2013) Corporate *waqf* model and its distinctive features: the future of Islamic philanthropy. Paper presented at the World Universities Islamic Philanthropy Conference 2013, Menara Bank Islam, Kuala Lumpur.

Chowdhury, S.R., Ghazali, M.F.B. and Ibrahim, M.F. (2011) Economics of cash *waqf* management in Malaysia: a proposed cash *waqf* model for practitioners and future researchers. *African Journal of Business Management.* 5(30), pp. 12155–12163.

Çizakça, M. (1998) *Awqaf* in history and its implications for modern Islamic economies. *Islamic Economic Studies.* 6(1), pp. 43–70.

Çizakça, M. (2013) The new *waqf* law prepared by IDB/IRTI and the Kuwait Public Foundation: a critical assessment. *Fourth Draft of the Paper submitted at the PNB Paribas-INCEIF Centre for Islamic Wealth Management Inaugural Colloquium*, 19 December 2013, Kuala Lumpur.

Dreksler, S., *et al.* (2013) *Solvency II Technical Provisions for General Insurers.* London: Institute and Faculty of Actuaries.

Gaudiosi, M.M. (1988) The influence of the Islamic law of *waqf* on the development of the trust in England: the case of Merton College. *University of Pennsylvania Law Review.* 136, pp. 1231–1261.

IFSB (Islamic Financial Services Board) (2009) *Guiding Principles on Governance for* Takaful *(Islamic Insurance) Undertakings* [online]. Available from: www.ifsb.org/standard/ED8Takaful%20Governance%20Standard.pdf [Accessed 12 August 2017]. Kuala Lumpur: Islamic Finance Services Board, pp. 1–30.

Jalil, M.I.A., Yahya, S. and Pitchay, A.A. (2016) The contemporary model of *waqf* structure. Conference paper presented at the International Conference on Islamic Leadership and Management 2016, Universiti Islam Sultan Sharif Ali, Brunei. *Research Gate.* [online; accessed 24 August 2017].

Kahf, M. (2004) *Shari'ah* and historical aspects of *zakah* and *awqaf*. Paper presented at the Islamic Research and Training Institute, Islamic Development Bank, Jeddah.

Kuran, T. (2001) The provision of public goods under Islamic law: origins, impact, and limitations of the *waqf* system. *Law & Society Review.* 35(4), pp. 841–898.

Mohammad, M.T., and Iman, A.H. (2010) *Obstacles of the current concept of* waqf *to the development of* waqf *properties and the recommended alternative* [online]. Available from: http://eprints.utm.my/501/1/27–38.pdf [Accessed 20 August 2017], pp. 27–38.

Nizamoglu, C. (undated) The institution of *waqf* as a solution to the economic crisis. *Muslim Heritage* [online]. Available from: muslimheritage.com/article/institution-waqf-solution-economic-crisis [Accessed 24 August 2017].

Norton Rose Fulbright (2017) *2017: Insurance Regulation in Asia Pacific. Ten Things to Know about 20 Countries.* Norton Rose Fulbright.

Raimi, L., Patel, A. and Adelopo, I. (2014) Corporate social responsibility, *waqf* system and *zakat* system as faith-based model for poverty reduction. *World Journal of Entrepreneurship, Management and Sustainable Development.* 10(3), pp. 228–242.

Salarzehi, H., Armesh, H. and Nikbin, D. (2010) *Waqf* as a social entrepreneurship model in Islam. *International Journal of Business and Management.* 5(7), pp. 179–186.

Salman, S.A., and Htay, S.N.N. (2012) Introducing *waqf* based *takaful* model in India. *Tazkia Islamic Finance & Business Review.* 7(2), pp. 234–255.

Salman, S.A., Rashid, H.M.R. and Htay, S.N.N. (2015) *Takaful* (Islamic insurance): when we started and where we are now. *International Journal of Economics, Finance and Management Sciences.* Special Issue: Islamic Finance System and Economic Growth: Theory and Empirical Studies. 3(5–2), pp. 7–15.

Shirazi, N.S., Obaidullah, M. and Haneef, M.A. (2015) Integration of *waqf* and Islamic microfinance for poverty reduction: case of Pakistan. *IRTI Working Papers Series*, Working Paper 1436–05, pp. 1–37.

Takaful Act (1984) Laws of Malaysia, Act 312.

Zainol, F.A., Norhayate, W., Daud, W., Abdullah, Z. and Yaacob, M.R. (2014) Social entrepreneurship via corporate *waqf*: a case of Islamic Chamber of Commerce (ICC) in Malaysia. *Global Journal of Commerce & Management Perspective.* 3(5), pp. 50–53.

Zakaria, A.A.M., Samad, R.R.A. and Shafii, Z. (2012) Venture philanthropy – *Waqf* practices and its implementation: scenario in Malaysia. *International Journal of Business, Economics and Law.* 1, pp. 108–115.

12 *Zakat*: its micro-entrepreneurship model and socio-humanitarian impact

Mohd Ma'Sum Billah

1. Introduction

Today's world is dominated by a self-oriented capitalism, while half of its population live on less than $2.50 a day (Global Issues, 2013). Numerous strategic steps have been undertaken by several governments, international organizations, NGOs and individuals through different schemes (namely social finance, social business, micro-credit, trusts, foundations, ethical funds, charity and the like) aiming at poverty eradication by meeting one's basic needs with food, shelter, health care and education. But the true objective of poverty eradication, that is to say, promoting sustainable development by making everyone economically self-reliant, also through micro-entrepreneurship and socio-humanitarian tools, unfortunately, has not been achieved yet.

This chapter looks at *zakat* as a divine obligatory tax in Islam (Shad, 1986, p. 13) which is imposed on the wealthier and is aimed at poverty eradication. In particular it argues that *zakat*, when conceptualized within the general objectives of Islamic law (*maqasid al-Shari'ah*) (Section 2), can be seen as an instrument for general human welfare for all the members of the community, where economic development is fostered also through micro-entrepreneurial mechanisms with an underlying humanitarian impact.

Accordingly, after indicating the recipients of *zakat* according to the *Qur'an* (Section 3), the chapter shows how *zakat* is not a mere charity to satisfy the beggars in their short-term needs with no plan, but it is indeed a potential platform to promote micro-entrepreneurship (Section 4) with a socio-humanitarian impact within the community, able to achieve a sustainable long-term objective of poverty eradication (Section 5).

In this light, the study indicates the mechanisms to facilitate the implementation of *zakat* in relation to entrepreneurial objectives also through cooperatives, *takaful* and capacity building, and provides some final recommendations to this objective (Section 6).

2. *Zakat* sources, *maqasid al-Shari'ah* and human welfare

Zakat (alms) is among the five tenets of Islam, and is divinely ruled as an obligatory tax (Mannan, 1970, p. 220; Saud, 1988, p. 193) aiming at purifying one's soul and wealth leading to a socio-economic justice for all with sharing and caring concern (Muhammad, 1993, p. 1). The recipients with beneficial interest of *zakat* are categorized in the *Qur'an* as a divine guideline for just distribution (see Section 3).[1]

Zakat may play an important role in providing socio-economic security in the contemporary society, with its sources deriving from income over commercial businesses, savings, shares, gold and silver, wealth, asset and property in form of agro-products.[2]

To determine whether the goods and wealth in issue are indeed *zakatable* (i.e. able to be subject to *zakat*), it is important to apply, *inter alia*, the tradable test by the doctrine of *qiyas* (analogy) and *masalih al-mursalah* (public interest), so to arrive to an appropriate estimation. This is to enable the recipients to maximize with the benefit from *zakat* in ways recognized by the *Shari'ah*. *Zakatable* wealth must be a net after deduction for one's self expenditures, family maintenance and settlement of debts and dues.

It is important to note that, while the modern social security system offers only material assistance to the needy, *zakat* provides a socio-humanitarian economic support, since in Islam it does not represent a mere physical act of philanthropy to satisfy the beggars temporarily, but it goes beyond that limit by embodying spiritual, moral and educational values besides socio-economic and humanitarian concern and related welfare sustainability.

Furthermore, an effective management of *zakat* in the light of the *maqasid al-Shari'ah* (the 'purposes of the divine *Shari'ah*') can represent an alternative to today's capitalism and its debt-based economy with no risk-sharing mechanism (Mannan, 1970, p. 220).

In fact, *zakat* is not merely a form of philanthropy, but is a divine mandatory tax collected from those who are wealthy, and distributed among the recipients as described in the Holy *Qur'an* (see Section 3). The prime objective of *zakat* is not only to reduce the rate of poverty in the society by economic distribution, but to purify one's soul and wealth, towards socio-economic and humanitarian concerns: accordingly, it represents a socio-humanitarian model of general human welfare, which is actually alternative to mainstream capitalism.[3]

It is thus important to analyse and understand the true mechanism of *zakat* as per *maqasid al-Shari'ah*. *Zakat* is imposed on wealth and income at a customary rate of 2.5 per cent, but on agricultural products, precious metals, minerals and livestock, the *zakat* is payable at a rate varying between 2.5 per cent and 20 per cent, depending on the type of *zakatable* goods and products. *Zakat* does not only provide financial assistance for the needy, but also purifies one's soul so as to make one closer to Allah and also purifies one's property and wealth so as to eliminate one from any sense of selfishness while creating an environment with socio-humanitarian care and concern. In this way, as previously remarked, its rationale constitutes an alternative paradigm to conventional capitalism for collective welfare.

The scope of *zakat* needs to be rationally interpreted today by looking at the socio-economic needs of the contemporary society, while referring to the guidance and practices of the golden era of the Prophet (PBUH). In the early Islamic period, the idea of levying *zakat* was on an annual savings of a prescribed amount, after deducting self and family maintenance and settlement of one's debts. Today, the notion of *zakatable* properties has to be interpreted in relation to the doctrine of *masalih al-mursalah* (public interest), hence enabling *zakat* to be practised with a wider scope in view of providing a solution to the destitute in today's reality. Thus, '*zakatable* wealth' should also include today any annual savings against the amount prescribed by the *Shari'ah*, be it in the form of currency or otherwise legitimate net income.

Next to the collection, also the distribution of *zakat* needs to be interpreted in relation to a long-term plan of socio-entrepreneurship environment based on its welfare model.

On the one side, *zakat* is an institution aimed at eradicating poverty by providing financial protection to the needy. It is in fact ruled by Allah that in everyone's wealth there is a right for the persons in need: 'And in their properties there was the right of the *sa'il* [the beggar who asks] and the *mahrum* [the poor who does not ask others]' (Q. 51:19).

On the other side, in the light of the *maqasid al-Shari'ah*, not only do *zakat* rules aim at providing social security for the poor and needy, but also to develop a balanced economic growth (al-Harran, 1993, p. 121), as well as to become a vehicle of spiritual purity and development.

Considering all this, the objectives of *zakat* can be summed up as follows.

First and foremost, *zakat* is an act of purifying one's soul by enabling one to become closer to Allah. It is in this sense that the Holy *Qur'an* states: 'it is righteousness ... to spend your wealth ... for your kin, for orphans, for the needy, for the wayfarer, for beggars and for the ransom of captives ... and practice regular charity (*zakat*)' (Q. 2:177).

Second, it is meant to be an act of protecting the poor and the needy from any type of financial and material constraints. Accordingly, *zakat* strongly opposes the system of contemporary capitalism (Mannan, 1970, p. 220) and does not allow one to practise the habit of hoarding goods and wealth. Allah indeed warns against capitalism in the following verses:

> Woe to every scandalmonger and backbiters. Who piled up wealth and layeth it by. He thinks that his wealth would make him last forever! By no means he will be sure to be thrown into the crushing Fire. And what will explain to you what the crushing Fire is? The fire of Allah kindled [to a blaze], which leaps up over the hearts. Verily, it shall be closed upon them, in pillars stretched forth [i.e. they will be punished in the Fire with pillars].
> (Q. 104:1–9)

Third, as much as the poor and the destitute benefit from the financial and material assistance obtained from the rich, the wealthy will be handsomely rewarded by Allah in the hereafter for their act of obedience (El-Gouri, 1982, pp. 251 ff.).

Fourth, *zakat* plays a vital role in the progress of a socio-humanitarian economy. While *zakat* functions as a mean to eradicate poverty in the society, it also simultaneously moulds the individuals into responsible and caring persons, who are always ready to help the poor and those who are helpless (Mannan, 1970, p. 284). The institution of *zakat* inculcates the spirit of brotherhood (Saud, 1988, p. 40) in upholding socio-solidarity in the community. It ensures an ideal sustainable social security for the poor, needy, elderly, disabled, regardless of one's religious belief, language, status, race or gender. Furthermore, *zakat* develops creative individuals who are non-materialistic, self-sufficient and grateful for the bounty of Allah, and are enabled to experience and enjoy vast spiritual development, social solidarity and material prosperity as well.

3. Recipients of *zakat*

The eight categories of recipients of *zakat* are indicated in Q. 9:60 as follows:

> *As-sadaqat* [here in the sense of *zakat*] are only for the *fuqara'*, and *al-masakin*, and those employed to collect [the funds], and to attract the hearts of those who have been inclined [to Islam], and to free the captives, and for those in debt, and for Allah's cause, and for the wayfarer [a traveller who is cut off from everything]; a duty imposed by Allah. And Allah is All-Knower, All-Wise.

(a) (b) *Fuqara'* (the needy) are those with income less than half of their needs while *al-masakin* (the poor) are those with income more than half of their needs, but still not enough for subsistence. These two categories of people may receive *zakat* for the following purposes: food; financial aid; health care; education; assistance during the month of Ramadan; shelter; emergency aid; parents' care; marriage assistance; skills and training aids; building/repairing basic home issues; assistance for the disabled; clothing aids; *qard hasan* for entrepreneurship.

(c) The category of *amil-zakat* includes collectors and administrators of *zakat*, with related costs of administration, and more specifically: *zakat* collectors (individual or organization); accountants of *zakat* money; administrators, managers, clerical workers or secretaries; *zakat* distributors; auditors over *zakat* management and administration; office and other related management costs involving *zakat* administration.

(d) *Mu'allaf*, the non-Muslim who convert to Islam may receive *zakat*. The purposes for this category are among the following: education; training; printing and publishing; preaching activities; shelter; emergency aids; strengthening one's faith; assistance to the Muslims who stay at the border of an enemy's country.

(e) *al-Riqab*, those who want to free themselves from slavery, may receive *zakat*. Money is employed here for the following purposes: freeing oneself from slavery; freeing a Muslim from being held captive by the enemy;

freeing a prostitute from being a hostage; freeing oneself from being forced into becoming a hostage.

(f) *al-Gharimin*, those in bondage with debt (insolvent) who may receive *zakat* for the settlement of their monetary debts or to be discharged from insolvency.

(g) *Fi-Sabilillah*, activities done in the cause of Allah. The *zakat* may be received for the following causes: individual preaching (*da'wah*); educational assistance; development of Islamic teachings and divine ethical values; health care; public utilities; skills and professional development; socio-cultural and moral buildings within the *Shari'ah* values.

(h) *Ibnu Sabil*, the wayfarer regardless of whether one is rich or poor, but the situation compels oneself to seek financial help, may receive *zakat* in the following situation and purposes: assistance for those who cannot afford to go back to their original country; aids for those who cannot afford to continue with the journey.

3.1. Multi-religion destitution and zakat

A common misconception about *zakat* is that, being a divine provision for Muslims, non-Muslims shall not be eligible to enjoy any benefit from it (Qudama, as quoted by Doi, 1990, p. 111). But, in fact, several scholars accept the idea that the institution of *zakat* provides benefit for both Muslims and non-Muslims, such as al-Tabari (*ibidem*, in Doi). It is thus concluded that *zakat* provides a practical solution to the problems faced by the poor and the needy in the contemporary society regardless of one's religious background. Accordingly, Mannan remarks that

> *zakat* acts as a unique measure provided by Islam to abolish poverty from the society by making the rich live to the social responsibilities they have. In the economic sphere, *zakat* prevents the morbid accumulation of wealth in a few hands and to defuse it before it assumes threatening proportions in the hands of its possessors, as it is a compulsory contribution of the Muslims to the state exchequer.
>
> (Mannan, 1970, p. 284)

Zakat is a divine compulsory tax imposed on those whose income and property has reached a certain regulatory limit. The recipients are classified, as seen above, in Q. 9:60. The majority of the *'ulama* are of the view that *zakat* is a divine institution with universal character, which does not provide social security for Muslims only, but also for non-Muslims who are poor and needy, regardless of differences in religion, colour, race or gender. This view is indeed justified by the following evidences.

- The words *faqir* and *miskin* mentioned in the verse Q. 9:60 are *'amm* (general), and include any poor or needy, be one Muslim or non-Muslim. It is indeed justified by the case when the second Caliph of Islam 'Umar once saw a Jew begging from other people due to old age and financial constraint. He upon witnessing this situation recited the Holy verse (Q. 9:60) and said that the recipient of *zakat* may not be necessarily Muslims only, but should also be extended to non-Muslims (see Doi, 1990, p. 111).

- Once, the second Caliph on another occasion saw some Christian lepers. He ordered that they should be given *zakat* and be looked after (*ibidem*, p. 117).
- During the period of Abu Bakr, the first Caliph, Khalid ibn Walid wrote in respect of the Christian inhabitants of al-Hira in Iraq, saying that:

Any old man incapable of work or anyone who has suffered from any calamity, or any person who was rich and suddenly became a pauper asking for charity from his people, *jizyah* [i.e. tax levied on non-Muslims] must not be collected from him. He and his family, as the contrary, should be maintained through the *bait al-mal* of Muslims.

(see Doi, 1990, p. 117)

- The first and second Caliphs had also established an organization for social security, which functioned for the betterment of the needy, which covered both Muslims and non-Muslims. Imam Zufar ruled that non-Muslims who are needy should also be helped out of the *zakat* fund, which may bring them closer to Muslims (*ibidem*).
- The Maliki and Zaidi Schools of law are also of the opinion that non-Muslims who are poor should also be given the opportunity to share the benefit of the *zakat* fund, so as to soften their hearts in order to become more friendly and closer to Muslims.
- Al-Nawawi (quoted by Doi, 1990, p. 118) also opined that it is a common obligation to help the needy and feed the hungry regardless of one's religion. Ramli, meanwhile, acknowledged that:

The non-Muslims are like Muslims when it comes to relieving them from their sufferings. It is essential for all Muslims to remove any harm coming to them. Apart from food or clothing of the needy non-Muslims, it is also *fardu al-kifayah* to help them in the treatment of their sickness and giving fees to the doctors, and buying medicine etc.

(quoted by Doi, 1990, *ibidem*)

4. Mechanisms and strategies for a shared development through *zakat* and micro-entrepreneurship

4.1. *Mechanisms to promote* zakat *understanding*

Given that the institution of *zakat* provides financial assistance for the needy individual, family and society regardless of one's religious belief, colour, race, gender or status (so long as one falls within the scope of recipients identified in Q. 9:60), how can it constitute a model for a collective welfare alternative to mainstream capitalism in the light of the *maqasid al-Shari'ah*? The following mechanisms are suggested.

4.1.1. *Diffusion of the significance of* zakat

Zakat provides significant results for mankind that are not limited to material solutions, but also more social, moral and spiritual benefits for the society when compared to what is offered under modern capitalism. Hence, in order to educate and inculcate the value and importance of *zakat* awareness, exhibitions, seminars and dialogues should be organized for the public and government officials around the globe. This effort should always be accompanied by appropriate scholarly writing, sharing and publishing.

4.1.2. *Waiver of misconceptions about* zakat *and micro-entrepreneurship*

The popular and common misconception about the institution of *zakat* is that it is a mere charitable platform to give a bit of charity to beggars just for making them satisfied temporarily with no long-term plan as to 'poverty eradication'. Such a misconception shall be rebutted by upholding in reality that *zakat* is a form of socio-humanitarian model provided for those who are poor and needy aiming at transforming them into self-reliant actors, able to participate in the market, eventually becoming micro-entrepreneurs. Such material and financial sharing of resources, also in the light of mutual entrepreneurship, is indeed a duty upon those who are financially sound, aiming at assisting and accommodating those needy members of the society in a collective welfare community.

4.1.3. *Implementation of* zakat *by complying with the* maqasid al-Shari'ah

Another fundamental aspect is the implementation of the *zakat* model within a model of government in line with the principle of *Shari'ah* (*siyyasah al-Shari'ah*), through the doctrine of *qiyas* (analogy) and *masalih al-mursalah* (public interest). Such a move is important in order to ensure a successful application of the rules of *zakat* and provide a financial and material helping-hand for the poor, the needy and the helpless, hence embracing the *maqasid*, the objectives of *Shari'ah*.

4.2. Zakat *long-term micro-entrepreneurship and cooperative model*

Zakat funds shall not be treated with a short-term objective: indeed, only a long-term strategic plan over the *zakat* funds may truly lead to an achievement of sustainable development goals. Thus, *zakat* funds should be managed strategically with long-term objectives to achieve good social security for all in ensuring a true spirit of collective welfare. To this aim, the following strategies are recommended.

4.2.1. Cooperative micro-entrepreneurship

In view of poverty eradication by creating economic stability among the needy with long-term effect through a micro-entrepreneurship model, the *zakat* funds may provide a required financing facility in the form of *qard al-hasan* (benevolent loan) for the identified poor and destitute, encouraging them to become entrepreneurs as per their interest. The facility may be for a period of three to five years depending on the business venture. The identified recipient shall establish and operate an agreed enterprise, which may be monitored with possible strategies by the *zakat* management office.

The entrepreneur shall be provided with a refund schedule, where the repayment may take place on an agreed instalment basis, payable out of the income generated in the venture. For the risk management over the venture, an appropriate venture *takaful* coverage on a short-term basis is recommended to be held, where the premium shall be payable either by the *zakat* fund or by the entrepreneur. Through this scheme, the *zakat* fund may be able to enrich its capacity with greater outcomes for poverty eradication. For a long-term sustainable plan, the targeted entrepreneurs shall be required to enrich themselves with appropriate skill development by training, which shall be facilitated and organized by the *zakat* board. Last but not least, a standard policy or guidelines shall be established in regulating the total scheme professionally.

4.2.2. Cooperation in training, education and capacity-building

Financial assistance may be awarded as a *qard al-hasan* (benevolent loan) out of *zakat* funds for the poor and needy students, which shall be refundable out of the income generated only upon one's graduation and during employment. The objective of the refund is to enrich the *zakat* funds to help strategically other ones in need, which may ultimately contribute to the start of a more sound local development.

4.2.3. Group health care

A group health care insurance scheme (*takaful*) may be designed for the poor and destitute, in which the premium shall be payable out of the *zakat* fund, aiming at opening an opportunity for the poor and helpless patients enabling them to enjoy basic health care rights.

4.2.4. Cooperative housing scheme

Financing facility may be awarded as a *qard al-hasan* (benevolent loan) out of the *zakat* fund for poor and helpless families to purchase a reasonably comfortable house enabling them to enjoy with their basic right to live in their own shelter. This *qard al-hasan* shall be refundable within an agreed affordable duration. If in case the house owner fails to complete the refund because of his or her death or disablement, the legal heirs of the owner shall settle it or a mortgage *takaful* plan on the house may take care of it or the *zakat* fund may issue a waiver note to the house owner.

4.2.5. Immunity insolvency plan

There are many poor living in society who suffer from unsettled debts, resulting in them being declared bankrupt or facing other disastrous consequences. *Zakat* funds may provide financing facility as a *qard al-hasan* (benevolent loan) for those bad debtors or insolvents in relieving them from the unexpected suffering due to unsettlement of debts. The *qard al-hasan* shall be refundable within an agreed affordable period. Also in this situation, if the borrower fails to complete the refund because of his or her death or disablement, the legal heirs of the borrower shall settle it or the *zakat* fund may issue a waiver note to the borrower.

5. *Zakat* funds and socio-humanitarian impact

As already mentioned in this text, it has been a traditional mindset that *zakat*, as mandatory charity, shall be given to the recipients by having no objective of commercial gain or income generation for their own benefit and with a long-term eco-sustainability. But this mindset may ensure only short-term satisfaction, while the true divine objective of *zakat* (*maqasid al-Shari'ah*) is to care about poverty eradication with sustainable and long-term results.

In Section 4, this chapter highlighted a list of mechanisms and strategies to promote a shared development thanks to *zakat* and micro-entrepreneurship. Accordingly, also the mindset of the management authorities shall be shifted towards a socio-humanitarian approach able to foster a longer-term eco-sustainability of *zakat* funds and to create added opportunities for the poor and the needy. In other words, investing *zakat* funds should not be seen as a *Shari'ah* contradiction, rather it should be encouraged strategically in view of expanding the scope of the humanitarian well-being with sustainable and long-term goals, hence fully embracing the rationale underlying the link between *zakat* and *maqasid al-Shari'ah*.

The possibilities of investment of *zakat* funds have recently been emphasized by Mohammad Sahyabani in a presentation held at the Islamic Economics Institute, King Abdul Aziz University, Saudi Arabia (Sahyabani, 2016). The investment of *zakat* funds can be structured through *mudarabah*, *musharakah* and other *Shari'ah* tools.

The only risk may be in the case of a deficit encountered by the principal (*zakat* fund) in the course of the investment. Who shall take the responsibility, then? The state or the *zakat* foundation or the project owner (investee)? And how should the issue be resolved? In this light, it is recommended that an investment of *zakat* fund should be securitized by a mutual insurance company (*takaful*) against any risk of deficit. At the same time it has been noted that the investment of *zakat* funds may be allowed only over the outstanding fund available in the account at the end of the annual closing upon settlement of the recipients. In summary, for any type of micro-entrepreneurship or cooperative plan through *qard al-hasan* or investment plan over *zakat* funds, the risk factor requires an appropriate *takaful* policy to cover it.[4] Such policy shall be among the prerequisite for any disbursement of *zakat* fund for any of the above causes. The policy may be named as the deposit or investment or venture *takaful*.

5.1. Contemporary security system and the role of zakat

It is undeniable that the contemporary security system aims to help the poor and the needy in society to live comfortably and with dignity. Nevertheless, there are still some aspects of it which may be questioned.

First of all, the modern security system fails to cater for the insolvent in providing financial assistance to settle one's debts. Second, even though it helps the unemployed by offering them assistance, such a move may be unwise as it does not offer incentives for personal effort to solve one's economic crisis. Hence, instead of providing such assistance, it may be better to offer short-term loans to allow the poor to open their own businesses, which may be more beneficial in the long term.

Zakat, as compulsory tax paid by those who are financially able, can be addressed to solve both these limits (help to insolvent people; support of micro-entrepreneurship). Furthermore, a more comprehensive social security system can be ensured under the *zakat* model in comparison to what we observe today in the modern security system, with regard to retirement pensions,[5] the support of widows,[6] invalidity and unemployment benefits,[7] as well help for medical and health treatment.

In fact, while the modern security system usually specifies its beneficiaries according to strict parameters, the institution of *zakat* covers an unlimited category of beneficiaries under the broad application of the words *fuqara'* and *masakin* (Q. 9:60).

Furthermore, the idea of providing a free health service for those who are unable to pay for medical and health treatments (such as by providing medicines, ambulance, healthcare subsidies, sick-beds at clinics and hospitals, food for those who are hospitalized, etc.) is certainly in line with *Shari'ah* humanitarian principles. The institution of *zakat* may provide total exclusion from medical expenses and other health care for the needy.[8]

Last but not least, also other types of beneficiaries under the modern social security system who are entitled to obtain benefits such as attendance allowance, mobility allowance, invalid care allowance, housing benefits, social funds and so on, may be recognized under *zakat*.

5.2. *The general socio-humanitarian model grounded on* zakat

The institution of *zakat* does not only provide the basis for social security, it simultaneously offers a general framework for a socio-economic environment grounded on a results-oriented humanitarian concern.

In fact, as seen throughout the pages of this chapter, it provides society with soul and wealth purity, and moulds the rich into being responsible and caring about the poor. At the same time it develops the spirit of brotherhood and cooperation based on goodwill and tolerance in society. Moreover, it benefits both the rich and the poor, whereby the rich will be rewarded by Allah in the hereafter, and the poor will be thankful for the material assistance rendered to them under the divine law of Allah.

In summary, it can be said that the *zakat* model can play a central socio-humanitarian role as an alternative to contemporary capitalism, through the realization of the *maqasid al-Shari'ah* (see Section 2) and viable mechanisms and strategies of micro-entrepreneurship (Section 4) towards the recipients indicated by the *Qur'an* (Section 3).

In conclusion, *zakat* positions itself as a unique platform in providing socio-humanitarian well-being for all the members of society, especially when funds are streamed towards a model of long-term eco-sustainability through micro-entrepreneurship.

6. Conclusions and final recommendations

This chapter has shown how the institution of *zakat* is unique and capable of providing practical solutions as an alternative to the modern social security system and the contemporary capitalism paradigm. In fact, the proper application and administration of *zakat* does not only guarantee a meaningful social security and solidarity but also provides an alternative way out of today's most common threat of capitalism in developing an entrepreneurship spirit deprived of solidarity (for further reflection on the point, see recently Clarke and Tittensor, 2014; Ramadani *et al.*, 2017).

To face the effort of poverty eradication through a *zakat* micro-entrepreneurship model compliant with the *maqasid al-Shari'ah* (aiming at a result-oriented socio-humanitarian impact with long-term economic sustainability), the following are recommended.

It is important that the institution of *zakat*, besides being able to provide for the needy with material and financial security, also contributes to everyone's socio-moral and spiritual achievement (whether the person is rich or poor, Muslim or non-Muslim).

Hence, it is timely to inculcate the value of *zakat* with its significant results for humanity through writings, talks, debates and views to prove that it is not merely a charitable platform, but it also potentially creates an atmosphere of poverty eradication with community entrepreneurship for everybody.

Accordingly, to upgrade the lives of the poor through a shared spirit of brotherhood, solidarity, cooperation and concern, the funds of *zakat* should not be disbursed exclusively as a traditional charity to the poor, but should be utilized by micro-entrepreneurship schemes (hence strengthening the spirit of brotherhood between the rich and the poor) to boost entrepreneurship and make the needy eventually financially self-reliant. This strategy may bring success to the objective of poverty eradication in the long-term.

More in general, the administration and application of the rules of *zakat* should be done on the basis of *siyyasah al-Shari'ah* in an effort to meet the legitimate demands of the needy. Such a move is aimed at ensuring that *zakat* is managed as a practical solution for society by structuring it as a micro-entrepreneurship model, benefiting all needy citizens in upgrading their socio-economic status, regardless of one's religion, race, colour or gender.

To conclude, *zakat* may with gradual effect gain the recognition of a practical solution in helping the poor and the needy with micro-entrepreneurship schemes in the contemporary socio-economic reality, and positions itself as a better alternative to the contemporary micro-credit, social business, social finance, charitable trust, social security system and the like in view of true poverty eradication. Such aspiration is not only related to Islamic teaching, but to the nature of *zakat* as operating on the ground of a brotherhood strengthening the unity of all mankind.

Notes

1 See, in particular, Q. 9:60; 7:156; 19:31; 19:55; 21:73; 23:4; 24:56; 27:3; 30:39; 31:4 and 41:7. Some of these passages of the *Qur'an* will be explained in more detail in the chapter.

2 More precisely, *zakatable* wealth or income are: gold, silver, diamond, monetary savings, salary, premiums obtained from legal transactions, assets and capitals of any company or business firms, stocks and shares, animals, business licence, hoarded articles or properties, agricultural products such as paddy, palm oil, cocoa, etc., wealth obtained from mines such as tin, petrol, natural gas, etc. (see in this regard Saud, 1988, pp. 68, 70 and 72; Aliyu, 1993; Muhammad, 1993, p. 1).

3 In this light, it is unfortunate that the notion of *zakat* is often reduced by many people to a form of traditional charity given away by the rich to the poor and the needy, and not as an alternative model of collective welfare.

4 The premium shall be payable either by the receiver or recipient of the *zakat* fund or out of the *zakat* fund.

5 As regards to the concept of retirement pension, it had been even practised 1,500 years ago during the era of the second Caliph 'Umar, who set up a special *diwan* or department. He even once ordered the government to pay a regular pension to both Muslims and non-Muslims.

6 As regards the widows' benefits, it is one of the great virtues to look after the welfare of the widows as the Holy Prophet (PBUH) once said to this effect: 'The one who looks after and works for a widow and for a poor person is like a warrior fighting for Allah or like a person who fasts during the day and prays all the night' (*Sahih al-Bukhari*).

7 Unemployment benefits are meant for those who are unemployed due to retrenchment in the job market or underqualification. It is a moral obligation to help those
who are unemployed and face difficulties resulting from retrenchment and alike.
The Holy Prophet (PBUH) said to this effect: 'Whoever solves the worldly difficulties of a believer, Allah will remove from him one of the grieves of the Day of
Judgment. Whosoever alleviates [the lot of] a needy person, Allah will alleviate [his
lot] in this world and the next' (*Sahih Muslim*).

8 It may be suggested that, for a better healthcare service for the needy and helpless
groups, a group healthcare *takaful* policy may be the solution. In this idea, the
policy may be a group healthcare *takaful* where the premium shall be payable
from the *zakat* fund with a needs-based test. This idea may be undertaken and
implemented under any wing of the government and be treated as an alternative to
social insurance that exists in the traditional model (see Section 4.2).

References

al-Harran, S.A.S. (1993) *Islamic Finance: Partnership Financing.* Malaysia: Pelanduk
Publications.

Aliyu, C.U. (1993) *Fiqh al muamalat* and the need for Islamic economics: a clarifica-
tion of misconception. *Journal of Objective Studies.* **5**(1).

Al-Nawawi, *Al-Minhaj.*

Al-Tabari, *Tafsir al-Tabari.* Vol. 2, Cairo.

Clarke, M., and Tittensor, D. (eds, 2014) *Islam and Development: Exploring the Invisible
Aid Economy.* London: Routledge.

Doi, A.R.I. (1990) *Non-Muslims Under Shari'ah.* Kuala Lumpur: A.S. Noordeen.

El-Gouri, A.M. (1982) *Riba, Islamic Law and Interest.* Unpublished manuscript.
Temple University.

Global Issues (2013) *Poverty Facts and Stats* [online]. Available from: www.globalissues.
org/article/26/poverty-facts-and-stats [Accessed 25 August 2017].

Mannan, M.A. (1970) *Islamic Economics, Theories and Practices.* Lahore: Muhammad
Ashraf Publishers.

Muhammad, A.A.B. (1993) *Zakat and Rural Development in Malaysia.* Kuala
Lumpur: Berita Publishing.

Qudama, I. (1348 AH) *Al-Mughni*, Cairo, Vol. 11.

Ramadani, V., Dana, L.-P., Gërguri-Rashiti, S. and Ratten, V. (eds, 2017)
Entrepreneurship and Management in an Islamic Context. Switzerland: Springer
International.

Ramli, S. (1292 AH) *Nihayatul Muhtajila Shahrul Minhaj, Bulaq.* Vol. 8.

Sahih al-Bukhari (trans. Khan, M.M., 1983) Lahore: Kazi Publications.

Sahih Muslim (as compiled in Al-Nawawi's *Forty Hadith*) (English trans. Ibrahim,
E., 1985).

Sahyabani, M. (2016) *Zakatus Sanadiq al-Istithmariyah.* Paper presentation at
the Islamic Economics Institute, King Abdul Aziz University, Saudi Arabia, 2
November 2016. Unpublished.

Saud, M.A. (1988) *Contemporary Zakat.* Ohio: Zakat and Research Foundation.

Shad, A.R. (1986) *Zakat and Usher.* Lahore: Kazi Publications.

Index